Imperial Pilgrims

Imperial Pilgrims

A Theological Account of Augustine, Empire, and the "Just War on Terror"

Shawn A. Aghajan

◆PICKWICK *Publications* • Eugene, Oregon

IMPERIAL PILGRIMS
A Theological Account of Augustine, Empire, and the "Just War on Terror"

Copyright © 2022 Shawn A. Aghajan. All rights reserved. Except for brief quotations in critical publications or reviews, no part of this book may be reproduced in any manner without prior written permission from the publisher. Write: Permissions, Wipf and Stock Publishers, 199 W. 8th Ave., Suite 3, Eugene, OR 97401.

Pickwick Publications
An Imprint of Wipf and Stock Publishers
199 W. 8th Ave., Suite 3
Eugene, OR 97401

www.wipfandstock.com

PAPERBACK ISBN: 978-1-6667-0393-1
HARDCOVER ISBN: 978-1-6667-0394-8
EBOOK ISBN: 978-1-6667-0395-5

Cataloguing-in-Publication data:

Names: Aghajan, Shawn A., author.

Title: Imperial pilgrims : a theological account of Augustine, empire, and the "just war on terror" / by Shawn A. Aghajan.

Description: Eugene, OR : Pickwick Publications, 2022 | Includes bibliographical references and index(es).

Identifiers: ISBN 978-1-6667-0393-1 (paperback) | ISBN 978-1-6667-0394-8 (hardcover) | ISBN 978-1-6667-0395-5 (ebook)

Subjects: LCSH: Christianity and politics. | History of doctrines. | Christianity and culture. | Power (Christian theology).

Classification: BR170 .A35 2022 (print) | BR170 .A35 (ebook)

03/25/22

Scripture quotations are from The ESV® Bible (The Holy Bible, English Standard Version®), copyright © 2001 by Crossway, a publishing ministry of Good News Publishers. Used by permission. All rights reserved.

To my many teachers—from my mother to Brian—each who bore with great patience the questions and grievances of a headstrong child and, in turn, made me a better ~~teacher~~ man.

I was taught from my childhood that Christ is God and that His teaching is divine and authoritative; while, on the other hand, I was also told to respect those institutions that, by means of violence, secured my safety from evil; I was taught to honor those institutions as being sacred. I was taught to resist evil; and it was instilled into me that it was humiliating and dishonorable to submit to evil and to suffer from it; and that it was praiseworthy to resist evil. I was taught to condemn and to execute. I was taught to make war, i.e., to resist evil by murder . . . I was taught to resist an offender by violence and to avenge a private insult, or one against my native land, by violence. All this was never regarded as wrong, but, on the contrary, I was told that it was perfectly right and in no way contrary to Christ's doctrine. All surrounding interests, such as the peace and safety of my family, my property, and myself were based on the law that was rejected by Christ—on the law of a "tooth for a tooth" . . . I imbibed such a notion of the practical impossibility of following the divine doctrine gradually and almost imperceptibly. I was so accustomed to it, it coincided so well with all my animal feelings, that I had never observed the contradiction in which I lived. I did not see that it was impossible to admit the Godhead of Christ—the basis of whose teaching is non-resistance of evil—and, at the same time, to work consciously and calmly for the institutions of property, courts of law, kingdoms, the army, and so on. It could not be consistent for us to regulate our lives contrary to the doctrine of Christ, and then pray to the same Christ that we might be enabled to keep His commandments—to "forgive," and not to "resist evil." It did not then occur to me, as it does now, that it would be much simpler to regulate our lives according to the doctrine of Christ; and then, if courts of law, executions, and war were found to be indispensably necessary for our welfare, we might pray to have them too. And I understood from where my error arose. It arose from my professing Christ in words and denying Him in deed.

—Leo Tolstoy, "What I Believe"

Contents

Acknowledgments | ix

    Introduction—"Whose Side are You on Son?" | 1
I America as Unconventional Empire | 18
II Augustine on Empires and their "Just Wars" | 65
III A "Just War on Terror?" | 111
IV Imperial Pilgrims | 165
    Conclusion—Who Would Jesus Drone? | 195

Bibliography | 205
Subject Index | 219
Scripture Index | 247

Acknowledgments

I learned fairly early on in my childhood that many people are born on third base and think they hit a triple to get there. I did not realize that I was one of those near-sighted ingrates until my mid-thirties. One of the most sobering pearls of wisdom a colleague offered me shortly after my family arrived in Aberdeen was that earning a PhD does not mean you are smarter than anyone else; it merely means you had more time and money than most. With all due respect to the brilliant people I have had the pleasure of learning with and from, I am inclined to think my friend was right.

I am grateful for my mother and Aunt Kaye who embodied the truth that I read in Maya Angelou: "That some people, unable to go to school, were more intelligent and more educated than college professors." I believe growing up learning from their tireless work ethic has made me a better steward of my "excess time and money." These lessons were supplemented by many teachers who loved Jesus by loving me and a principal who disciplined me with a patient and persistent grace despite my rebelliousness.

I am blessed to have been a part of church communities that have broadened my understanding of the "already" of God's kingdom. I am particularly thankful to Aberdeen Vineyard and Alliance Bible Church for being genuine surrogate families to our family over the course of this project during which we said goodbye to my mother and hello to four daughters.

The Lord has also been far more gracious than I deserve in providing a partner, a faithful friend who has been mother to our girls, head teacher to the differently abled, and chief encourager to me particularly during the times when I would have preferred to throw in the towel rather than write another word. To that end, I am also indebted to friends like David, Richard, Steven, and Doug who have encouraged me by reading and commenting on this work in its various stages.

Finally, I would be remiss if I did not extend my most profound gratitude to the men and women of the University of Aberdeen's College of Arts and Sciences Normativity Project who were kind enough to see some glimmer of potential in this project and back it with funding. I pray that this book is a fair return on your investment.

Baytown, Texas
March 2020

Introduction—"Whose Side Are You on Son?"

"I beseech thee therefore Brethren!" The problem of ethics is presented once again as a great disturbance. How, indeed, can it be otherwise? For human behavior must inevitably be disturbed by the thought of God. Every conversation about Him ends in disharmony, since it is undertaken by men lacking sufficient perception to enable them to keep a firm hold upon the subject about which they are talking. The fact that ethics constitutes a problem reminds us that the object about which we are conversing has no objectivity, that is to say, it is not a concrete world existing above or behind our world; it is not a treasury of our spiritual experiences; it is not even some transcendental vastness: for we are not metaphysicians. Our conversation is about men living in the world of nature and of civilization; and, moreover, we ourselves are also men living of necessity from minute to minute a quite concrete life . . . To be sincere, our thought must share in the tension of human life, in its criss-cross lines, and in its kaleidoscopic movements. And life is neither simple, nor straightforward, nor obvious. Things are simple and straightforward and obvious only when they are detached from their context and then treated "superficially."[1]

—Karl Barth

1. Barth, *Epistle to The Romans*, XII/1–2. Barth admonishes me to remember the particular kind of moral imagining I *think* I am practicing when I call my work "theological ethics." Such a bold reminder is necessary because I concur with Barth and Bonhoeffer's claim that the serpent's invitation to "be like God, knowing good and evil" heralded the birth of ethics and sin, conjoined twins that presume to stand in judgement over God's word rather than to lay prostrate before the Word of God to be

I grew up about twenty-five miles east of Houston, Texas—a particularly violent part of an exceptionally violent country. Texans are *not* just quintessentially American; we pride ourselves on being exceedingly so. If the stereotypical American is big, brash, and bombastic, the Texan is bigger, brasher, and more bombastic. In short, Texans are a hyperbolic incarnation of the American caricature. The American obsession with violence is just one way this axiom manifests itself. In the nation that holds more than 40 percent of the world's firearms—few will be surprised to learn that the US has more guns than citizens—Texans own the lion's share of them.[2] According to the Texas Department of Public Safety, there are nearly 1.4 million Texans that are licensed to carry a firearm. Due to the inordinate strength of the National Rifle Association's political lobby, these weapons can legally be carried, openly or concealed, nearly everywhere in the state from church to a university's classroom.

The United States is one of only two post-industrialized nations that still utilizes capital punishment.[3] Thirty of the United States' fifty states actively employ the death penalty. The "Lone Star State" shines brighter than its neighbors yet again by excelling in its use of killing to ostensibly curb its citizenry's desire to murder one another. In 2018, the US executed 25 prisoners, over half of whom were killed in Texas. Moreover, of the 1,498 executions that have taken place in the United States since the Supreme Court approved new capital punishment laws in 1976, ending a four-year moratorium on the practice, over one-third (563) of the sanctioned executions have occurred in the sleepy little Texas college town of Huntsville.[4]

---

judged by it. My teachers, Barth, Bonhoeffer, and Brian Brock, have helped me develop a healthy aversion to the moral arrogance that tempts me to use theological ethics as a means of justifying myself rather than viewing it as an instrument of God's Holy Spirit by which I am exposed as guilty but declared righteous. If there are claims made in the following lines that seem ignorant of the tension created by the intersection of concrete, human lives or conclusions written as though they are immune from being disturbed by God's ethical thought, these deficiencies can only be attributed to my shortcomings for my teachers have trained me to do more carefully nuanced work. See Bonhoeffer, *Creation and Fall*, 103 and Barth, *Church Dogmatics*, IV/1.

2. Schaeffer, "US Citizens Own 40% of All Guns in World."

3. Japan is the other nation with this dubious distinction.

4. Over one-third of those death sentences originated in Harris County, the county in which I was raised and still live. In fact, Harris County alone hands out more capital punishment convictions than every other state in the Union besides Texas. That courts and juries so precariously play god might be made somewhat more tolerable if they did so judiciously, but in Texas this is not the case. Over the last five years, more than 70 percent of death sentences have been imposed on people of color in Texas. Although African Americans comprise less than 13 percent of the Texas's population, they comprise 43.4 percent of death row inmates, according to the Texas Department of Criminal

Introduction—"Whose Side Are You On Son?"

The American experience is profoundly tempered by immersion in violence. Our history is rife with examples of how well we impose our collective will upon other people. Even our most popular pastime, football, is a celebration of violently choreographed coercion and, consequently, leaves bodies and minds similarly mangled. Mass shootings occur with such frequency[5] that they have ceased to surprise many when they occur. Such is the baptism of Cain; it can anesthetize citizens against ritualized violence and elicits a perverse pleasure instead of repulsion.

Yet there are few Americans for whom this convoluted relationship with violence seems to cause much moral dissonance, even among Christians. We tell ourselves many small myths and half-truths to reconcile what is seemingly incongruous. Those within the American Church are proud to declare that the US was founded upon Christian principles. Principles that have produced a justice system that protects good people from bad people, rather than an inherently biased system that disproportionately favors the wealthy and white. We have guns to protect ourselves when other good people are too far away to help, rather than munitions to guard the idols of our affluence that we have amassed. The national violence that we disseminate to all corners of the globe is called freedom, rather than imperialism. This system suffices to more or less assuage our collective conscience until someone dares to question our national self-perception.

The lines that follow are my attempt to reconcile my dual citizenships in the heavenly and earthly cities—how to rightly navigate my pilgrimage as a follower of Jesus through a country that is at *best* indifferent to violence but at worst worships it. My intent is to interrogate the American Christian story from within, without being forced to abdicate either identity. Following Augustine and the Prophet Isaiah before him, these first few pages are my *Confessions* that I am but one of many men among a people of unclean hands and lips. The early context is necessarily autobiographical since in order to clearly consider the ethical implications of being a contemporary Christian and imperial citizen I had to push back against much of what I was taught explicitly and implicitly that good American Christians hold as sacrosanct.

Justice. Hispanics comprise 26.8 percent and whites comprise 27.6 percent of the death row population. Texas Department of Criminal Justice, *Death Row Information*.

5. In 2018 alone, the US Center for Homeland Security and Defense and the Federal Emergency Management Agency (FEMA) tallied ninety-four gun incidents in American schools with 114 people killed or injured. With the typical American school year lasting 180 days, there was, on average, a gun fired on a US school campus more frequently than every other school day. Coughlan, *2018 "Worst Year for US School Shootings."*

My first forays outside my myopic perspective were provided by my father, an Iranian immigrant to the US. My parents divorced when I was two years old. I typically saw my father once a month when I was in grade school. Consequently, the most prominent childhood memories I have of him are attributed to his absence rather than his presence.[6] However, I remember July 4, 1991, as clearly as any memory I can recall. I was ten, and he had taken me to a local amusement park to spend Independence Day. The culmination of the celebration was Lee Greenwood's performance of "God Bless the USA" complete with fireworks illuminating the muggy Houston skyline above him. It is unlikely that Greenwood's lyrics were intended to be read as political theology. However, his chorus is as tidy of a synopsis of American morality that frequently ties the god of our forefathers to its national history by conflating pride, freedom, sacrifice, inalienable rights, self-defense, and unflappable love for the nation with a god who pardons all sins committed in its defense.

It was not the rollercoasters, concert, or fireworks that left an indelible impression on me that day. Instead, I recall how angry I was with my father for refusing to stand and place his hand over heart during the song. I could not understand why he was not overflowing with pride, as the rest of us were. July 4, 1991, was an exceptionally good time to be an American. Not only were we celebrating our David over Goliath-esque victory over the British Empire in 1776, but we were also less than six months removed from leading a team of nations to liberate Kuwait from Saddam Hussein. Things were even better than I had realized at the time. Though I knew the Berlin Wall had fallen, how profoundly the collapse of the Soviet Union would come to shape the United States' self-perception and role as the world's sole remaining superpower were lost upon me at the age of ten.

My hasty assessment of my father's lack of patriotism was missing a great deal of context—not only about him and his immigration to the US but also around the tense history between the US and Iran and the underlying causes of their mutually deep-seated distrust. Given the US policy of "plausible deniability" and most nations' penchant for selectively retelling their histories to cast a flattering light on their policies, I did not know that many other nations in which the US had been involved shared Iran's enmity

---

6. I realize that I cannot write the previous sentence without it sounding pejorative. I want to assure readers—particularly if they include my father—that it is not. It is merely a statement of fact that highlights why I find my recollection of the following story so remarkable. I understand that there were many reasons for my father's absence from my childhood, not the least of which was his contentious relationship with my mother. For greater insight into my daddy issues, see Harry Chapin's ballad, "Cat's in the Cradle."

for the "home of the free and the land of the brave." That night was seminal in my questioning of patriotism, specifically when mixed with theology as in Greenwood's song. What did it mean to "be American" and why was I so certain that I was proud enough of whatever it meant that I would openly disparage my father for not sharing this pride? How did I know I was free and what was I free *from* or free *for*? What was the relationship between the men who died, the "rights" their deaths imputed to me, and the implicit pledge that I would reciprocate in kind by gladly defending the land? These questions deserve more reflection than the well-rehearsed answers usually given. They are complicated further when they are considered by Christians who believe in a God who meaningfully and intentionally participates in the history of His people and their nations.

As I progressed through the American educational system in both public and private schools, each time I questioned this narrative I saw another disconcerting hole gouged into the story of what I had previously thought an impenetrably righteous national biography. The "self-evident truths" that I had been taught to hold—that my country, wealthy yet benevolent and powerful but restrained, was the guardian of global freedom and justice—increasingly seemed to resemble an overly charitable, self-interested, and coerced revision rather than a truthful and responsible historical account.[7] This discrepancy would have likely caused no more cognitive dissonance in me than it had in most Americans had Jesus not began a new work in me the following summer. As I started to "work out my salvation with fear and trembling,"[8] I experienced the truth of what I would later read in Barth's commentary on Romans quoted above: God has a peculiar habit of confounding even the most earnest attempts at Christian moral self-justification.

The lines that follow are the products of these "divine disturbances" in my thoughts about Christian complicity with their governing authority's use of coercive violence on behalf of its citizens. I cannot feign neutrality, objectively pontificating in the realm of casuistry about occasional ethics for perpetual wars, judgment, patriotism, and violence. We are not so easily parsed apart from our historical and theological contexts. Anyone who tries to convince you otherwise is selling you a false bill of goods.

Instead, I write as a baptized Christian and citizen of the United States. Undoubtedly, both profoundly influence how I read and interpret history and the present political and theological *saeculum*. I have watched my country—at times proudly, at others shamefully—as it has engaged

---

7. The idea that the church is only visible to the world to the extent that the church is able to speak to the world truthfully about Christ and the gospel frequently appears in the work of Dietrich Bonhoeffer, John Howard Yoder, and Stanley Hauerwas.

8. Phil 2:12.

with other nations. Through all its engagements my government reminds me and the world that both the US's action and inaction have my freedom and security as their chief mission. This is welcomed by most as good news. However, among Christians, "good news" or gospel has a substantially thicker quality. The gospel complicates my rights as a US citizen because baptism is more determinative of my home than is my birth certificate. Statecraft has distilled many violent moral quandaries into different proofs of relative good or evil. The discussion of whether the US engages in relatively more or less evil practices than other countries is not a fruitful one for Christians who, "are empowered [by the Holy Spirit] not to settle for lesser evils but to inhabit the good."[9]

I am aware that this runs counter to the widespread conviction among American Christians who are primarily conditioned by Niebuhrian realist sensibilities that favor Paul Ramsey's assessment that every sort of "doing evil" is not wickedness—as most actions, whether personal, political, or military, have multiple consequences that cannot be reduced down to one effect. The Christian's responsibility in Ramsey's assessment is this: "To choose the least evil that can be done is to choose the good that alone is possible."[10] Ramsey's tone is pointed and has been used by many to skewer Christian pacifists as naïve at best, or wicked because of their inaction at worst.

However, if the only witness the church can offer a world faced with evil is indistinguishable from secular conventional wisdom conditioned by the consequentialist confession that dilutes the common good down to "the least evil for the most people," then the church has nothing of consequence to contribute to the global public discourse on war. The world does not need the church to proclaim, "An eye for an eye and a tooth for a tooth," because this sensibility already resonates with the humanistic idea of justice. The church's witness is impotent if it cannot echo and embody Christ's command to "not resist the one who is evil."[11]

To read scripture earnestly and attempt to obey the teaching of Christ found in the gospels unearths tension between his disciples and the mechanisms of power that are seen by unbelievers as well. Marcellinus and Volusianus, two of Augustine's nonbelieving Roman contemporaries, recognized that if the gospel were taken at face value, the Church and state would make strange bedfellows indeed. They could not reconcile the functions of a government as compatible with Jesus's commands to

---

9. Bell, *Just War as Christian Discipleship*, 88.

10. Ramsey, "How Shall the Counter-Insurgency War Be Conducted Justly?" 427–64.

11. Matt 5:39.

repay no one with evil for evil or to turn the other cheek when struck.[12] In Augustine's response, we find some of the fledgling accommodations the Bishop introduced. He tacitly agrees that Rome would not fully obey Christ, but to the extent that Rome would embrace Christ's examples of pardoning injuries received rather than avenging them, Rome would be a greater empire rather than diminished.

He then blunts the gravitas of Jesus's Sermon on the Mount by relegating them to "dispositions of the heart" rather than external actions despite what seem to be concrete examples rather than metaphors. He notes that Jesus and Paul did not offer the other cheek when struck.[13] This is a questionable claim as Augustine seems to make no distinction between the "resistance" of objecting to being unjustly beaten and the "resistance" of returning a physically violent response of like kind to the one received. He seems to equate questioning the grounds on which someone has taken your sight to gouging out the offender's eye in return. For all the clarity that Augustine's writing has brought the church, here his exegesis obscures the truth and inadvertently provides the groundwork for Christian participation in violence without remorse.[14]

In the epigraph to this book, Tolstoy described how the meaning of "do not resist evil" he was taught by the church (which was Augustine's interpretation) enabled him to hold opposed truth claims made by the gospel and his country without noticing the contradiction.[15] Though he wrote in a cultural and political context far removed from our own, Tolstoy's is an accurate depiction of the moral incongruences with which many Christians in America are content to live. One of the aims of this work is to push back against this dichotomy and make it less comfortable for Christians to accept the inevitability of violence as self-evident.

To be clear, I am not arguing for the church to abstain from political participation to preserve some feigned moral purity. Instead, I am advocating for the church to participate *better* in the political sphere by confessing and repenting of its complicity with the American use of coercive

12. Augustine, *Letters*, 136/2.

13. Jesus's response in John 18:23, "If I have spoken evil, rebuke me for the evil, but if I have spoken well, why do you hit me?" and Paul's in Acts 23:3, "God will strike you, you whitewashed wall. You sit to judge me according to the law, and against the law, you order me to be struck!"

14. I use inadvertently because having read Augustine's letters to judges pleading for mercy and for them to exact only as much punishment as necessary to reform the offender, it would be mendacious to paint him as an advocate for unfettered violence. However, less scrupulous readers of Augustine who followed would use a few lines from his massive corpus to justify all manner of abuse.

15. Tolstoy, "What I Believe."

violence. If the church refused to approve of and participate in the violent pursuit of the American dream of amassing as much wealth as possible, it would be a substantially greater witness to the world of the transformative power of the gospel.

Stanley Hauerwas has described American Christians as people caught between two conflicting stories. The stories cannot simultaneously be true as they require "two entirely different kinds of people with equally incompatible understandings of reality."[16] These two competing stories are those of Christianity and America, and we cannot deny that both stories intensely grip our lives. In framing the discussion as he does, Hauerwas accurately describes identification with one's homeland as inextricably formative yet not determinative of one's identity. He concludes that by confessing our complicity with what he calls "the death-avoidance practices of America," we can at least offer an alternative to our neighbors.[17]

This moral dissonance caused by competing allegiances is not a peculiarly American dilemma. Every regime's exercise of power over its citizens and foreigners is fertile ground for Christian theological reflection. What is distinctly American is that despite its explicit declaration of the separation of church from state and state from empire, the three coalesce profoundly.

The central research question this project intends to work out is how Christian Americans are to reconcile the competing claims of their faith and citizenship. It is an old question asked of a new people in a specific place and time. This struggle is more than an intellectual attempt to reconcile two incongruous identities. The Church's relationship to power and those who wield it over them is long and complicated. Analyzing theological accounts of Christian responsibility for inhabiting empire will prove beneficial for discerning what fidelity to Christ may look like in this contemporary American context.

This book will examine some of the formative texts of the Christian tradition to seek out points of analogy that help American Christians think through an uniquely contemporary question: What does it mean to be a Christian citizen, in robustly theological terms, of a political entity that wages a "war on terror" in her defense? Furthermore, the book probes the field of political theology by engaging popular themes of Augustinian interpretation. By reading Augustine pastorally, one is more likely to find an opponent rather than an advocate of the "war on terror." The result is an Augustinian critique of American empire and its perpetual "war on terror."

---

16. Hauerwas, *Performing the Faith*, 29.
17. Hauerwas, *Performing the Faith*, 29.

The fact that the phrase, "this contemporary American context," though meant to limit the scope of this project, may still be too ambitious is not lost upon me. Nonetheless, this caveat is a necessary qualifier given the amorphous nature of the war on terror's "combatants." When the research for this book began in 2012, the destruction of al Qaeda was still the most prominent US "war" objective. As the US is currently in its nineteenth year of fighting the "war on terror," al Qaeda has been replaced by Islamic State (IS) as the embodiment of the terror against which the US fights.

By naming the enemy "terror," Bush Jr.'s White House laid the furtive groundwork for justifying war in perpetuity. The Bush and subsequent administrations circumvented international laws by authorizing torture, indefinitely detained those whom it refused to identify as combatants or criminals to deny them the legal protections of either classification, and used drones to pre-emptively kill those it deemed "terrorists." Though Congress ordered the end of detainee torture in 2007, the next Commander in Chief and Nobel Peace laureate, Barack Obama, continued the CIA's use of "black sites" for illegal detention and widened the US use of drones. Though those classified as "enemies" and "defenders" of freedom may change, the justification for war without end has been a consistent tenet of American foreign policy since it was founded.

Chapter 1—America as an Unconventional Empire

The first chapter will be a brief and critical deconstruction of American history. Like all histories, this one is necessarily selective. It intentionally chooses illustrations that cast doubt on the predominant American self-perception as the benevolent primary arbiter of global peace and democracy. When cast in a less charitable light, a rather different mosaic emerges. In this study the forces that manipulated the free-market economy remained unseen, not because the hand was invisible, but because it was cloaked in the stars and stripes replete with the military muscle to apply pressure to the scales when the political realities on the ground did not coincide with American capitalist ambitions.

While American imperialism may seem like a thoroughly trodden trope that need not be revisited, the fact that the question of American empire is firmly answered in the minds of many as either glaringly self-evident or absurdly implausible requires it to be re-examined. Rather than retire empire to an obsolete governing relic of the twentieth century, the United States has evolved into an unconventional empire that is better suited to survive in today's geopolitical landscape. The United States has undergirded its fiscal and military clout with ubiquitous technology and military bases to solve what was, heretofore, the congenital birth defect that led to the demise of all great empires: imperial overstretch.

Throughout American history, this tripartite backbone of economic influence, military dominance, and political power emerges as the locus of foreign policy decision-making even when they diametrically opposed freedom, democracy, and liberty—the publicly professed core of the American ethos. This triad that governs a people through the convergence of financial, military, and political coercion did not originate in the United States but is instead the distinctively conspicuous earmark of classical imperialism.

The US history of engaging the "other" whether they were the indigenous inhabitants of the American continent or distant peoples belies its imperial premonitions. The chapter outlines a brief history of the American use of its military strength to advance its economic interests that challenge the United States' more popular and beneficent self-narrative as the chief guarantor of world peace, freedom, and justice. Understanding the "war on terror" as a peculiarly imperial endeavor will enable the reader to draw more from Augustine's *City of God* and *Letters* than a mere nascent just-war account. The primary aim of chapter 2 is to understand these works as pastoral theology (as opposed to systematic theology or theological ethics) that potentially illuminate the contemporary American Christian milieu.

Chapter 2—Augustine on Empires and Their Just War

Augustine devoted a great deal of thought to reconciling his dual citizenships in the Roman empire and the kingdom of heaven. Despite the depth of his insights, the questions posed to the Church by its imperial context and *vice versa* are necessarily unique to each emerging era. For this reason, Augustine's work has been mined anew by each subsequent generation of Christians for wisdom that would shine a light on contemporary issues.

Post September 11 America is no exception. However, the size of Augustine's corpus of work and the expanding historical distance between the context in which he wrote and new frameworks to which his teaching is applied have meant that Augustine has been pressed into service to justify activities that would seem foreign to him. For example, those who have appealed to Augustine and found an advocate of the US "war on terror" may have begged the question of whether he would see any visage of his burgeoning just-war account in the American response. How might Augustine, as a Roman citizen and Bishop of Hippo, asses America's leveraging of its ubiquitous military and economic dominance to dismantle *al*

Qaeda, overthrow Saddam Hussein, assassinate Osama bin Laden, occupy Afghanistan, and torture its presumed enemies? Is the US simply fulfilling God's providential role for earthly authorities, which Augustine describes as restraining the wicked in order to enable the good among its citizens to more fully enjoy their lives and liberties? Or would Augustine less sympathetically liken the US to Rome, which became so discontent with its domestic peace and security that it succumbed to what he called the "lust to dominate" (*libido dominandi*), which has manifested itself in the explicit yet clandestine means that the US employs to manipulate international relations among its friends and foes alike? This book will seek to answer these questions and others by thinking with Augustine, inhabiting his theology to gain fresh purchase on the present.

Chapter 3—A "Just War on Terror?"

The third chapter will more closely examine how contemporary theologians have utilized Augustine to interpret the "war on terror." However, this project will diverge from the current consensus in the field because it will not use the baton handed down from Augustine to beat the just war drum or, more precisely, to bludgeon terrorists.[18] This concern will be focused by engaging the most formidable contributions to Christian ethics to engage both Augustine and the "war on terror" since 9/11. The chapter will look at contributions from Jean Bethke Elshtain, Nigel Biggar, Charles Mathewes, Daniel Bell, Lisa Sowle Cahill, R. A. Markus, and John Milbank.

I will also ask my own questions of Augustine. For example, how might he appraise President Bush's authorization of "enhanced interrogation techniques" at various CIA black sites given Augustine's reflections on the lamentable yet indispensable task of the judge who must torture to assess guilt without any certainty that he has reached the correct verdict.[19] Would George W. Bush cry out to God like King David and Augustine's judge: "Deliver me from my necessities!"?[20]

---

18. "Terrorist" is a term so subjective and malleable in the hands of powerful governments that the term is nearly vacuous. For example, when the US armed the *mujahideen* to kill the occupying Soviets, Americans called them "freedom fighters," but when they began killing occupying Americans the *mujahideen* became "terrorists."

19. Augustine, *City of God*, XIX/6.

20. Psalm 25:17.

Chapter 4—Imperial Pilgrims

The fourth chapter will seek to properly orient American Christians within the contemporary American context. It identifies repentance as the opening move in Christian political engagement. Public confession of complicity with national sin is a humbling and disarming political posture. This chapter will also consider ways that a democratic republic complicates repentance and its necessary corollary: witness. This section will also attempt to broaden the conventional understanding of patriotism by including critical dissent as an act of fidelity to one's nation.

Patriotism is multifaceted. Former Secretary of State John Kerry embodied this sentiment when in a mere five years from 1966 to 1971 he gave a graduation speech denouncing the US policies in Vietnam, voluntarily enlisted in the Navy, requested to serve in Vietnam, earned three Purple Hearts and a Silver Star while there,[21] and became the most prominent spokesman for the organization Vietnam Veterans Against the War. His example reminds us that patriotism is more nuanced than unquestioned devotion. He says of the time, "I saw courage both in the Vietnam War and in the struggle to stop it. I learned that patriotism includes protest, not just military service. But you don't have to go halfway around the world or march on Washington to learn about bravery or love of country."[22] From this position, Christians can witness to the gospel truth by imitating the work of Jesus, particularly the work of enabling justice. The starkest example of justice-centered witness to a violent nation is to be *holistically* pro-life. This notion further develops the meaning of pro-life beyond the discussion of the unborn to include responsibility for the disadvantaged neighbor and the enemy combatant.

Educated by Augustine's distillation of Roman imperial history through the gospel that calls its disciples to interrogate competing claims of sovereignty, this book imagines itself doing work similar to Augustine's in the contemporary American context where the *libido dominandi* is flourishing. It is through the crucibles of scripture, historical candor, and Augustinian pastoral theology that this book seeks to challenge the American moral memory and contemporary governing praxis, neither of which is as beatific as is widely rehearsed.

---

21. Kerry captained two Swift boats in Vietnam and brought back all his men alive. The Purple Heart is awarded to soldiers wounded or killed in combat. The Silver Star is the third-highest military decoration that can be awarded to the US Armed Forces. It is awarded for gallantry in action when engaged with a US enemy.

22. Kerry, "Announcement Speech."

Such a rearticulating necessitates that Christian citizens ask themselves, their church elders, and confessing government representatives pointed questions, like is it possible to fight a just war, as Augustine would recognize it, against terror? If so, is that the kind of war that United States is waging? Are American calls for freedom and justice rendered invalid by the dehumanization of its enemy by torture, indefinite detainment without charge, and preemptive execution without trial by drones, most of which are remotely controlled by operators safely thousands of miles away peering into screens with images more closely resembling a poorly made video game than war? Christianity that has been seduced by American exceptionalism and co-opted by political power loathes to engage in this type of discourse. If seriously engaged, these questions problematize unfettered fidelity to the American project and the perpetual state of war required to maintain it. Against this backdrop, it would be helpful for Christian pilgrims to consider whether ideologies and practices of nationalism, patriotism, and civil obedience are faithful to Christ's gospel.

Conclusion—Who Would Jesus Drone?

One cannot coherently read the gospel's description of how male and female authentically inhabit the *imago Dei* or how they fulfil the entirety of the law or are responsible to their neighbors apart from a substantial understanding of love. Similarly, one cannot read Augustine's description of judgment, coercion, capital punishment, or war unless it is through the metaphor of the loving father who, though he would prefer to correct the malevolent child through verbal reasoning, would rather physically discipline his son than see the boy ruined by harsher punishment, torture, or death that vacates any space for repentance. Both aspects of love will be addressed in fuller detail below. They are only broached here to make two brief points.

Foremost, Christians can neither obey the commandments Jesus called the greatest nor discuss just war in an Augustinian sense without a thick account of love. Conversely, human loves are easily misappropriated to objects unworthy of love, as Augustine readily attested. Even objects rightly loved like children or justice can be loved wrongly as ends in themselves rather than for God's sake. When one loves a proper thing inordinately, the virtue of love spoils and becomes vice. On Augustine's reading of Roman history, it was Rome's disproportionate love of being free that quickly metastasized into its lust to dominate its neighbors.

Despite the Christian consensus that love is the primary driver behind obedience and right action toward one another, there is little agreement among Christians as to what constitutes a proportionate and rightly ordered love of one's homeland and government. It is surprising to find the strength of many people's conviction that patriotism is a non-negotiable article of faith and the suspicion with which they view those who doubt the moral strength of their government's claim on the allegiance of its citizens, particularly Christian citizens.

I am aware that making "critical remarks about America is a very American thing to do."[23] However, my criticisms of the US "war on terror" and Christian support or apathy for it have led some to question my allegiances. I do not love my country unconditionally as I love Christ, my family, or the church. These covenantal loves place an irrevocable claim on my life that a country with violently manipulated and arbitrarily drawn borders simply cannot. The deaths of military servicemen and women before me do not compel me to lay down my life for the survival of my country the same way that my love for the gospel or family would.

Statements like this are often met with derision and the accusation that the cost of this moral high ground is no less than the lives of soldiers who are willing to get their hands dirty in the ethically sordid business of war so that I can keep my conscience clean.[24] Can civilians, particularly nonviolent ones, contribute anything of worth to their nation's war discourse or are they, as a curmudgeonly old sergeant once remarked, "virgins studying sex, [with] nothing to go on but porno movies"?[25]

Nigel Biggar, professor of moral and pastoral theology at Oxford University, is certainly not a pacifist. However, he points out that lack of familiarity from at least one vantage point would disqualify everyone from all ethical decision making because "if moral judgements are to be made at all, then any judge must shoulder risks in making them, by entering territory where he is not entirely expert."[26] The academic lacks the politician's experience in public decision-making. However, the politician lacks the academic's time for mature reflection. While the ethicist is likely deficient in her understanding

---

23. Hauerwas, *War and the American Difference*, 13.

24. For a prominent and recent advance of this thesis, see Biggar, *In Defence of War* with which I engage in chapter 3. I must also readily confess that, save for the blood of Jesus, this pacifist no less than any soldier has both stained hands and conscience.

25. Grossman, *On Killing*, 2. Grossman concurs with the old sergeant. The studies of killing and sex are quite similar. The destructive and procreative acts are private and intimate encounters of immense intensity. The uninitiated may be able to learn some of the mechanics of sex or murder from a film, but the medium is incapable of conveying the intimacy and intensity of either act.

26. Biggar, *In Defence of War*, 333.

of the diplomatic relations between nations, the ambassador is just as likely to lack knowledge of the Christian just war tradition.

Oliver O'Donovan acknowledges private contributions to public political debates are limited because the civilian lacks the authority to decide or even offer precise policy recommendations. However, O'Donovan also notes there is significance in adding one's voice to the conversation. Following the lead of his teacher Paul Ramsey, O'Donovan encourages Christians to exemplify the utility of the just war proposal by employing it as a *tool* with which to help others think about their responsibilities before God and neighbors.[27]

It is difficult to deny that most American Christians understand their nation's role in world affairs to be generally benevolent. The fact that this book questions the moral integrity of this account of American security or the coercive means by which it must be safeguarded may lead some to call it un-American. That is an appraisal I can endure. However, one criticism I will not tolerate silently is that this work is anti-service member. Hauerwas has said the military is the last US institution that still has an honor code, and I am inclined to believe him. Many members of the armed services anguish over moral decisions from drone use to protecting foreign translators and their families. My quarrel will always be with the greedy imperial mechanisms that sacrifice its children on the altar of (in)security rather than with the pawns who are lost or maimed in the process. It is not insignificant that a disproportionate number of these soldiers are poor, uneducated, and various shades of brown.[28]

Perhaps it *is* audacious to question the manner in which our freedom is provided, but this is what Christian witnesses must do if we understand freedom to be a spiritual reality won by martyrdom suffered on a cross and not a political position won by violence perpetrated on our behalf by the government in the name of national security. Refusing to conflate these two disparate meanings of freedom makes it difficult to merely say "thank you" and go on about our lives or pick up a weapon and stand a post. As it has since its inception, baptism continues to complicate Christian understandings of citizenship since implicit in both baptism and citizenship are contradictory allegiances and obligations. As an American Christian, it is important to remember which is the noun—the genuine creature as eternal being—and which is the adjective—the ordinary description of a fairly recent phenomenon.

---

27. O'Donovan, *Just War Revisited*, 127.

28. Department of Defense Joint Advertising, Market Research and Studies, "Reports: Youth Poll 20."

It is an onerous chore for Christians to defend the US preoccupation with its national defense, particularly when our obsession with security imperils the lives of vulnerable neighbors. The subsequent faith Americans have in our military supremacy to guarantee our well-being and the premium we are willing to pay for it comes precariously close to idolatry. Can Christians inhabit the state, particularly the American security state, without being idolatrous? It may be feasible, but it necessitates the refashioning of how we understand patriotism and citizenship. It requires more witnesses to the gospel, in the original sense of the word as both martyr and truthful testifier before an unbelieving authority, and fewer blind partisans.

War inevitably provokes a robust moral reaction in those who experience it. It is a communal ethical praxis whose ends and means are determined by people with common objects of love and fear. Were this not so, there would no need to continually justify to soldiers and citizens that the war is being fought for morally sound reasons. American enthusiasm for the liberal use of war as a moral and political firewall is likely bolstered by the fact that we have not hosted a battle since the Civil War. For this reason, days like December 7, 1942, and September 11, 2001, live in infamy in the American conscience; they provided rare, eyewitness glimpses of the horror of the murder of innocents to achieve political ends.

The most poignant murder on 9/11 was that of the United States's sense of invincibility.[29] For there to be tangible objection against the nation-state's assumption that war is normative and even a communal good when held far away from its borders, the challenge must come from a community within the nation whose common objects of love and fear and moral practices are so profoundly different than those of the state that their witness in such a proximity to power would create enough friction to overcome the state's moral inertia and affect change. The church is the only community in America with the potential of playing the moral foil I have described. However, two centuries of collusion among self-interested governors and ministers have significantly blurred the distinctions between the church and nation's competing loves.

Stan Goff's analysis in *Borderline: Reflections on War, Sex, and Church* is helpful to Christians navigating these competing loves. After retiring from 30 years of military service and converting to Christianity, Goff came to understand nonviolence as a nonnegotiable part of Christian faith. He writes that among the many things that distinguish Christian citizens from those who would enthusiastically wield power or pay others to do so in

---

29. In this manner, 9/11 resembles the sack of Rome in 410. Though a relatively small loss of life and property, both attacks caused great fear and vulnerability to spread throughout the empires.

their stead to underwrite their safety is that Christians "are not called to be *powerful*. We are not called to be *respectable*. We are not called to be *patriotic*. We are not called to be *masculine*. We are called to be holy."[30] If Goff's elucidation of the unique way Christians inhabit the state is accurate, Jesus's disciples should be wary of petitioning the same golden calves we have fashioned from our treasure because in doing so we call down judgment upon ourselves.

---

30. Goff, *Borderline*, 400. Emphases in the original.

I

America as Unconventional Empire

America has never been an empire. We may be the only great power in history that had the chance and refused, preferring greatness to power and justice to glory. The story of America is the story of expanding liberty, an ever-widening circle, constantly growing to reach further and include more. Our nation's founding commitment is still our deepest commitment: In our world, and here at home, we will extend the frontiers of freedom.[1]

—George W. Bush

Whether or not the United States can rightly be considered an empire depends largely on how one frames the concept. If one understands empire to mean "classically imperial" of the variety the world knew from the first-century Roman through the twentieth-century British varieties, it is difficult to muster an unambiguous answer. In fact, it is this very notion of classical imperialism, which has been an anathema to the American conscience since the nation's founding, that President Bush is pushing back against in the epigraph above.

It would be beneficial to focus on what is intended when this book uses terms like empire and imperialism that are burdened by cumbersome historical baggage and fiercely contested meanings. Stephen Howe's definition of empire as a "large, composite, multi-ethnic or multinational political unit, usually created by conquest, and divided between a dominant center

1. Bush, "Acceptance Speech to the Republican National Convention."

and subordinate, sometimes far distant, peripheries"[2] is a suitably broad point of departure. In addition to the connotation of size, there is also a sense of absolute sovereignty and aspirations of universality.

If empire is the proper noun for this political reality, imperialism describes the processes and ideologies required to maintain the apparatuses of the empire. The mechanisms of imperialism are domination through and dissemination of military strength, economic control, and cultural influence. Classical empires are ones that fit this traditional understanding as framed above: those that expanded by conquering their neighbors or by colonizing people in faraway places. The lines that follow will argue that for over half of its history the US has acted much like classical empires. It ceased to do so only when the geopolitical landscape was indelibly reconfigured by the deep scars of World War II. The second great war was the catalyst that disassembled classical empires and colonialism and yet provided the stimulus and means the United States would need to metamorphosize into an "unconventional empire." It maintained the classically imperial earmarks of military, economic, and cultural coercion, but it did so in more subtle and untraditional ways.

The US founding fathers helped lead thirteen colonies in the first successful anti-colonial revolution, and they were not eager to replicate the practice by entangling their fledgling nation in the monarchical entrapments of foreign conquest. John Quincy Adams wrote that America would always encourage those who pursue the freedom to live independently according to the consent of the governed, but it would not go abroad "in search of monsters to destroy" to guarantee the freedom and liberty of any people but its own.[3] This isolationist heritage was developed so the US would not become inextricably ensconced in one freedom fight after another. Essentially the framers of the constitution sought to resist the temptation of imperial overstretch.

However, the US desire for isolation from global conflicts was also accompanied by an expansionist spirit. The US added settlers and territory at an exponential rate. The ill-fated Roanoke Colony notwithstanding, the British colonization of the Americas began in 1607 with nearly 100 settlers inhabiting a 1-acre fort at Jamestown. On the eve of the revolutionary war in 1775, 2.5 million colonists were living on 430,000 square miles (275.2 million acres) of land in the new world. After winning its independence, Americans would fight and buy (usually in that order) their way across the continent

---

2. Howe, *Empire*, 30.

3. Adams, "She Goes Not Abroad in Search of Monsters to Destroy," cited in Immerman, *Empire for Liberty*, 88.

until it had secured all of what is now the continental United States by 1853 with an estimated residential population of about 23.2 million at the time.[4] The American ethos of moral and racial superiority justified its telos to rule from coast to coast, even if doing so necessitated the US renege on numerous treaties with Native Americans, forcing the land's original inhabitants to relocate or assimilate.[5] This is also a classically imperial trope.

The settlers's realization of their "manifest destiny" to inhabit the land from shore to shore often followed a familiar script. American settlers would move into foreign-owned territory with the permission of the local sovereign. As the settlers encroached farther and farther into foreign lands, conflicts with the natives unsurprisingly developed. The settlers would then appeal to the US military to mount an armed defense and do what the local rulers were ostensibly unable or unwilling to do—protect the American settlers from the natives. Inevitably a power struggle would ensue for control of the land. Once the superior American military gained the upper hand the conflict was usually resolved through a lopsided real-estate transaction skewed heavily in the Americans' favor.

---

4. United States Census Bureau, *Pop Culture: 1850*.

5. The Native Americans' experience was much different than their European settler neighbors. Rather than a population boom, natives saw their numbers decline by 90 percent from an estimated five million before Europeans arrived to a mere half million by 1800. Their lands disappeared just as quickly as their people. Native Americans were pushed further and further west to an ill-defined "Indian Territory" with fluid and diminishing boundaries until the little land that remained was absorbed by the state of Oklahoma. For a fuller account of the Native Americans' plight during westward expansion, see Immerwahr, *How to Hide an Empire*, 36–45.

Table 1: Buying an Empire: Major American Territorial Acquisitions, 1803–1898[6]

Date	Treaty or Act	Property	Acquired from	Total Area (Acres)	Price ($)	Price per Acre (Cents)
1803	Louisiana Purchase	Louisiana	France	559,513,600	15,000,000	3
1819	Adams-Onis Treaty	East Florida	Spain	46,144,640	15,000,000	33
1846	Oregon Treaty	Pacific Northwest south of 49th parallel	Great Britain	192,000,000	–	0
1848	Guadalupe-Hidalgo	Texas, California, New Mexico etc.	Mexico	336,660,960	15,000,000 +5,000,000	6
1850	Texas Cession	New Mexico	Texas	78,926,720	10,000,000	13
1853	Gadsden Purchase	Southern Arizona, New Mexican border	Mexico	18,988,800	10,000,000	53
1867	Alaska Purchase	Alaska	Russia	375,296,000	7,200,000	2
1898	Treaty of Paris	Philippines	Spain	74,112,000	20,000,000	27

The manner in which the Republic came to occupy what is now the continental US is but one example of why the American imperial question is a challenging one. At this point in its history, was the US an empire in the traditional sense of the word? The US militarily, financially, and diplomatically engaged with foreign powers to enlarge its territory, but does the fact that the acquired land was bordering the republic's original boundaries rather than half a world away make the means of acquisition less imperial? These questions are further encumbered by the clear reality that the Native people were unquestionably being governed *without* their consent. Does the

6. Richard B. Morris, ed., *Encyclopedia of American History*, 599; Charles Arnold Baker, *The Companion to British History*; from *Colossus: The Price of America's Empire* by Niall Ferguson. Used by permission of Penguin Press, an imprint of Penguin Publishing Group, a division of Penguin Random House LLC. All rights reserved.

fact that it occurred in a neighboring territory rather than a distant colony make it less imperial? The US treatment of the Native peoples and the manner it acquired territory were the epitome of imperial, yet it does not seem fitting to call 1850s America a fully-fledged empire. It had the demeanor and adolescent trappings of an empire but was still shy with respect to the breadth of its domain. However, as the nineteenth century drew to a close the US would replicate this pattern of military and fiscal manipulation away from its shores on the islands of Hawaii, Puerto Rico, Cuba, and the Philippines, making it difficult to continue to equivocate on the imperial question.

The "war on terror" has caused many to revisit the imperial question regarding the United States. Since September 11, the manner in which the US has waged the "war on terror" has provided plenty of fodder to keep publishers churning out critiques as well as apologias for American imperialism, with some loathe to identify the US as an empire and others who do so quite facilely.[7] Whether one calls it an empire, a hegemon, or the last remaining superpower, these are all pseudonyms for a distinct political *modus operandi*.

Classical Empire may have breathed its last with the dismantling of the British Empire after World War II, nonetheless what Augustine called the "lust to dominate" continued to flourish as malignantly and intensely as ever in Washington and Moscow. Though they were not burdened by an imperial moniker, their nuclearly charged DNA was unmistakably imperial. The Cold War between the US and the Soviet Union would kindle many hot conflicts in smaller nations as the two juggernauts jockeyed for global supremacy. It was during this period that the US pivoted from its classically imperial predilections to what can most appropriately be characterized as an "unconventional empire."

I call it unconventional, but it is the only empire that could survive in the aftermath of World War II. Just as racism in America did not die with the Civil Rights Act of 1964 but was pushed underground and took on subtler means, World War II forced imperialism to evolve into more discrete and subversive forms since blatant colonialism and flagrant transgressions of borders remained the most egregious violations of international law that would provoke a military response from the global community.

This chapter will cover the United States' burgeoning experimentation with classical imperialism at the twilight of the nineteenth century. This is followed by instances of the US's metamorphosis into an unconventional empire during the Cold War and "war on terror."

---

7. In his offering on American imperialism, Peter Leithart sardonically conjectures, "Publishers seemed to have discovered that adding 'empire' to a title will pique interest in an otherwise unrelated book." Leithart, *Between Babel and Beast*, ix.

Histories are necessarily selective by nature, and this chapter is no exception. These snapshots of US history have been chosen for two reasons: 1) the stories are widely unknown by many Americans because the events are not taught in many schools, and 2) the stories challenge the overwhelmingly positive American self-perception as global defender of freedom and democracy by casting US policies and practices in a critical and unflattering light. Napoleon may have accurately called history a "set of agreed upon lies,"[8] but the accounts given below do not resonate with the US history upon which many of its citizens agree. I have purposefully avoided rehashing at any substantial length the US's involvement in either World War because these wars are thoroughly trodden territory for most Americans. This chapter will focus on some of the United States' more obscure history to make the concept of an American empire more plausible.

1893—Hawaii

Ask almost any American why the United States entered War World II and they will likely respond "the Japanese bombing of Pearl Harbor."[9] However, few are able to answer the seldom asked, yet crucial, follow-up question: Why did the United States have a military base on an island nearly 2,500 miles from the US mainland and not one of its states in the first place?

With its mainland secured by 1853, the US looked for other ways to enlarge its sphere of economic influence. John Stevens, the US Ambassador to Hawaii, led a group of wealthy businessmen and sugar plantation owners in a *coup d'état* against Hawaiian Queen Liliuokalani after she expressed her intention to restrict voting rights to native Hawaiians. The white minority[10] controlled 80 percent of Hawaii's arable land with their sugar plantations and were leery of the possible repercussions representative democracy would have on their business interests. Foreign-owned sugar plantations were ubiquitous for the same reason 120 US Marines were immediately available to help "protect American life and property" during the coup.

In 1876, Queen Liliuokalani's brother and predecessor, King Kalakaua, had been duped into signing the "Reciprocity Treaty" guaranteeing

---

8. De Las Cases, *Napoleon at Saint Helena*, Vol. 4/7, 250–52.

9. During the siege, Lt. Howell M. Forge, the chaplain aboard the USS New Orleans, encouraged the crew members to keep up the fight by shouting, "Praise the Lord and pass the ammunition!" Naturally, the line was turned into a hit song, only finishing behind Bing Crosby's "White Christmas" on 1942's American music charts—thus completing its representation of the Holy American Trinity of God, guns, and glory.

10. According to the 1890 census there were 40,612 native Hawaiians, 27,391 Chinese and Japanese laborers, and 6,220 foreign born whites. Kinzer, *Overthrow*, 18.

the US exclusive rights to maintain commercial and military bases on the islands in exchange for removing the high tariffs on Hawaiian sugar imports. Reciprocity proved to be a profound misnomer as the only beneficiaries were the American military and white plantation owners. By any honest metric, Hawaii was annexed economically long before it became a US state.[11] When American commercial interests were threatened by democracy, the US military was there to subvert the latter to protect the former. When a government's soldiers are used to undermine the will of a foreign majority to benefit a few of its own citizens, it is the embodiment of classic imperialism. The scene that played out in Hawaii was not an aberration but the new normal for US foreign policy. Beginning at the turn of the twentieth century, the United States would use its military to secure and leverage favorable market conditions in foreign lands.

1898—Cuba

Although the US had discussed various ways (including purchasing) to wrest Cuba away from Spanish control as early as 1850, no tangible progress was made until American troops arrived on the island to aid Cuban rebels in their fight against their colonial rulers.[12] The US quickly routed Spain and acquired Guam, Puerto Rico, and the Philippines from Spain for its

---

11. Though Hawaii was not yet a state, the Japanese attack on Pearl Harbor provided the iron-clad provocation for America's entry into World War II. US trade with China had grown so rapidly in the nineteenth century that the US felt the need to expand its presence in the South Pacific to sure up trade routes. The US used its intimidating Navy to forcefully open ports in Fiji, Samoa, the Marshall Islands, and Japan in order to further leverage its trade with China. These trading posts were also useful refueling stations when the US went to war in the Philippines at the end of the nineteenth century.

12. This is merely the first chapter in a long, complicated history between Cuba and the United States—a history that includes the fact that Fidel Castro failed to overthrow Cuban President Fulgencio Batista until the US government withdrew its military support from the Batista regime in 1959. Though Batista was a corrupt and repressive dictator, he was firmly anti-Communist and pro-American business, making him the ideal American shill. Before Batista fled, US companies owned nearly half of Cuba's sugar plantations and the majority of its cattle ranches, mines, and utilities—attributes that made him more than tolerable from Uncle Sam's perspective. Less than a year after seizing power, Castro nationalized all US businesses in Cuba without compensation. The US responded with the first iteration of its trade embargo, a failed invasion at the Bay of Pigs by 1,400 CIA trained Cuban expatriates, and multiple plans to assassinate Castro under the code name "Operation Mongoose." As the US and Cuba alienated each other, Havana grew closer to Moscow leading to the precipice of nuclear war during the Cuban missile crisis in 1962.

troubles. Spain renounced its claim to Cuba and received $20 million as compensation for the Philippines.

Imagine the Cubans' surprise when their American liberators refused to leave.[13] The rebels were dejected because they had certainly not fought for nearly half a century to replace one colonial master with another. The Platt Amendment passed in 1901 established the terms under which the United States would end its military occupation of the island. The first condition was that Cuba would not enter into any international treaty that would compromise its independence or allow foreign powers to use its land for military purposes. The US also reserved the right to intervene in Cuban affairs to defend Cuban independence and to maintain "a government adequate for the protection of life, property, and individual liberty."[14]

Another clause required the Cuban government to sell or lease land to the United States for naval stations.[15] It is not overly cynical to question the hypocrisy of the US's strong arming of Cuba to denounce foreign treaties and military occupation by imposing a treaty with the caveat that allowed the US to do both of these very acts the treaty forbade. The US's State Department did not even bother to put a charitable gloss on its occupation of Cuba, stating that, "The rationale behind the Platt Amendment was straightforward. The United States Government had intervened in Cuba to safeguard its significant commercial interests on the island in the wake of Spain's inability to preserve law and order."[16] The events in Cuba were the first confirmation that the conflation of commercial and military interests seen in the Hawaiian coup had not been an anomaly. The *modus operandi* of the US government moving forward, like the empires that had preceded it, would be to use its military strength to bolster its fiscal interests by forcing open and manipulating foreign markets. The next American imperial excursion would be in yet another island nation, however this one was quite literally half a world away.

---

13. Niall Ferguson argues that American distaste for occupying and ruling foreign lands makes the US *insufficiently* imperial. While America excels at changing regimes, it does not adequately maintain them as did the British. Ferguson, *Colossus*, VIII/1.

14. Platt, "Milestones: 1899-1913."

15. Hence the US military has not left Guantanamo Bay since it first arrived in 1898. Guantanamo is a geopolitical unicorn since, "it is the only place where the US military forcefully occupies a foreign land on an open-ended basis, against the wishes of the host nation." Miroff, *Why the US Base at Cuba's Guantanamo Bay Is Probably Doomed*.

16. Platt, "Milestones:1899-1913." The US relinquished its right to intervene in Cuban affairs in 1934 but maintains the military base much to the chagrin of the Cuban government. Each month, the US sends Cuba a check for the base's rent, though the Castros have refused to cash them.

1899—The Philippines

Filipino nationalists, like their Cuban counterparts, mistakenly thought they had struggled to secure their independence, not merely affect the emergence of a new colonial ruler. Unlike Cuba however, the Philippines was not fortunate enough to receive conditions under which the American military would end its occupation. The US Congress voted instead to annex the Philippines, given its proximity to Asian commercial markets, perceived (or projected) lack of Filipino ability to self-govern, and the ever increasing American paranoia that if it did not guide a country's decision making the Soviet Union would.

The war[17] that ensued saw the Filipino fighters deploy guerrilla tactics in an attempt to mitigate the advantage of the superiorly trained and equipped American military. According to the US Department of State, 200,000 Filipino civilians died from violence, disease, or famine in just three years of conflict.[18] The US burned villages and re-concentrated their residents. Both sides tortured suspected enemy collaborators. In 1916, the US promised Filipinos independence it would not grant them until three decades later. The Philippine-American War was but a brief preview of a much lengthier and deadlier war just 910 miles west across the South China Sea in Vietnam, in which the US would not fare nearly as well. The US, like many empires before it, killed masses of foreigners with no greater justification than the American desire to create a more proximate trading post to Asian markets.

1904—The Monroe Doctrine and Roosevelt Corollary

In 1823, President James Monroe presented Congress with what would become the cornerstone of official US foreign policy for some time to come. The Monroe Doctrine maintained three core tenets: separate spheres of influence for Europe and the Americas, non-colonization, and non-intervention. When wed to the ideology of "Manifest Destiny" and administered through the US's increasing economic and military influence, the Monroe

---

17. Even the description of it as a war was debated since "Americans tended to refer to the ensuing conflict as an 'insurrection' rather than acknowledge the Filipinos' contention that they were fighting to ward off a foreign invader.'" US Department of State, *Philippine-American War*.

18. US Department of State, *Philippine-American War*.

Doctrine provided the auspices for protecting unfettered US expansion throughout the Western Hemisphere.

Soon after, another president created a loophole that obliged the US to intervene under certain "exceptional circumstances." The Roosevelt Corollary was not an extension of the Monroe Doctrine as much as it was a holistic inversion of it. Theodore Roosevelt explained the corollary in the following manner. If countries were socially responsible and politically decent neighbors in the Americas, they "need fear no interference from the United States."[19] However, flagrant or chronic wrongdoing, whether domestic or international, would provide the US with a justification for intervention as it assumed international policing power in the Western Hemisphere.

Roosevelt's Corollary was a repudiation of the Monroe Doctrine that would authorize the United States' "search abroad for monsters to destroy" that Adams had admonished the young republic against. The US would avail itself of "exceptional cases to act" in Cuba, Haiti, Nicaragua, and the Dominican Republic.

Current US foreign policy and prevailing public opinion continue to resonate with Roosevelt's corollary. The conspicuous difference in the twenty-first century finds the US exercising its international police prerogative over a jurisdiction substantially larger than the Western Hemisphere wherever it deems nations to be "poor stewards" of their independence or perceives American interests are threatened. When a country unilaterally anoints itself the reluctant international judge, arbiter, and law enforcement arm among nations it has assumed a distinctively imperial disposition.

1947—The Truman Doctrine

President Truman augmented Roosevelt's Corollary as America's predilection to endure as global guardian was intensely bolstered by victories in two world wars and the looming specter of nuclear conflict with the Soviet Union. The Truman Doctrine obliged the US to assist politically, economically, and militarily any democracy threatened by communism. This promise was less demure and more forthright than Roosevelt's pledge that the US would only grudgingly be provoked to act by the most brazen of injustices. The National Security Act of 1947 followed four months later and outlined the forms the United States assistance would take.

The act restructured the US armed forces and created the National Security Council (NSC) and Central Intelligence Agency (CIA). Comprised of the President, Vice President, Secretary of State, Secretary of Defense,

---

19. Roosevelt, "Transcript to Theodore Roosevelt's Corollary."

Chairman of the Joint Chiefs of Staff, and director of the CIA, the NSC became the President's principal forum for deliberating foreign policy and national security issues. The chief onus of the NSC was to appraise US military objectives, commitments, and liabilities and make recommendations to the President based upon their findings.

One of its earliest recommendations was NSC 10/2, which declared "in the interests of world peace and US national security, the overt foreign activities of the US government must be supplemented by covert operations."[20] The directive granted the CIA the autonomy with which to carry out these covert operations, which it described as:

> [A]ll activities . . . which are conducted or sponsored by this Government against hostile foreign states or groups or in support of friendly foreign states or groups but which are so planned and executed that any US Government responsibility for them is not evident to unauthorized persons and that if uncovered the US Government can plausibly disclaim any responsibility for them. Specifically, such operations shall include any covert activities related to: propaganda, economic warfare; preventive direct action, including sabotage, anti-sabotage, demolition and evacuation measures; subversion against hostile states, including assistance to underground resistance movements, guerrillas and refugee liberation groups, and support of indigenous anti-communist elements in threatened countries of the free world.[21]

---

20. US Department of the State, "Foreign Relations of the United States, 1945–1950."

21. US Department of the State, "Foreign Relations of the United States, 1945–1950." NSC 10/2 exemplified the US penchant for enacting consequentialist policies, particularly when it defined its military campaigns as struggles between "good" and "evil"—as it did in the Cold War and would again in the "war against terror." The Lieber Code, signed by President Lincoln at the height of the Civil War, provided the historical precedent for authorizing legally and morally dubious means of warfare if they enhanced the likelihood of victory. Ostensibly, the document was written to reign in unjust practices that had become commonplace in the war. However, any constraints the law placed on generals and soldiers were hamstrung by the caveat that sanctioned the circumvention of laws due to "military necessity." This exception, vaguely delimited as "that which is indispensable for securing the ends of the war," could outflank any moral criticism of questionable practices in war if the tactics were indispensable to victory. Stan Goff, a US special operations sergeant who became a pacifist upon his conversion to Christianity, observed that the Lieber Code was the elastic boundary that was stretched to cover any multitude of transgressions. Inevitably it became, "the loophole through which Sherman would ravage Southern farms in 1864, and through which twenty-two thousand Dresden civilians would be firebombed to death in 1944, and through which fell two atomic bombs on Japanese cities." Goff, *Borderline*, 168. The Lieber Code like other attempts to write ethical warfare into law tacitly formalized the belief that war could either be just *or* effective but not both.

NSC 10/2 was the origin of the Cold War policy of "plausible deniability"—the US attempt to imperceptibly orchestrate the outcomes of global affairs in a profitable manner for American interests.[22] It also represents the moment the US pivoted from openly classical imperial expressions to surreptitiously unconventional imperial ones.

This memo gave political consent to civil servants to resort to illicit behaviors like abductions, domestic surveillance, infiltration of anti-war movements, tapping journalists' phones, and sub-contracting assassinations of political enemies to the Mafia. Anonymity was a clear prerequisite for the execution of such nefarious means of statecraft as they were opposed to America's self-perception of global standard-bearer of freedom and liberty. What the Truman administration had created was an organization replete with the President's blessing to covertly carry out reprehensible war crimes with complete impunity. Consider the CIA's manual on political assassinations as an example:

> Murder is not morally justifiable. Self-defense may be argued if the victim has knowledge which may destroy the resistance organization if divulged. Assassination of persons responsible for atrocities or reprisals may be regarded as just punishment. Killing a political leader whose burgeoning career is a clear and present danger to the cause of freedom may be held necessary. But assassination can seldom be employed with a clear conscience. Persons who are morally squeamish should not attempt it.[23]

---

22. James Douglas called NSC 10/2 the creation of a Frankenstein monster because it often required the CIA to act without the oversight of other branches of the government to maintain plausible deniability. Douglas argues that an agency willing to assassinate foreign leaders abroad and disavow any involvement to secure its objectives would have little aversion to performing similar duties at home. Douglas has argued that the CIA was responsible for the murders of John F. Kennedy, Robert Kennedy, Martin Luther King Jr., and Malcolm X. Whether one agrees with Douglas's thesis or not, the treachery to which the CIA has admitted committing abroad should at least raise questions of its plausible culpability at home. See Douglas, *JFK and the Unspeakable*.

23. Central Intelligence Agency, "CIA and Assassinations." This CIA file is a nineteen-page training manual for assassins. It describes the rationale, techniques, tools, and procedures employed in political killing in lurid detail: "[T]he simplest local tools are often much the most efficient means of assassination. A hammer, axe, wrench, screwdriver, fire poker, kitchen knife, lamp stand, or anything hard, heavy and handy will suffice. A length of rope or wire or a belt will do if the assassin is strong and agile. All such improvised weapons have the important advantage of availability and apparent innocence. The obviously lethal machine gun failed to kill Trotsky where an item of sporting goods succeeded." It was declassified along with other files from Operation PBSUCCESS—the CIA's code name for its covert action in 1954 to overthrow the democratically elected president of Guatemala Jacobo Arbenz.

The US's defense of liberty and freedom metastasized to preemptive murder under the auspices of politically expedient causes. That this information is widely available to those who seek to learn US history seems to have engendered little to no public "moral squeamishness" at all.

The Truman Doctrine merely formalized what had been the *de facto* practice since at least the turn of the twentieth century—the US had become a full-fledged empire. Why identify the Truman doctrine as the imperial Rubicon? Previously the US had paid lip service to moral standards in its self-assumed role of international police. NSC 10/2 is written proof that the US would advance its self-interests by *any* means necessary. This is the dark heart of the imperial lust to dominate. While the Truman Doctrine pledged to overtly fight communism from spreading to more countries, NSC 10/2 sought to clandestinely and decapitate heads of states that were accused of having capitulated to Moscow's influence. The US began to exercise this newfound moral flexibility almost immediately.

1953—Iran

One of the earliest applications of NSC 10/2 occurred in Iran. From 1901 until the election of Prime Minister Mohammad Mossadegh in 1951, the British-owned Anglo-Iranian Oil Company, the predecessor of British Petroleum, held a monopoly over every aspect of oil production in Iran. Iran retained a paltry 16 percent of the revenue from the sale of its oil.

Mossadegh sought to nationalize the oil industry while compensating Britain for its investment in building Iran's oil infrastructure. The loss of British dividends alone did not sufficiently warrant the US's intervention. Unfortunately for Mossadegh, Secretary of State John Dulles and his brother Allen, the director of the CIA, shared two correlated and mutually reinforcing lifelong obsessions, "fighting Communism and protecting the rights of multinational corporations."[24] Together the Dulles brothers convinced a reticent President Eisenhower that Mossadegh's failure would create a political vacuum that would open the door wide for Communist control of the Middle East and its oil, which accounted for 60 percent of the world's proven crude oil reserves.

To preempt this potential catastrophe, the Dulles brothers sought to expedite and control the parameters of the Iranian Prime Minister's removal from power by affecting the collapse of his government through the aforementioned legal, or quasi-legal, methods and replacing him with a head of state who was more amenable to Western political and economic meddling

---

24. Kinzer, *Overthrow*, 122.

in Iran.[25] The Dulles brothers found a willing co-conspirator in the Shah Mohammed Reza Pahlavi who was no fan of Mossadegh. Pahlavi had clashed with the Prime Minister over nationalizing oil production and felt increasingly marginalized into being little more than a figurehead by Mossadegh. The animosity between the two men led Mossadegh to resign in July of 1952 only to have Pahlavi reinstate him three days later after riots ensued.

In March of 1953, the NSC resolved to funnel $1 million through the CIA station in Tehran for the express purpose of organizing a coup against Mossadegh. This influx of US cash into Iran's capitol was used to bribe nearly anyone with their hands out. The press, military generals, Islamic preachers, protestors, and other opinion leaders were placed on the US's payroll to "create, extend and enhance public hostility and distrust and fear of Mossadegh and his government."[26] The money was also used to hire unsavory characters to carry out attacks on religious figures and other prominent Iranians under the guise that the henchmen were acting at the behest of Mossadegh. Additional funds were used to fund waves of protests against Mossadegh. Religious leaders on the CIA's payroll gave sermons accusing Mossadegh of being an atheist, Jew, or infidel.

The bribes were used to influence journalists in both Iran and the United States. However, the lies they wrote were unique to their respective contexts. The Iranian newspapers printed articles and drew cartoons depicting the Prime Minister as a homosexual and British puppet while American papers called him a Communist dictator. An additional $11,000 per week was earmarked to bribe members of the Iranian parliament who not only withdrew their support from Mossadegh but also denounced him with wildly fabricated accusations. By August, the US-sown chaos would come to fruition as the Shah signed royal decrees dismissing Mossadegh from his position and installing retired general Fazlollah Zahedi in his stead.

The US's overthrow of the only democratically elected government in Iranian history and subsequent support[27] of the Shah's repressive regime

---

25. The quotation and summary of the US involvement in the coup are from an internal CIA history declassified in 2013. Central Intelligence Agency, *National Security Archive*. More surprising than the US government's confirmation of its role in the plot that many had long suspected was how imperceptible the American public's response to its government's confession was. The admission hardly registered in the American new's cycle. There was little to no embarrassment, outrage, or apology.

26. Kinzer, *Overthrow*, 122.

27. By the time Richard Nixon arrived in the Oval Office in 1969, Iran was already the largest purchaser of American-manufactured weapons. When Nixon signed an arms agreement with Tehran in 1972, the Shah was given a blank check to purchase any quantity of every non-nuclear US weapons system he desired. The Shah's desire and oil-backed purchasing power were indeed great. After the arms agreements, the Shah's

sowed the seeds from which the Islamic revolution would emerge in 1979.[28] The prognosticators at the State Department and CIA had thoroughly misread the Iranian geopolitical situation; it was Iranian nationalism, rather than Soviet Communism, that would arrest the US's imperial interests in the country.

1954—Guatemala

Jacobo Arbenz was elected president of Guatemala in 1950. His nationalistic socio-economic reforms did little to ingratiate himself to the US. Arbenz's most provocative policy from Washington's perspective was his agrarian reform that legalized the expropriation of uncultivated land for redistribution among the landless poor. The previous landowners were compensated with government bonds equal to the taxable value of the land. Unsurprisingly, the reform was popular among Guatemalans as one and a half million acres were given to roughly one hundred thousand families. However, the American-owned United Fruit Company (UFC) was less than enamored with the amendment. The government had seized nearly 40 percent (210,000 acres) of UFC's uncultivated land and offered the company $2.99 per acre in recompense based on the company's tax filings. Within a month, the US State Department sent a letter of protest claiming the land was more properly valued at $75 per acre. This swift and robust intercession by the US government on behalf of American business was no accident of history.

The aforementioned Dulles brothers had a great deal of conflicting interests in Guatemala. Former UFC president, Allen Dulles remained on the company's board of directors when he became the director of the CIA. John Dulles was a partner in the law firm that negotiated the contract between the UFC and Guatemala and remained on the company's payroll when he was confirmed as Secretary of State. Emboldened by their success in Iran, the Dulles brothers followed a nearly identical script in Guatemala.

After Arbenz's government refused to pay the State Department's inflated valuation for UFC's holdings in the country, President Truman's successor, Dwight Eisenhower, authorized "Operation PBSUCCESS," which allocated $2.7 million to the CIA to pursue "psychological warfare, political

---

purchases of US weapons rose 10-fold annually, consuming as much of 80 percent of Iran's oil revenue—a fact that did not endear him to all but the wealthiest Iranians. See McGlinchey, "Richard Nixon's Road to Tehran."

28. Stephen Kinzer argues that the consanguinity of 1953's coup and 1979's Islamic revolution serve as an admonition that the violent reshaping of Iran to suit US interests may have affected the opposite result—gravely undermining American national security. See Kinzer, *All the Shah's Men.*

action, and subversion"[29] in Guatemala. As they had with Mossadegh in Iran, the Dulles brothers had convinced the President that toppling the democratically elected leader was a matter of international security because the country was vulnerable to Communist influence.

Two years into Arbenz's tenure, Truman had approved the CIA's plan to replace Arbenz's government by supporting a military junta led by Carlos Castillo Armas. Despite the support of Nicaragua, Venezuela, and the Dominican Republic[30] the NSC was skeptical of the probability of success and terminated its plan. However, the CIA's historical analysis of its role in the coup, "sanitized for release" in 1997, disclosed that "until the day that Arbenz resigned in June 1954 the option of assassination was still being considered."[31]

The following day, John Foster Dulles delivered the State Department's official analysis of the events in Guatemala.[32] Dulles began by alleging that Soviet despotism's intrusion in Guatemala had challenged the United States' "first and foremost foreign policy," the Monroe Doctrine. Despite providing prevarications for US intervention, he was silent on the US involvement in Guatemala. He obscured the US support for the military junta by praising the Guatemalan "patriots" who single-handedly spoiled "the evil purposes of the Kremlin"—to secure an ideological beachhead in their country from which the Soviets would advance Communism throughout the Western Hemisphere. Dulles further accused Arbenz of serving the "Communist lust for power"[33] by suppressing dissent through

---

29. US psychological warfare included sending leading Communists death threats, coffins, hangmen's nooses, fake bombs, as well as painting slogans like "Here lives a spy" or "Only 5 days to live" on their homes.

30. The United Fruit Company expressed its gratitude to Uncle Sam by retrofitting one of its freighters to smuggle weapons to the rebels under the guise of agricultural equipment.

31. Haines, "CIA and Guatemala Assassination Proposals." The CIA, in conjunction with Armas, had compiled lists of political adversaries who would be disposed of during the operation. One group would be removed through "executive action" (a trite government euphemism for murder), and the other group would be imprisoned or exiled. The analysis also maintains that the CIA never implemented the assassination strategy, but since both lists were declassified with the targets' names redacted, there is no way to verify this claim.

32. Dulles, "Radio and Television Address." The following quotes are from the same source. For an illuminating analysis of the Dulles brothers formative roles in early US Cold War strategies, see Kinzer, *The Brothers*.

33. The phrase "lust for power" (*libido dominandi*) originated in Augustine's *City of God* and will feature prominently in the following chapter's discussion of his assessment of empire. Dulles' allusion is likely intentional since he was an elder in the Presbyterian Church and on the board of directors of Union Theological Seminary. Before he chose

"mass arrests, suppression of constitutional guarantees, killing opposition leaders, and other brutal tactics normally employed by communism to secure the consolidation of power." Purportedly Dulles was able to keep a straight face while he publicly accused Arbenz of brazenly employing the same means to secure the consolidation of his power that the US was clandestinely utilizing to maintain its own.

Dulles denigrated critics who said the United States' sole priority was securing its business interests in Guatemala. He would reply that "Communist imperialism," not American capitalism, was the debilitating cancer in Guatemala that, if not excised, would rapidly metastasize throughout the Americas. Dulles dismissed the United Fruit Company's role as quickly as he had acknowledged it by claiming that it was, "relatively unimportant" in light of the overriding concern: "namely the endangering by international communism of the peace and security of this hemisphere."

Dulles concluded that the courage of loyal Guatemalans had overcome terrorism, violence, and insuperable odds to add "a new and glorious chapter to the already great tradition of the American States." Save for the restoration of the United Fruit Company's land that guaranteed Guatemala's continued economic subservience, the alleged "new and glorious chapter" had not gone as the CIA planned. Armas, whom the CIA had cast as its liberating protagonist, disenfranchised the illiterate (two thirds of the voting population), banned all political parties, annulled the constitution, and declared that he held exclusive executive and legislative authority.

The CIA's internal history of Operation PBSUCCESS explained why the US could not prevent the proxies it installed for leftist heads of state from drifting brutally to the far right. The US was so too heavily invested in Armas's success to allow him to fail, a fact of which he was well aware. In Guatemala, "US officials learned a lesson they would relearn in Vietnam, Iran, [Chile], and other countries: intervention usually produces 'allies' that are stubborn, aid hungry and corrupt."[34]

Armas used the powers he bestowed upon himself to seize and kill hundreds of Guatemalans he deemed enemies of the state before he was assassinated by his palace guard in 1957. The US legacy in Guatemala is that of a foreign usurper that turned a young democracy into the first of many successive military regimes that would go on to murder over one hundred thousand civilians between 1954 and 1990. As it had in Iran, the

---

to study law at Princeton University, Dulles had planned to enter into the clergy as his father had.

34. Cullather, "Operation PBSUCESS," 91. The name of the third country was redacted in the CIA's declassified documents. For reasons that will become apparent below, I believe Chile to be the redacted nation.

US secured its short-term objective at the expense of sabotaging its long-term one: the US had secured the removal of Jacobo Arbenz by ultimately undermining the prospects of producing a stable Guatemala impervious to Communist influence.

1954–1963—Vietnam

The convoluted political developments in Vietnam after World War II further belied the United States' priorities. Within hours of Japan's formal surrender, Vietnam declared its independence from France. Instead of bolstering Vietnam's claim to liberty, the US backed France's attempt to reassert its colonial authority over Vietnam. Although the US refused to recognize Vietnam's independence, the US had already unwittingly contributed to it by equipping and training the *Viet Minh* to expel the country's common enemy Japan. The *Viet Minh* would use their American resources to evict America's ally France and subsequently the Americans themselves to gain independence for Vietnam thirty years after the end of World War II.[35]

Despite the US support of the French effort,[36] the French withdrew from Vietnam in 1954. The Geneva Accords divided Vietnam along the 17th parallel for two years until an election could be held to reunify the country. The US faced two unsavory options: either allow the whole of Vietnam to become communist under the likely election of Ho Chi Minh or pick up the French burden of resistance to the *Viet Minh*. Fearing that the "Communist domino effect" would bring southeast Asia, from Japan to the Suez Canal, under Communist influence, the US threw its support behind Ngo Dinh Diem as president of South Vietnam.

Though supporting Diem was replete with its own set of problems, the US had no alternatives for a surrogate leader. The US propped him up despite the fact that he lacked a popular base, was a Catholic in a 90 percent Buddhist country, appointed venal family members to high offices, and showed little interest in the daily work of government. Stephen Kinzer assessed America's Vietnam dilemma in this way, "As in so many other countries, the Americans looked in South Vietnam for a leader who would be a

---

35. The scenario would be repeated in Afghanistan in the 80s as the US armed and trained the *mujahideen* to expel the Soviets—an aim which it accomplished, while introducing conditions fertile for reaping the unanticipated fruit that elements of the *mujahideen* would become *al Qaeda*.

36. At the urging of Secretary of State John Dulles, the US had committed $400 million to the French in late 1953 to persuade it to stay the course in Vietnam. Central Intelligence Agency, *CIA and the House of NGO*.

crowd-pleasing nationalist and also do what Washington wished, only to discover that they could not have both."[37]

In 1964, as it became increasingly clear that Diem was neither popular among his people nor effective at achieving US objectives in Vietnam, the Kennedy administration removed its protective hand from Diem. The suspension of a $14 million loan to South Vietnam and Kennedy's statement in an interview with Walter Cronkite that the war could not be won without changes in policies and personnel gave the conspirators the implicit green light they needed to initiate their coup. Having outlived his usefulness to the US, "the first Catholic ever to become a Vietnamese chief of state was dead, assassinated because of a policy authorized by the first American Catholic president."[38] The US intervention in Vietnam would languish on for nearly another decade after this before the US would concede its first military defeat. However, like the traditional empires it had replaced, the United States did not let setbacks in one foreign frontier deter it from exploring others.

1963—Chile

While still embroiled in an unwinnable war in Vietnam, the US government and business interests found another common enemy in Chile's President-elect Salvador Allende. Like Armas had in Guatemala, Allende promised to nationalize American-owned companies that dominated his country's economy.[39] The CIA had been successfully resisting an Allende presidency for the better part a decade by funding his opponents in previous elections, but its intervention in 1970 was not influential enough to prevent the socialist's election.

Having failed to keep Allende from winning the election, the CIA sought to enact a pre-emptive coup to keep him from assuming office. US officials knew any successful coup attempt would require the binding of Army Commander Rene Schneider, who felt deeply that the Constitution required that the Army allow the democratically elected Allende to assume power.

37. Kinzer, Overthrow, 155.

38. Hammer, quoted in Kinzer, Overthrow, 169.

39. The conflation of the economic and geopolitical interest was evidenced by the International Telephone and Telegraph's (ITT) offer of $1 million to the US State Department and subsequently the CIA to bolster the opposition to Allende. The offer was delivered directly to Secretary of State Henry Kissinger and CIA Director Richard Helms by ITT board member and former director of CIA John McCone. Though the government refused to reallocate the money on behalf of ITT, the government advised ITT on exactly how it could securely do so without the government's help. Kinzer, Overthrow, 171. See also Central Intelligence Agency, CIA Activities in Chile.

Though the CIA provided tear gas, submachineguns, and ammunition to a group of plotters, the US government disingenuously seemed surprised when Schneider was mortally wounded in a kidnapping attempt. Following Schneider's death, the US shelved its plans for military intervention but did not relent in its effort to undermine Allende's administration.

The US administration has acknowledged that it was aware of (but denies involvement in) the impending coup that replaced Allende with the leader of the military junta, Augusto Pinochet. Allende took his own life rather than accept the rebels' offer of free passage out of the country in exchange for his resignation.[40] In his last address, Allende assessed with disarming clarity the invisible foreign hand that had orchestrated the coup and set it into motion:

> [F]oreign capital, imperialism, united with reaction, created the climate for the Armed Forces to break their tradition, that which they were taught by General Schneider which was reaffirmed by Commander Araya, victims of the same social sector that today will be expecting with an alien hand to reconquer the power to continue defending their profits and their privileges.[41]

The cruel irony is that Chile thrived economically under Pinochet even as he squashed any dissent by killing, torturing, and exiling tens of thousands of Chileans.[42] The US government knew of the body count Pinochet was amassing but refused to withdraw its military aid out of fear the regime would collapse and a Marxist government would replace it. Washington clearly preferred an economic and political hegemon to a more just and representative one.

Then–Secretary of State Henry Kissinger summarized the US perspective on Pinochet's humanitarian crimes, "I agree that we should not knock down stories that later prove to be true, nor should we be in the position of defending what they are doing in Santiago. But I think we should understand our policy—that however unpleasant they act, the government is better for us than Allende was."[43] Pinochet was preferable to Allende from the US government's perspective because Pinochet kept Chile from falling into Communists' hands. The cost of securing its interests in Chile required the US turn a blind eye to the kidnappings and a deaf ear to screams of

---

40. An offer that tape recordings would later prove was a lie as Pinochet planned to shoot down Allende's plane in Chilean airspace.

41. Allende, "Last Words of Salvador Allende."

42. For a thoroughly theological account of Pinochet's murderous reign, see Cavanaugh, *Torture and Eucharist*.

43. US Department of State, "SECRET/NODIS, 'Secretary's Staff Meeting.'"

the systematically tortured Chileans branded "enemies of the state." Chile may have been saved from the godless Communists, but it was governed by "enemies of the cross of Christ, whose end was destruction, whose god was their appetites, and whose glory was their shame."[44]

1980–1992—The Reagan and Bush Sr. Years

Saddam Hussein had good reason to be surprised by the US response to his invasion of Kuwait in 1990. Only ten years earlier, he had made the same aggressive move east into Iran without incurring the US's resistance. The US response in 1980 was to reward rather than reprimand Hussein as it blessed his invasion by providing funds, armaments, and ignoring Iranian protests over Iraq's use of chemical weapons. As an ally, Hussein left a lot to be desired but juxtaposed against Ayatollah Khomeini, the Iranian revolution, and the US embassy hostage crisis, President Reagan thought Saddam the lesser evil.

This moral calculus was further complicated by Reagan's support of the Nicaraguan Contras' attempts to overthrow the Marxist-leaning Sandinista government. After Congress passed legislation that explicitly prohibited military or intelligence aid for the Contras, Reagan and his chief advisors began discretely seeking foreign backers. When these clandestine overtures did not yield enough support, NSC member Oliver North was authorized to divert revenues from illicit weapons sales to Iran, which were part of US negotiations for American hostages held in Lebanon.

The Reagan administration had orchestrated a convoluted shell game by selling munitions to opposing sides of an eight-year blood bath in the Middle East to gain leverage in hostage negotiations in Lebanon, the proceeds from which would be invested in overthrowing a foreign government in Central America. Although both major political parties praise Ronald Reagan as the gold standard of presidential political success, the aura that *should* emanate from his tenure in office is that of man who only escaped impeachment because his underlings fell on their collective swords to protect him.

Reagan's Vice President and successor, George H. W. Bush, only emerged unscathed from the scandal because he refused to turn over documents to the independent counsel and pardoned two other men indicted by the counsel's investigation before they could go to trial. Bush would have his own famous intervention in Iraq as would his son George Jr. ten years later. Both wars emerged as the result of the US attempt to play the

---

44. Phil 3:18–19.

2001—The "War on Terror"

The most cogent demonstration of how US imperial praxis undermines its widely marketed mythos as the "leader of the free world" is the way it has defended itself since September 11, 2001. To assert that the US has played fast and loose with the boundaries of international law, the Geneva Conventions in particular, is an understatement. In January 2002, helped by some legal maneuvering from Attorney General Alberto Gonzalez and the Vice President Dick Cheney's attorney David Addington, the Bush White House determined that the Geneva Conventions did not apply to terrorists, actual or accused, because they were deemed "illegal enemy combatants."[45]

Almost immediately afterwards, the Pentagon contracted with James Mitchell and Bruce Jessen, two military psychologists to design a crash course in "enhanced interrogation techniques" for CIA and military personnel heading to the US's detention center in Guantanamo Bay, Cuba.[46] Neither psychologist had any experience as an interrogator, nor did either have specialized knowledge of *al Qaeda*, a background in counterterrorism, or any relevant cultural or linguistic expertise.

Before implementing Mitchell and Jessen's program, the US had been practicing what the administration called "extraordinary renditions" in which it kidnapped suspects and outsourced their torture to US allies in Egypt, Jordan, and Pakistan. The early 2002 order gave the CIA quasi-legal cover to tacitly oversee the torture. The detention and torture of detainees remained overseas lest its victims attempt to claim any protections afforded them by the US Constitution.

What precisely is encompassed by the term "enhanced interrogation"? The Senate Select Committee on Intelligence's (SSCI) report[47] on torture listed such actions as rectal feeding and rehydration without medical warrant, walling (throwing prisoners against their cell walls), mock burials where detainees were confined to wooden boxes with no room to move, sleep deprivation for up to 180 hours, auditory overload, total darkness, and stripping detainees nude and dousing them with cold water while they were

---

45. Mayer, *Dark* Side, 101. To his credit, then–Secretary of State Colin Powell fought the rest of the administration vehemently over this issue.
46. Siems, *Torture Report*.
47. Senate Select Comittee on Intelligence, *Senate Torture Report*.

chained to their cell's wall or ceiling.[48] This last technique led to the death of an innocent man from hypothermia. CIA officers also threatened at least three detainees with harm to their families—including threats to harm the children of a detainee, threats to sexually abuse the mother of a detainee, and a threat to cut a detainee's mother's throat.[49] Perhaps the most widely deplored tactic is that of waterboarding or simulated drowning. Prisoners are strapped to an inclined board with their feet above their heads. A cloth is placed over the victim's mouth and nose, and water is poured over his face for up to 40 seconds. One Guantanamo prisoner, Khalid Sheikh Mohammed, was waterboarded 183 times.

The lamentable irony is that rather than punish the men and women responsible for ordering and implementing torture as war criminals, the United States has promoted them. The recently appointed head of the CIA, Gina Haspel, oversaw the US black site in Thailand. She was also responsible for destroying ninety-two videos of the torture that occurred at her site. These American practices without compunction have ceded any moral high ground that the US may have once claimed as defender of human rights.[50]

Further adding insults to injuries is the fact that the SSCI's report concluded that the CIA's use of its enhanced interrogation techniques was not an effective means of acquiring intelligence or gaining cooperation from detainees. Furthermore, the CIA's justification for its enhanced interrogation techniques rested on inaccurate claims of their effectiveness.[51] The SSCI reviewed twenty of the CIA's most frequently and prominently cited terrorist plots purportedly thwarted by enhanced interrogation techniques. The Committee found the claims to be fundamentally wrong, reporting that:

> In some cases, there was no relationship between the cited counterterrorism success and any information provided by detainees during or after the use of the CIA's enhanced interrogation techniques. In the remaining cases, the CIA inaccurately claimed that specific, otherwise unavailable information was acquired from a CIA detainee "as a result" of the CIA's enhanced interrogation techniques, when in fact the information was either: (1) corroborative of information already available to the

---

48. The events at the US Prison at Abu Ghraib were extraordinary even by "enhanced interrogation" standards and will be address specifically in light of Jean Bethke Elshtain's work in chapter three.

49. Senate Select Comittee on Intelligence, *Senate Torture Report*.

50. Another morally dubious part of the CIA's program was its detention of an intellectually challenged man who was solely detained as leverage to get a family member to provide information. Senate Select Comittee on Intelligence, *Senate Torture Report*.

51. Senate Select Comittee on Intelligence, *Senate Torture Report*.

CIA or other elements of the U.S. Intelligence Community from sources other than the CIA detainee, and was therefore not "otherwise unavailable"; or (2) acquired from the CIA detainee prior to the use of the CIA's enhanced interrogation techniques.[52]

Opponents of torture know that it is more likely to produce false rather than useful information. Khalid Sheikh Mohammed said that he simply told his interrogators what he thought they wanted to hear to make the torture stop. His fabricated plots included that *al Qaeda* was planning on conducting attacks on US gas stations using African American Muslim converts in Montana.[53]

Former international law counsel to George Bush Sr.'s State Department, Philip Bobbitt argues that operating outside the law also undermines the US strategic objective of protecting its citizens. He contends that the Bush administration's chief blunder was not giving its blessing to torture but rather that it failed to write such actions into law before doing so. He explains,

> Because international law has not caught up with the changes in the global strategic context, it seems to present states with an intolerable choice: either follow the rule of law and sacrifice one war aim (the protection of civilians) or dispense with law and sacrifice the legitimacy of the war effort (which is, after all, another war aim, namely the legitimation of market states as states of consent). The answer to the dilemma is to reject it: law must be reformed.[54]

On Bobbitt's reading, the US found itself acting illicitly because the law is currently ill-suited to address what he calls "market state terrorism."[55]

---

52. Senate Select Comittee on Intelligence, *Senate Torture Report*.

53. Senate Select Comittee on Intelligence, *Senate Torture Report*. Perhaps Mohammed meant this as a joke since only .6 percent (6,000) of Montana's one million residents are black and .03 percent (300) are Muslim. The thin overlap of these two groups does not provide very ample recruiting grounds from which to raise up a guerilla army of terrorists. United States Census Bureau, *Quick Facts: Montana*.

54. Bobbitt, *Terror and Consent*, 532.

55. For Bobbitt, the market-state is characterized by the privatization of many of the state's activities with the goal of maximizing the individual opportunities of its citizens as opposed to the nation-state that bases its legitimacy on the promise of improving the material wealth of its people. In Bobbitt's estimation, each emerging market-state will either be one of terror—a political state whose legitimacy is underwritten by fear of imminent violence—or of consent—where the rule of law exists to uphold individuals' liberties and rights. Both states of consent and terror are evolving into market-states as Bobbitt frames it: "al Qaeda no less than the United States and the European Union is becoming a devolved, decentralized, outsourcing, privatized, global, and networked entity." In each genus of market state, the locus of concern has shifted from the state

Whether the reader finds Bobbitt's line of argument for writing criminality into the code of law compelling or preposterous, it is not the first time this line of reasoning has been deployed. German philosopher Carl Schmitt introduced the same notion of the "state of exception" in which "the sovereign, during a state of emergency, would transcend the rule of law in the name of the public good."[56] As the "crown jurist of the Third Reich,"[57] Schmitt was eyewitness to the reality that those who assume such powers rarely relinquish them willingly.

Giorgio Agamben further developed Schmitt's "state of exception" in his book by the same name. Agamben argues that the state of exception is not necessarily anti-democratic at its core since its temporary and controlled use can be compatible with democratic constitutions. However, "[o]ne of the essential characteristics of the state of exception—the provisional abolition of the distinction among legislative, executive, and judicial powers—[is] its tendency to become a lasting practice of government."[58] He does concede that once the exception becomes the rule through the "systematic and regular exercise of the institution, [it] necessarily leads to the 'liquidation' of democracy."[59]

Rather than defend the untenable position that the only way for democracy to survive is to consistently forgo the will of the people, some will suggest, as Bobbitt has, writing the state of exception into law. Agamben's well-founded objection to legalizing the state of exception in the constitution or special law is that the state cannot give legal form to that which is by its very definition is extra-juridical, i.e. torture. He is critical of those

---

to the individual citizen. *Al Qaeda* is the prototype for the market state of terror. This "virtual state" is ideologically rather than geographically demarcated and "outsources terrorism" like venture capitalists for "start-up" terrorist cells. In contrast to the nation-state terrorists like the Irish Republican Army or *Hamas*, *al Qaeda* is not singularly seeking to wrest territorial sovereignty away from a larger, more powerful nation-state. Instead, it is seeking ideological power and authority that traverses international boundaries. Bobbitt emphasizes that market-state terror is both the product of and response to globalization. Osama bin Laden used globalization both as a "doctrinal spur" to foment anger against the West for its manipulation and exploitation of Muslim lands as well as an "organizational saddle" to galvanize the ideology of global Islam. The same technologies that have fostered a robust global e-commerce have also rendered the same market space more vulnerable to attack through intricate terrorist networks.

56. Its similarity to the Monroe Doctrine and Roosevelt Corollary is no accident of history.

57. Stirk, *Carl Schmitt*.

58. Agamben, *State of Exception*, 7.

59. Agamben, *State of Exception*, 7.

who like Bobbitt advocate for "the pretense of regulating by law what by definition cannot be put in norms."[60]

Agamben laments that the deliberate creation of permanent states of exception has become commonplace among modern-day states. This is true even among democratic states whose fundamental premise of representative authority derived from the people (Bobbitt's "states of consent") would seem antithetical to the idea. The United States would be reticent to confess that the "war on terror" has ushered in a permanent state of exception, but the fact that national security perpetually remains the preeminent American value belies this reality. Agamben highlights the duplicitous irony that "all such theories remain prisoners in the vicious circle in which the emergency measures they seek to justify in the name of defending the democratic constitution are the same ones that lead to its ruin."[61] The manner in which the US has fought its "war on terror" leaves the US vulnerable to Agamben's observation that, "At the very moment when it would like to give lessons in democracy to different traditions and cultures, the political culture of the West does not realize that it has entirely lost its canon."[62]

In his 2009 Nobel Peace lecture titled "A Just and Lasting Peace," then US President Obama paid lip service to both just-war norms and the cost of evading them.[63] While he detailed the origins and classical tenets of the just-war tradition, he confessed that they have been "rarely observed." However, he was not prepared to jettison the just-war criteria, convinced as he was that adhering to international standards "strengthen those who do, and isolates and weakens those who don't."[64] He continued by saying that:

> America—in fact, no nation—can insist that others follow the rules of the road if we refuse to follow them ourselves. For when we don't, our actions appear arbitrary and undercut the legitimacy of future interventions, no matter how justified . . . Where force is necessary, we have a moral and strategic interest in binding ourselves to certain rules of conduct. And even as we confront a vicious adversary that abides by no rules, I believe the United States of America must remain a standard bearer in the conduct of war. That is what makes us different from those whom we fight. That is a source of our strength . . .

---

60. Agamben, *State of Exception*, 10.
61. Agamben, *State of Exception*, 8.
62. Agamben, *State of Exception*, 18.
63. Obama, "Nobel Lecture."
64. Obama, "Nobel Lecture."

We lose ourselves when we compromise the very ideals that we fight to defend.[65]

Obama said the appropriate things despite the insincerity of doing so while his administration continued to utilize the state of exception to justify its use of drones to pre-emptively assassinate those it designated as enemies of the United States. The Nobel Peace Prize winning commander in chief authorized 542 drone strikes that killed about 3,797 people, including 324 civilians "outside areas of active hostility" (Afghanistan, Iraq, and Syria).[66]

One of the many difficulties with waging a "war on terror" is that one is never certain whether the war's objective has been met. Is the mission accomplished when no American is afraid or perhaps when all our enemies are dead? If either is the criterion for victory, then the war will last in perpetuity because fear is easily fomented among people who have no certitude of a life after this one and the manner in which the US has fought the war is more likely to fashion more terrorists than it eliminates.

War Is Merely the Continuation of Commerce by Other Means[67]

These glimpses of US history raise the question of whether the US can concurrently extend the borders of liberty and freedom while simultaneously pursuing its national interests. When foreign democracies develop their political agendas and economic priorities that inevitably compete with those of the US, the US has shown little creativity in developing alternatives to economic and violent coercion. Henry Chadwick concisely elaborates upon Jesus's teaching in the Sermon on the Mount by writing that, "If you want to understand the values of a society, look at (*a*) its criminal code, (*b*) what it spends its money on."[68]

65. Obama, "Nobel Lecture."

66. Director of National Intelligence, "Summary of Information Regarding U.S. Counterterrorism Strikes." In this report, the government admits that its estimate is much lower than those reported by non-governmental organizations and that determining non-combatant from combatant is an inexact science.

67. This section heading is my retooling of Carl von Clausewitz's famous dictum, "War is not merely an act of policy but a true political instrument, a continuation of political intercourse, carried on with other means." Clausewitz, *On War*, I/24. One would be hard pressed to find an account of war-making that has not referenced the maxim and then revised it to suit the author's thesis. The repurposing of the quote is faithful to Clausewitz's intentions because economics is a substantial political policy that is weaponized and usually maintained by military means.

68. Chadwick, *Augustine*, 2.

AMERICA AS UNCONVENTIONAL EMPIRE

The US has shown no aversion to prioritizing its economic welfare over foreign freedom and liberty while writing illicit practices into enduring official policy. America is not unique in navigating the geopolitical landscape with a purely self-interested gait. Nations are inherently self-centered entities; were they not they would not survive long. American exceptionalism maintains that in pursuing its interest, the US fosters the welfare of the world, as though the US were the tide that lifted all nations. What is peculiar to the US is its ability and willingness to sabotage self-determined governments when they rank their national interests over and against the US's. Though the superficial justifications varied from evangelization to liberation, the underlying motive was most typically economic. The Native Americans' land, Hawaiians' sugar, Iranians' oil, and Hondurans' bananas—were natural resources that the US brought into its sphere of influence by military means.

Steven Kinzer highlights how the benevolent narrative Americans tell ourselves to justify our foreign policy is but a thin veneer over our self-interest, since, "Spreading democracy, Christianizing the heathen nations, building a strong navy, establishing military bases around the world, and bringing foreign governments under American control were never ends in themselves."[69] These were always intended to be the means through which the United States guaranteed itself access to the markets, resources, and investment potential of distant lands. Each of these practices, particularly when economically driven, is the behavior of empires.

It is imperative to remember that the American Revolution was ignited, not unlike many divorces, by quarrels over money. Great Britain had been precipitously raising taxes on a variety of goods shipped to the colonies to replenish the empire's war chests that had been depleted by the costs of defending its colonists against the French and Native Americans. The colonists wanted a representative in parliament to advocate for the colonists' interests. The request was denied, but the revolt could have been avoided by lowering tariffs, as excessive taxation rather than the lack of representation drove an intractable wedge between Great Britain and her American colonies. The origins of the American Revolution offer insight into how tightly bound the ideas of money and sovereignty are and also how war is a justifiable means for securing them both. In this regard, there has never been a time when the US has not behaved imperially—either classically or unconventionally.

Niall Ferguson non-pejoratively affirms as much because he resists both the liberal tendency to demonize American empire and the

---

69. Kinzer, *Overthrow*, 34.

conservative propensity to deny its existence. He writes that "the United States has always been, functionally if not self-consciously, an empire [and it] might well be preferable to available alternatives."[70] According to Ferguson, the truth that Americans should hold to be self-evident is that the United States is an empire. The more interesting yet seldom asked question is what manner of empire is it? Is it the Colossus, towering over its imperial predecessors? Or is it Goliath, formidable yet vulnerable to a small and elusive foe? Alternatively, is America more analogous to Samson, "eyeless in Gaza, chained by irreconcilable commitments in the Middle East and ultimately capable only of blind destruction?"[71]

An honest assessment would admit that America has imitated all three characters—at times concurrently. It has manipulated the global markets to its advantage and developed weapons technology more effectively than its predecessor. However, in Vietnam and the "war on terror," it has seen its considerable advantages in military and financial resources mitigated by guerrilla and insurgent fighters who wage war asymmetrically.[72] At the same time, the US as self-appointed judge is chained, no less than Samson was, by its obligations in the Middle East as it bolsters some regimes while undermining or removing others.

Those still unconvinced that US is an empire may prefer Harold James's argument in *The Roman Predicament*. The second chapter is entitled "Mercury and Mars" after the respective gods of commerce and war. James correctly highlights that economic and military dominance are two unmistakable earmarks of empire. The "Roman predicament" James describes is distinctly American as well: "how can prosperity and markets be secured against 'barbarians'?"[73] He argues that the central question driving US foreign policy since 9/11 has been, "Should we fight or buy off the barbarians at the gate?"[74] Both options sound curiously like the Roman solution: conquer and provide prosperity, and neither answer is enduringly satisfactory.

---

70. Ferguson, *Colossus*, VIII/1.

71. Ferguson, *Colossus*, VIII/1.

72. Robert Taber describes the difficulty a state has in guerrilla warfare: "Analogically, the guerrilla fights the war of the flea, and his military enemy suffers the dog's disadvantages: too much to defend; too small, ubiquitous, and agile an enemy to come to grips with. If the war continues long enough—this is the theory—the dog succumbs to exhaustion and anemia without ever having found anything on which to close his jaws or to rake with his claws . . . In practice, the dog does not die of anemia. He merely becomes too weakened—in military terms, overextended; in political terms, too unpopular; in economic terms, too expensive—to defend himself." Taber, *War of the Flea*, 20.

73. James, *The Roman Predicament*, 99.

74. James, *The Roman Predicament*, 148.

Does the US buy off "barbarians"? The US allocates $24 billion annually for foreign aid in development, humanitarian, and military assistance. Whether it is the $4 billion doled out to allies like Israel or the $1.1 billion to less enthusiastic partners like Pakistan, the goal is to purchase influence. Rome took a similar tact with the Visigoths. Under Constantine I, the Visigoths were paid an annual tribute in exchange for their cooperation with the empire. When a later emperor refused to continue the subsidy, the Visigoths sacked Rome to recoup their losses.

The substantial economic influence that the US wields globally is one of the identifying marks of empire. If the 2008 financial crisis taught the world anything about the insidiousness of US fiscal policy, it is this: when America sneezes, the whole world catches a cold. Spurred by the US housing bubble that burst precipitously after a half-decade of predatory lending of sub-prime loans to the poor, global markets entered a recession.

US sanctions against oil-rich nations like Iran and Russia have more teeth because in 1973 Saudi Arabia agreed that all oil trade would be denominated in US dollars in exchange for Saudi access to American weapons. Despite Russia and Iran fighting back against this petrodollar monopoly by selling oil to China in *yuans*, the lion's share of oil trading is still tied precariously to the US dollar. Of this strategy Charles de Gaulle correctly remarked, "No domain escapes from American imperialism. It takes all forms. The most insidious is that of the dollar."[75]

Where the United States treasure is, there its heart must also be. In 2018, the US spent $623 billion, nearly half of discretionary spending, on defense.[76] The current budget proposal would raise that figure by nearly $60 billion.[77] The same budget allocates $25.8 billion for the State Department, a 26 percent decrease from the previous year. For every dollar the US invests in diplomacy, it spends over $24 on defense. This discrepancy helps account for the United States prioritizing of military solutions to its foreign problems over and against diplomacy. As Abraham Maslow wrote, "I suppose it is tempting, if the only tool you have is a hammer, to treat everything as if it were a nail."[78]

The US's defense budget is three times as great as China's, the second largest military spender, and more than the next 13 highest defense budgets

---

75. Peyrefitte, *C'était de Gaulle*, 603, 663, quoted in James, *The Roman Predicament*, 156.

76. Congressional Budget Office, *The Federal Budget in 2017*.

77. Office of Management and Budget, "Budget of the United States Government, Fiscal Year 2019."

78. Maslow, *Toward a Psychology of Being*.

combined.[79] One of the obvious dangers of maintaining imperial order is fiscal hyperextension. The US seems perilously close to such a hyperextension as China holds $1.2 trillion of US debt.[80] America has unabashedly mortgaged itself to the world's second-largest military so the United States can have the world's most expansive military.

The enemy of empire is size. History is rife with examples that show that whether empires spread through subjugation or incorporation, their demise is frequently facilitated by their getting too large and unwieldy to manage. No matter how great the military expenditures or prowess, history has shown that empires that grow too large inevitably collapse under their own weight as it they cannot defend themselves everywhere at once, even through proxy.

One US remedy to this problem is the military base. According to a 2010 Pentagon report, the US has 662 military bases in thirty-eight countries. This led Chalmers Johnson to conclude that America has merely replaced the colony with the military base.[81] Ostensibly, these bases exist to *prevent* the outbreak of war; but they seem far better situated to expedite it. The proliferation of military bases is a uniquely American strategy as Britain, France, and Russia have about thirty foreign bases combined.[82]

Where the US cannot control a region through its physical military presence or financial influence, monitoring of Internet traffic allows the US access to the decision-making centers of its enemies, allies, and own citizens. The US need not bomb an enemy's nuclear plant to knock it out of commission as Israel did in Iraq in 1981; it can send a cyber weapon like the computer virus it deployed in 2009 that caused 20 percent of Iran's nuclear centrifuges to spin out of control and fail. However, the same technology that allows the US to extend its reach also makes it more vulnerable to attack, as evidenced by the late-2016 hacking of Vermont's power grid and the Democratic National Committee's databases.

However, the margin of the US's technological advantage over its rivals is diminishing. Both China and Iran have captured US drones and produced models of their own. James comments that, historically, empires are most vulnerable at the fringe, and in the modern world the fringe is everywhere.[83] In a world of instant communication and rapid transport,

---

79. These include Saudi Arabia, Russia, India France, UK, Japan, Germany, South Korea, Brazil, Italy, Australia, Canada, and Turkey. Stockholm International Peace Research Institute, *Military Expenditure*.

80. McGregor and Greifeld, "China Holdings of U.S. Debt."

81. Johnson, "On Garrisoning the Planet."

82. Vine, "Where in the World is the U.S. Military?"

83. James, *Roman Predicament*, 99.

the proverbial frontier of an empire is indefinite, leaving the whole of it vulnerable. It is unquestionable that the last century of US foreign policy has created enemies and begrudging but opportunistic allies who would delight in exploiting the cracks in the juggernaut's armor.

The union of Mars and Venus in the US's policies is unlikely to cease in the foreseeable future. This is true, at least in part, because of the US Supreme Court's 2010 *Citizen's United* decision, which opened the floodgates ever wider to allow an influx of capital to influence the nation's political process. The court ruled that "corporations are people" and that donating money for political purposes is an act of free speech, the cap on donations was removed, and the special-interest floodgates were opened beyond their capacities. The hundreds of millions of dollars funneled anonymously through Super PACs are not only influencing who gets elected but also their obligations once in office.

One such example is the Freedom Partners Action Fund created by the Koch brothers expressly to help the Republicans recapture the Senate in the 2014-midterm elections. The PAC spent $25 million on advertising during the campaigns. This is just one of the half dozen groups that comprise the political arm of the Koch network that spent $400 million on campaign contributions during the 2012 presidential elections and $290 million in the 2014 midterms—more than either the Republican or Democratic National Committees did during the entire election cycle.[84]

The financial and military configuration of the United States looks familiarly imperial, and the domestic political rules seem stacked in favor of maintaining the status quo by strategic use of the US military to advance the interests of particularly generous corporate donors. Whether such an arrangement should cause citizens, specifically those who bear the name of Christ, any moral dissonance is a discussion well worth having. Fortunately, we are not the first inhabitants of empire to wrestle with this issue. Peter Leithart provides a theological response to Niall Ferguson's question of the nature of American empire, and it is worth considering at length.

---

84. Vogel and Allen, "Koch Donors Uncloaked." What motivates such philanthropy? Robert Mercer, the largest donor to the Freedom Partners Super PAC, contributed $2.5 million. Mercer is a leading donor to conservative Super PACs that have tried to defeat Rep. Peter DeFazio (Democrat-OR) after the congressman emerged as the leading voice in Congress for a financial transaction tax, which would hit hard hedge funds that rely on high-speed computer trading. Coincidentally, Mercer is also a top executive at the Long Island high-frequency trading fund Renaissance Technologies. Others are more open about the motives for their benevolence, like Arkansas poultry producer Ronnie Cameron who said that his $1 million contribution to the Super PAC was the result of his fear that his grandchildren could be living under Communism if the current leadership were allowed to remain in power.

Between Babel and Beast

Leithart argues the Bible is neither inherently *for* nor *against* the political construct of empire, since scripture, "does not concede that empire in the singular is a useful category of political analysis [, rather] [t]he key question for Scripture is, how does this political entity treat the people of God?"[85] Accordingly, he posits that empires exist on a spectrum, where at one pole they emulate Babel by seeking to make a great name for themselves and recreating the world in their own cultural and political images and at the opposite extremity they emulate *Revelation*'s Beast by spilling the blood of God's saints.[86] Both options seem to challenge Leithart's premise of empire as a theologically inert political construct.

Leithart concludes that United States of America stands more or less between these two imperial archetypes. The United States is Babelic when it uses its power to further its own national interests while maintaining that it is, in actuality, fostering the world's welfare. He surmises that the American penchant for prioritizing religious tolerance makes it unlikely to turn bestial, but that the country also has no qualms about collaborating with beasts when doing so serves American political ends. Persecution of Christians is common among many US allies and recipients of US foreign aid, like Egypt, Saudi Arabia, Iraq, Israel, Pakistan, and Afghanistan.

Leithart christens the US's civil religion "Americanism" and claims it provides the moral authority that enables the US to be an empire. Americanism is a heretical version of citizenship in which the nation supplants the church as the sacred community with the authority to call its people to lay down their lives. The "old lie" *dulce et decorum est pro Patria mori*[87] is neither peculiarly modern nor American, but it does resonate poignantly in a country that has unremittingly offered up its sons and daughters on the altars of wars that stretch back long before it was an independent nation.

This is the natural end of what Leithart calls "nihilistic politics." In the absence of competing deities, the state is sacralized by the blood of its citizens in an aberrant and counterfeit Eucharist. What distinguishes America's civil religion from patriotism common in most nation-states is that Americanism is profoundly *evangelical* in its desire to spread the "gospel" of liberal democratic capitalism. Charles Mathewes underscores this

---

85. Leithart, *Between Babel and Beast*, xi.

86. He also includes a third imperial category, "guardians" of the people of God, with quite an exclusive membership.

87. "It is sweet and right to die for one's country" is a line from the Roman poet Horace's *Odes*, III/2.13, from which Wilfred Owen derived his anti-World War I poem in which he called Horace's claim the "old lie."

discrepancy between the US and other democracies by contrasting America with its long-time Republic foil, France.

> America and France are often identified as the originally "modern" nation-states. But no French person would imagine that the rest of the world could ever be French. (The French may be cynical narcissists, but they are not naive megalomaniacs.) To traffic in stereotypes, what the French want is for everyone else to recognize French superiority while staying in their inferior state. The terror of Americans' genuinely welcoming attitude is that we can imagine no reason that the rest of the world would not want to be like America—and we are going to help them, by God, even if they don't want our help.[88]

Americanism's eschatology sees the United States as the "already" of the *Novus Ordo Seclorum* and the rest of the world as the "not yet."[89] Most US churches are ill-equipped to critique Americanism because they have not only embraced it but also unequivocally promote it.[90] The sacralization of national interest has provided the American government with the ostensible moral duty—an aberrant kind of "great commission"—to advance liberty and freedom throughout the globe by economic, political, and militarized coercion. Leithart concludes that in the manner the US disseminates liberty and freedom they have become what Augustine called "splendid vices"—idealized virtues that became spoiled because they were sought as ends unto themselves rather than for God's sake.[91]

It is duplicitous to deny that the United States has often pursued the notions of liberty and freedom with a missionary zeal and a thoroughly self-assured moral rectitude that it was at a minimum doing moral good in the world if not carrying out the very work of the Lord. However, the virtues of liberty and freedom became vices when they were secured only for a few, namely Americans—or more specifically wealthy, white, and landowning males—at everyone else's expense. Only a national identity that weds the violent pursuit of liberty and freedom with the Christian

---

88. Mathewes, *Republic of Grace*, 92.

89. Leithart, *Between Babel and Beast*, 75.

90. Both of Leithart's arguments here echo those of Michael Northcott: "[American cultural Christianity's] core values are more American than New Testament and include the curious combination of individual liberty and patriotism that requires individuals regularly commit themselves and their children, and the lion's share of the nation's public budget and hence their tax payments, to war and preparations for war." Northcott, *An Angel Directs the Storm*, 20.

91. Augustine, *City of God*, XIX/25.

gospel could create a song like *The Battle Hymn of the Republic* from the carnage of its own civil war:

> Mine eyes have seen the glory of the coming of the Lord;
> He is trampling out the vintage where the grapes of wrath are stored;
> He hath loosed the fateful lightning of His terrible swift sword,
> His truth is marching on.
>
> Chorus: Glory, glory, hallelujah!
>   Glory, glory, hallelujah!
>   Glory, glory, hallelujah!
>   His truth is marching on . . .
>
> . . . In the beauty of the lilies, Christ was born across the sea,
> With a glory in his bosom that transfigures you and me;
> *As he died to make men holy, let us die to make men free,*
> While God is marching on.[92]

These lyrics capture the enduring and conflated faith in American soldiers and its houses of worship. The cost of genuine freedom is no less than the sacrifice of the nation's children in "just wars." American service members, no less than Christ, are lambs whose blood covers a multitude of national transgressions. In as much as the citizen has faith in the efficacy of the substitutionary atonement secured by the soldier's martyrdom, it is credited to the civilian as righteousness—or at least genuine patriotism.

This reinterpretation of sacrifice should give Christians pause, as they are better equipped than most citizens to recognize the substantial gulf that exists between the liberty and freedom advocated by the principalities and powers of this world and those ideas as they are articulated in the Gospels. For governments, liberty consists of certain inalienable rights promised to their citizens but not extended to the "other." Market capitalism nuances freedom to include unencumbered choice and consumption among citizens' inalienable rights.

According to journalist George Will, this was no accident of history, but the Founders' will. He writes that the purpose behind America's political arrangements was to subordinate religion to the political order of democracy. The founders did not want to replicate Europe's religious conflicts in their country. Rather, they attempted to tame and domesticate religious fervor by establishing a commercial republic. The notion was that unfettered

---

92. Howe, *Battle Hymn of the Republic*. Emphasis mine.

capitalism would inhibit people's turbulent energies in self-interested pursuit of material comforts."[93]

It is under the auspices of defending this genus of freedom that the United States has frequently harnessed the same "turbulent energies" of its citizens that Will said would be diminished in order to advance its own "self-interested pursuits." The quarantine of religion to the personal realm and the elevation of *mammon* to civic idol combined to render the meaning of freedom malleable enough to assume a multitude of meanings. Although Stanley Hauerwas concurs with Will's assessment, he offers a more critical inspection of the Founding Fathers' intentions and their ability to constrain violence. Post-Enlightenment political philosophy aimed to create people who were incapable of killing in God's name. Hauerwas writes that the sadly ironic result of such efforts was merely the formation of new, though no less violent, peoples obliged to kill in the name of their countries. He elaborates, "Indeed, I think it can be suggested that the political achievement of the Enlightenment has been to create people who believe it is necessary to kill others in the interest of something called 'the nation,' which is allegedly protecting and ensuring their freedom as individuals."[94]

It is hard to dispute Hauerwas's conclusion that rather than expunging violence, post-Enlightenment political structures have merely repurposed forceful coercion to achieve different ends. In general, the citizenry is content with this arrangement as long as the repurposed violence is exported to other nations. Elsewhere, Hauerwas describes how the rejigging of freedom in this manner has affected the faith of many Americans who accept their symbiotic relationship with the state as at least natural if not altogether sanctified. He argues, "The god most Americans say they believe in is not interesting enough to deny, because it is only the god that has given them a country that ensures that they have the right to choose to believe in the god of their choosing."[95] If this is how Americans define theism, then the only kind of atheism that is genuinely provocative is one that does not believe in the state that lets them choose their own god.

For Hauerwas, America is the exemplification of the project of modernity, which he describes as,

> The attempt to produce a people that believes it should have no story except the story it chose when it had no story. That is what

93. Will, "Scalia Missed the Point."
94. Hauerwas, *After Christendom?*, 33.
95. Hauerwas, "How Real is America's Faith?" Elsewhere Hauerwas has equipped that Americans think freedom means being able to choose which brand of television to buy.

> Americans mean by freedom. The problem with that story is its central paradox: you did not choose the story that you should have no story except the story you chose when you had no story. Americans, however, are unable to acknowledge that they have been fated to be "free," which makes them all the more adamant that they have a right to choose the god that underwrites their "freedom"... The story that you should have no story except the story you chose when you had no story produces a people who say: "I believe that Jesus is Lord—but that is just my personal opinion." I hope that makes it understandable that Americans expect their presidents to believe in god. They do so because they are confident that the god presidents believe in is not a god that can call into question the American project.[96]

The freedom to worship the god of consumer choice, who can only affirm your moral premonitions but is too impotent to challenge your assumptions or allegiances is starkly opposed to the New Testament's depiction of the freedom that exists where the Spirit of the Lord is transforming his disciples' unveiled faces into his own image.[97] For those who have been set free by Jesus, liberty entails more than the worship of one's predilections. Christians are bound to a community of servants who must be watchful, so that their exercise of freedom does not hinder the growth of another. Christian freedom is necessarily formed by boundaries of obedience to God and responsibility to neighbors—not constrained by national or ethnic borders as the parable of the good Samaritan reminds us. Paradoxically, many will appeal to this same obligation to neighbor to justify violent intervention. Though the powerful may sanction their violence by coating it in a thin evangelical veneer, the cross is the only authentically redemptive violence in history. It is uniquely redemptive violence precisely because it was unjust violence *suffered* rather than "justified violence" perpetrated.

"The Eagle in the Mirror"[98]

Before the morning of September 11, 2001, was etched into our collective memories, the night of August 24, 410, left a similarly indelible mark on history. On that night, rebellious slaves opened Rome's gates to Alaric and his Visigoth army. It took the invaders three short days to plunder the city that remained the figurative heart, though no longer the head, of the empire in

---

96. Hauerwas, "How Real is America's Faith?"
97. 2 Cor 3:17–18.
98. This phrase is borrowed from Murphy, *Are We Rome*, 6.

decline.[99] Reading Jerome's description of the sack of Rome inevitably beckons my own horrid memories of watching people leap from the smoldering towers of the World Trade Center that would soon be reduced to mangled masses of concrete, steel, and humanity on 9/11:

> My voice sticks in my throat; and, as I dictate, sobs choke my utterance. The City which had taken the whole world was itself taken . . . Who can set forth the carnage of that night? What tears are equal to its agony? Of ancient date a sovran [sic] city falls; and lifeless in its streets and houses lie unnumbered bodies of its citizens. In many a ghastly shape does death appear.[100]

Both attacks rent wounds far deeper in the empires than their mere physical destruction. On these two analogously fateful days separated by over a millennium and a half the most spectacular collapses were neither of buildings nor of bodies but of two disparate empires's confidence in their respective invincibility and eternalness. As Augustine articulated it, "It was, after all, only stones and timbers that collapsed in Rome's ruin. In their form of life, however, it was not Rome's material but its moral fortifications and furnishings that fell to pieces, for their hearts were on fire with desires far more deadly than any flames licking at the city's houses."[101]

Invoking the concept of empire in the West, even an unconventional one as I have, will inevitably raise the specter of Rome: the quintessentially imperial standard-bearer against which all others are measured. While no comparison runs on all fours, there are many congruencies between the United States of America and the Roman Empire. Both empires were initially ruled by kings before their authority became too unpalatable to their subjects who cast off their collective yoke in favor of emerging republics that deliberately sought to balance governmental power in such a way as to resist the rise of another autonomous ruler.

For example, Rome's aristocratic senate was led by two consuls, elected annually, who wielded executive power to command armies, preside over the senate, and propose laws. The tripartite US equilibrium of power was crafted with intention that the oversight of laws that govern the lives of its citizens would not fall under the exclusive domain of any one of the three branches of government. The fundamental principles of

99. Augustine biographer Peter Brown notes that Rome had long ceased to be the political capital of the Roman Empire. He elaborates, "Above all, Rome was the symbol of a whole civilization; it was as if an army had been allowed to sack Westminster Abbey or the Louvre." Brown, *Augustine*, 287.

100. Jerome, "Letter 127."

101. Augustine, *City of God*, II/2.

jurisprudence may originate and evolve within the legislative branch, but their substantive interpretation is the prerogative of the judicial branch, and the ultimate purview of the genuine enforcement of these derived and interpreted principles, i.e., laws, is essentially constricted or broadened at the discretion of the executive branch.

Paul Burton has suggested plausibly that the catalyst for the revival of the Roman-American imperial comparisons was the rapid and intense accretion of American anxiety post-9/11. The post 9/11 reality was that Americans, like so many others in the world, would learn to live in a state of nearly perpetual fear and uncertainty. Any notion of the sanctity of our borders was jettisoned as every home, school, and office with a functioning television or computer screen was infiltrated by the unremitting loop of images of the ineffable murder of innocents that concurrently mortified Americans viewers yet also obligated them to be eyewitnesses to the repeated defilement of their security state. Burton concludes that after September 11 the increasingly timid American was less concerned with the question, "*who* is my enemy," and increasingly plagued by the more vexing query, "*where* is my enemy?"[102] The US's inability to unequivocally answer this question is at least partly attributable to the fact that it ambiguously identified its enemy as "terror," which only served to increase apprehension and anxiety among its citizens. The subsequently circuitous mission to eradicate terror has also invited responses from all political participants that reevaluate classically imperial and American analogues in light of the US's current "war on terror."

Predictably, the opposing political ideologies have produced disparate interpretations even though they are ostensibly distilling the same collection of facts. Politically right-leaning pundits, with few exceptions, envy the strength and stamina of Roman pre-eminence and view it favorably as an exemplar worthy of emulation by the US in the current geopolitical landscape. They may too casually dismiss the monikers "empire" or "imperial" opting for softer, more palatable superlatives like "global hegemon" or "guarantor of liberal international order," but the political machinations they are espousing are but attempts to recast the outmoded power structure in a more charitable light. Regardless of the imperial pseudonym one prefers, empires are erected upon comparable foundations buttressed by the convergence of three staunchly coercive and political pillars: economic, military, and cultural dominance.[103]

102. Burton, "Pax Romana/Pax Americana," 143.

103. The three pillars are often interlocked with one another. The same technology, for example, can be found to meander through all three spheres. The Roman innovation in engineering and road construction was sparked by the military necessity of

Those who lean towards the opposite side of the political spectrum, can demarcate these same three pillars as they extend from Ancient Rome through every polity with imperial premonitions since. From the left's perspective, the US is merely the most recent example of a polity that has efficaciously manipulated its governing ethos and telos to coincide with these three precarious loci. Those who lean further left politically are more likely to view the Roman imperial archetype as a more foreboding exemplar than one worthy of emulation. They more cynically interpret the pillars as the torturous rack that leads to imperial overstretch rather than the solid groundwork for global order. Instead of continuing to outline two competing metanarratives about whether Roman vestiges in American political structures and policies strengthen or destabilize the US, the remainder of this chapter will underscore congruencies between the empires and allow the reader to weigh the evidence herself.

When asked what kind of government the Constitutional Convention had chosen for the United States, Benjamin Franklin is anecdotally reported to have replied, "A republic, if you can keep it." The terseness of his retort does not belie its meaning. A republic is not merely born of the consent of its people, but its survival and maturation are contingent upon their *continued* collective will to engage with and develop their nascent nation. The Roman Republic endured for 500 years. Thus far, the US Republic has lasted less than half as long.

If Rome and the United States were initially christened Republics, they also evolved into empires as they came of age. For both republics, the catalyst that altered the balance of political wills was a civil war. In Rome, it was from the embers of the first-century BC civil war that ensued after Julius Caesar was murdered in the Senate by some sixty conspirators who took umbrage with Caesar designating himself "perpetual dictator."

Caesar Augustus made careful note of his Great Uncle Julius's hubris and fate and eschewed monarchical titles for himself preferring instead the more traditional moniker of *princeps*, or first citizen. Although he was an emperor in every sense of the word, Augustus was mindful to maintain at least a modicum of the Republican façade by treating the senate with deference and defending Republican social values.[104] In so doing, he created an efficient template for his imperial successors. Those who did not at least pay

---

moving many troops quickly throughout the empire. These same roads became the arteries through which trade flowed and the Latin language and culture were spread. Similarly, the US Department of Defense created the internet as a military communications tool, but it has become the core of American commerce and primary disseminator of American culture.

104. Gwynn, *The Roman Republic*, 117.

lip service to the empire's Republican past did not linger in power for long since "every Roman emperor of the first century AD who aspired to naked autocracy was cut down, from Caligula and Nero to Domitian."[105]

The emergence of the Roman Empire from within the Republic was not wrought by a political shift away from isolationism in favor of expansionism or a change in a military philosophy from defensive to domineering. Rather it was Augustus's consolidation of the governing powers of Roman citizens and the senate for himself. However, the transition from Roman Republic to Empire was not as jarring as one might expect. Paul Burton reminds his readers that before Augustus became Rome's first emperor, the city that was founded on a small Palatine hill already occupied the Mediterranean shoreline, modern day France (Gaul), Spain, Greece, and Turkey (Asia Minor). He explains that, "The Romans had been in effective possession of a territorial empire since the late third century BC, when Rome was formally and constitutionally a Republic."[106] Ironically, the primary era of Roman imperial expansion occurred under the Republic's rule while the Roman Empire functioned primarily to protect, consolidate, and maintain the territories it had already acquired.[107]

The previous pages of this chapter argued that the American Republic has emulated the Roman Republic's penchant for imperial expansion, particularly during its first seventy-five years as an independent republic. As it had also been for Roman rulers before Augustus, any suggestion by US politicians that their nation has ever been, in effect or actuality, anything other than the Republic described and demarcated in its founding documents is political heresy. Unlike Rome's civil wars, the US's Civil War did not provide a foothold from which an opportunistic despot could ascend and claim to be the unending embodiment of sovereignty. However, it did galvanize a nation previously more accurately described as a loose confederation of states with varied competing agendas.

Following the US Civil War, the Republican Congress rejected President Andrew Johnson's reconstruction plan and instead amended the constitution to federally centralize powers that were formerly the exclusive prerogative of state legislatures.[108] The US Republic bowed under the profound stress of its internal war, but it did not ultimately buckle. Yet, the crucible of the Civil War failed to animate support for a more equitable and just

---

105. Gwynn, *The Roman Republic*, 117.

106. Burton, "Pax Romana/Pax Americana," 72.

107. Burton, "Pax Romana/Pax Americana," 73.

108. Within five years of the Civil War's conclusion, Congress abolished slavery, required states to provide equal protection under the law to all persons (not only citizens) within their jurisdiction, and enfranchised Black Southerners.

republic[109] but instead the nation was galvanized into a more formidable and fiercer antagonist that would use its newfound collective strength to pry its way into foreign lands and markets as noted above. In this manner, the American Republic emulated her Roman predecessor.

However, the reality that nearly 250 years of US history has failed to produce even one opportunistic, totalitarian tyrant with the boldness to usurp governmental structures in an unadulterated power grab is no small point of incongruency between the US and Roman empires. Nevertheless, this neither nullifies the arguments for America as an unconventional empire nor undermines comparisons to the Roman empire. This claim can endure such scrutiny because there are but a few, meager degrees of separation between a functional monarchy and a de facto oligarchy.

It is no embellishment to call Rome an oligarchy before its emergence as an empire, as membership in the Senate was initially restricted to the aristocracy among the patrician class. The small detail that the Senate's begrudging acquiescence to becoming more inclusive coincided with the ceding of most of its tangible power is unlikely to be mere happenstance.

The small handful of Americans who wield fiscal, political, and/or cultural clout are no more enthusiastic than their Roman counterparts had been to hasten the enfranchisement and empowerment of poorer classes. Some may find this claim ostentatious or irresponsible, written, as it is, from within borders of a republic with a democratically elected and ostensibly representative government. It also endows every natural-born citizen aged thirty-five or older with the opportunity to become president and commander-in-chief should she so wish. Even citizens who hold no political ambitions of their own are encouraged to participate in the routine reshuffling of the composition of the representative portions of their governing bodies by voting for advocates who they believe will most faithfully and fervently prioritize their constituency's primary concerns so that they are not scuttled beneath the cacophony of competing agendas inherent within a democratic republic.

However, the fine print on this social contract is decidedly less inspiring than advertised. Many with political aspirations to serve the common good by holding public office are often disillusioned to learn that the price tag on

---

109. This is evidenced by the fact that the freedoms that were promised to Black Americans by the thirteenth, fourteenth, and fifteenth amendments were not realized in actuality for one hundred years. Southern municipalities thwarted Congress's intentions by enacting "Jim Crow Laws"—a collection of state and local statutes that legalized racial segregation. These laws were meant to return Southern states to an antebellum class structure by marginalizing black Americans. Black citizens that defied Jim Crow laws often suffered violent lynchings at the hands of the Ku Klux Klan or similar racist mobs.

their candidacy is prohibitively high unless they are already independently wealthy or well-travelled in the circles of those that are.

At least each citizen gets to participate by voting. Although her vote is likely to be rendered futile by some combination of highly gerrymandered and partisan configuration of her voting district, or the nation's refusal to abandon the antiquated electoral college that has twice in the last two decades awarded the presidency to an unpopularly elected candidate, or the influx of corporate money into the electoral process that guarantees the continued prioritization of the will of the wealthy, or the tyranny of the two-party cartel that silences all but the most moderate of voices from within their own ranks. American democracy ensures that only a small handful of particular kinds of people are able to fully participate in the selection process of what we dare call a representative government while maintaining a straight face. Nevertheless, any American with the audacity to openly question to what extent her government is genuinely either representative or a Republic courts the accusations of being seditious and unpatriotic.

For Burton, the US Republic's attempts to fulfil its "manifest destiny"—the Divine auspices under which it sought to expand its dominion, democracy, and capitalism throughout North America, the Western Hemisphere, and eventually the world—is not the most compelling argument for a US imperium. He argues that in lieu of a territorial empire (i.e., what has been characterized as classically imperial above), twenty-first-century America "possesses a largely informal, non-territorial empire of influence primarily by virtue of its unmatched military power, its unrivalled ability to project its power beyond its borders, the attractiveness of its cultural production, and its ability to persuade other states to follow its lead."[110] Essentially, Burton argues that the abundance of US "hard (militarily or economically coercive) power" and "soft (culturally or ideologically seductive)[111] power" are the most persuasive points of departure for investigating an American imperial trope.

Ancient Rome also possessed ample amounts of its own "hard" and "soft" powers that it was rarely reticent to employ in either its defense or expansion. The Roman Republic–turned–Empire survived over 1,200 years and at its height stretched from Hadrian's Wall in North Britain to the

---

110. Burton, "Pax Romana/Pax Americana," 75–6.

111. The term "soft power" was coined by Joseph Nye, and he describes it as "getting others to want the outcomes that you want— [soft power] co-opts rather than coerces them." It is the attractive and seductive qualities of a country that rest primarily in three resources: "its culture (where it is attractive to others), its political values (when it lives up to them at home and abroad), and its foreign policies (when they are seen as legitimate and having moral authority)." Nye, *Soft Power*, 5, 11.

Fertile Crescent in the Middle East. Rome's army originally consisted of four legions, between four to six thousand men each, drawn from tax-paying Romans who could afford to arm themselves.

As the Republic grew, so did its need for soldiers. Thus, citizenship and the right to serve was extended to all Italian men who could meet military requirements. As need arose, the ranks were filled with conscripts since volunteers were not always forthcoming quickly enough to meet the demands of the empire. The second century BC would find the Roman army stressed nearly beyond its limits by lengthy conflicts with Carthage. The Roman solution was to reorganize its soldiers into the world's first professional army. Rome trained, equipped, and paid these men in exchange for twenty-five years of service.

To supplement its infantry and as a prophylactic against insurgence among conquered peoples, Rome also contracted with foreign soldiers to fight predominantly at the empire's peripheries, where they would pose little threat to Rome itself. Once their service was completed, they were granted Roman citizenship and a parcel of land. These "auxiliaries," as the foreign fighters were known, were not only employed by Rome, they were often hired by native Italians to serve in their stead. What began as a true citizen's army slowly metamorphosized into a mercenary force with little affinity for or loyalty to the land, people, and culture they were paid to defend. The problematic precedents such practices established were easy to anticipate.

The United States' military has undergone an uncannily similar military evolution. Before he became the Republic's first President, General George Washington had hoped to fend off the British during the Revolutionary War with a conventional army raised by offering enlisted men cash bonuses and a promise of free western land after the war was over. However, these incentives did not attract enough soldiers, so Washington had to call upon the poorly trained and ill-equipped militias that were the vanguards of colonial defense.

The second tilt between the US and Great Britain, the War of 1812, presented a similar problem for then-President James Madison. After the promise of an enlistment bonus of sixteen dollars plus three months' salary and one hundred sixty acres of land after service could not raise an adequate army, Madison was authorized by Congress to supplement the standing army by calling up one hundred thousand additional state militia men.[112]

---

112. Part of the recruitment problem for Madison was that the war was largely unpopular among New England's Federalists. In fact, Connecticut, Massachusetts, and Rhode Island refused to send their militias because the states opposed the war as they were leery of the impact it would have on their commerce as Atlantic-bordering states.

Like Rome had before it, the US also did not hesitate to fill its military with conscripted soldiers when the numbers of volunteers proved insufficient. The United States first instituted a military draft during its Civil War.[113] Although both sides of the conflict implemented the draft, the Confederate Army, suffering from heavier losses and dwindling morale, resorted to enlisting slaves to fight against their own freedom. Conscription remained the manner by which the US would routinely and controversially staff its sparse military rolls until 1973 when the military officially became a professional, all-volunteer force.[114]

The US military has also adopted aspects of the Roman auxiliary model. As less than roughly 1 percent of eligible Americans volunteer for military service, the US has increasingly relied on foreign and domestic defense contractors to perform its military duties. While defense contractors do not engage in direct combat, since 2001 the US has outsourced the government's monopoly on force to private military firms such as Blackwater, which alone has won billions in federal contracts,[115] to guard officials and military installations, train the Iraqi army and police forces, and provide other support for the armed services.[116]

Like their Roman auxiliary counterparts, these defense contractors are hired for a specific term of service and task. Unlike the Roman auxiliaries, however, foreign personnel hired as defense contractors are not eligible to gain citizenship at the end of their contract.[117] Without hiring

---

113. To characterize the draft as unpopular is a gross understatement. President Lincoln's draft calls for more New Yorkers to fight for the Union Army sparked three days of race riots in New York City that killed 120 people. The draft riots are appropriately understood as class warfare as well, as the poor were angry at an exemption clause that allowed the wealthy to buy their way out of service for three hundred dollars—the equivalent of approximately five thousand dollars in today's currency.

114. Following the Civil War, the draft would be activated for the Spanish American War, World Wars I and II, the wars in Korea and Vietnam, as well as during the Cold War. Today, nearly every man in the United States between the ages of eighteen and twenty-five is still required to register with the "Selective Service System" as the government maintains the power to reinstate the draft in the event of a "national emergency."

115. More than half of which were awarded without full and open competitive bidding.

116. US Congressional Committee on Oversight and Government Reform, "House Hearing, 110th Congress - BLACKWATER USA." Also see Scahill, *Blackwater*.

117. Non-citizens *can* become naturalized citizens by honorably serving at least a year in the US armed services, though this path to citizenship has recently become more difficult. Despite the fact that only 25 percent of the US population is eligible to serve, due to academic, health or behavioral issues, recent data from the US Citizenship and Immigration Services suggests that military applications for citizenship are rejected at a *higher* rate (16.6 percent) than their foreign-born civilian counterparts (11.2 percent). This trend is the result of the Trump administration's 2017 changes to

large numbers of contract personnel, the US military, like their Roman counterparts, would have great difficulty maintaining the military necessities of so vast an empire.

Neither Rome nor the United States established and maintained an empire by might alone. Despite the military dominance displayed by Rome and the United States, both have had apologists who argue that the empires were based on the consent of the ruled rather than force. Aristides made this claim in the second century AD in an oration in the Athenaeum in Rome. His objectivity is open to question as he was a panegyrist, a court littérateur whose job was to extol people in power, and he we most likely speaking in the presence of the emperor.[118] Nonetheless, Aristides has contemporary voices like Arthur Eckstein who concur with him. Eckstein makes his case succinctly: "It is not the stern militarism but Rome's ability to assimilate outsiders and to create a large and stable territorial hegemony that makes Rome stand out from [its international competitors and rivals]."[119]

The US is not without similar advocates who argue, as Philip Bobbitt has above, that the United States is a "nation of consent."[120] Paul Burton has also argued that, at least in this respect, the US's resemblance to Rome is unmistakable. He maintains that the US has "built its post-war hegemony through consultative, multilateral institutions (NATO, the U.N.) and invited others to join the coalition of western nations opposed to the Warsaw Pact nations, which, by contrast, were more or less coerced into the Soviet empire and held there by force during the same period."[121] Burton contends that the United States, like Rome before it, is a "predominantly passive, reactive, and opportunistic power, lacking any meaningful long-term grand strategy of conquest."[122] He also argues that both ancient Roman and contemporary American imperial pundits have delusions of grandeur with respect to their empire's size and salience.[123]

Comparative mass and import aside, the US is not impervious to suffering the same subtle and meandering decline as its Roman predecessor.

---

the way the Pentagon vets and clears foreign-born recruits. Copp, "Immigrant Soldiers Now Denied US Citizenship at Higher Rate than Civilians."

118. Aristides, *Orations*, 26/22.
119. Eckstein, *Mediterranean Anarchy*, 245.
120. See discussion of Bobbitt in n. 55 above.
121. Burton, "Pax Romana/Pax Americana," 95.
122. Burton, "Pax Romana/Pax Americana," 94.
123. America's peculiar hegemony fails to exert sufficient pressure on others to have its will automatically done. Rome's "rule over the entire world" only covered 15 percent of the land mass known to ancient Mediterranean civilizations—and was almost 30 percent smaller than the contemporary Han Chinese empire.

In describing the aftermath of the sack of Rome in 410, Peter Brown perspicaciously articulates the fear that inundated the Roman world and is also echoed by vigilant critics of the American empire. For Brown, at its innermost depths "Rome symbolized the security of a whole civilized way of life. To an educated man [of the fifth century], the history of the known world culminated quite naturally in the Roman Empire, just as, to a nineteenth century man, the history of civilization culminated in the supremacy of Europe."[124] His last sentence could have just as compellingly read "twentieth century person" and the "United States of America."[125] Brown continues, "The sack of Rome by the Goths, then, was an ominous reminder of the fact that the even the most valuable societies might die."[126] Twenty-first century American citizens would do well to contemplate Jerome's rhetorically ominous question, "If Rome can perish, what can be safe?"[127]

Whether one classifies the US as an unconventional empire, representative republic, fortuitous hegemon, or some amalgamation of the three, it is indisputable that US's history is rife with lapses in its professed republican principles. This is acutely evident since September 11, 2001, as warrantless wiretapping, "enhanced interrogation techniques," denying *habeas corpus* to enemy combatants, and drone assassinations have calcified, as Agamben predicted they would, into the US's enduring procedural dogma rather than transient states of exception that the government promised that they would be. Such a society is not easily navigated by Christian citizens who are concurrently disciples of an atypical king, whose kingdom is "not of this world." Fortunately for American Christians, the juxtaposition of the church and empire is as old Christianity itself. Chapter 2 will seek to provide some bearings for contemporary American Christians by mining the writings of the Roman Bishop Augustine as some of the earliest yet most enduring contemplations of the competing allegiances of Christian discipleship and imperial citizenship.

---

124. Brown, *Augustine*, 287–8.

125. For evidence that this is not hyperbolic perspective, see Fukuyama, *The End of History*.

126. Brown, *Augustine*, 288.

127. Jerome, *Letters*, 123/16.

II

Augustine on Empires and Their "Just Wars"

> Like a mountain that assumes different shapes when seen from different angles yet always dominates the landscape, Augustine towers over the development of Christian political thought in the West, as he towers over much else.[1]
>
> —Oliver & Joan O'Donovan

The intention of the previous chapter was to erect a robust foundation for authentic American Christian engagement with her nation's political edifices by unambiguously excavating their imperial propensities from rarely discussed fissures within American history. Within this framework, chapter 2 will endeavor to deconstruct the political and theological reflections of a fourth-century North African Bishop and Roman citizen. This move may appear to be a peculiar pivot. Perhaps readers are wondering what implications can the millennium-and-a-half-old ruminations of an African cleric from a "stagnant backwater"[2] have for contemporary American Christians?

The question is a valid one and deserves an answer. Despite the comparisons between the two contexts that concluded the previous

---

1. Oliver O'Donovan and Joan Lockwood O'Donovan, eds., *From Irenaeus to Grotius*, 104.

2. This is Peter Brown's assessment of fourth-century North Africa in the Roman Empire: "Somehow, the superabundant energies of the second and third centuries had come to a halt: the Africa of the fourth century had become a stagnant and affluent backwater." Brown, *Augustine*, 12.

chapter, there are incalculable and substantial apertures (temporal, physical, theological—to name but a few) between fourth-century North Africa and twenty-first-century United States. In the interim, it is sufficient to recognize that Augustine was neither a typical minister nor did he serve during an uneventful age. It is difficult to overstate Augustine's enduring imprint upon Christian and Western thought. Henry Chadwick, one of Augustine's biographers, expresses this thought succinctly, writing that, "[Augustine] has left a permanent mark on the general consciousness of humanity."[3] Were the same grandiose pronouncement written about anyone else outside of scripture it would either be viewed as innocuous hyperbole or sinister puffery.

How did this boy born in 354 AD in Thagaste (modern-day Algeria) as the son of a poor pagan small-time farmer and a devoutly Christian but "all-absorbing"[4] mother come to occupy such a prominent place in history? The confines of this book only allow space for a synopsis that relegates most of the finer details to obscurity.[5] Augustine was motivated by his father's "pig-headed resolution"[6] to see his son educated and his mother's borderline idolatrous love and ambition for him. This inherited determination would drive Augustine to become Professor of Rhetoric in Milan where he would meet and be baptized by Ambrose before resigning his university post and returning to North Africa where he would eventually be compelled, "despite his profound reluctance,"[7] to become presbyter and successor to Valerius, Bishop of Hippo.[8]

3. Chadwick, *Augustine*, 1.

4. Brown, *Augustine*, 18.

5. Given the nature and scope of this book, an exhaustive biography is ill-suited to achieve its objectives. Fortunately, for those among us with a vested interest in fleshing out a fuller account of Augustine's life, there are thoroughly erudite volumes that have already been penned. In addition to the biographies written by Peter Brown and Henry Chadwick that have been cited above, there is the shorter and oldest Augustine biography written by his contemporary, friend, pupil, and Bishop of Calama, Possidius, *Life of Saint Augustine*. Chadwick describes Possidius's biography as a portrait "not of a great theologian . . . but of a heroic pastor of his people." Chadwick, *Augustine*, 4. Possidius's biography is preceded (chronologically) and exceeded (in depth of supple insight into Augustinian thought) by Augustine's autobiography *The Confessions*, which details the evolution of Augustine's heart from his childhood until his conversion to Christianity at age thirty-three. Chadwick also offers a glowing recommendation of Le Nain de Tillemont's biography originally published in 1700 calling it "the brilliant and most indispensable of [Augustine's] biographies."

6. Brown, *Augustine*, 19.

7. Chadwick, *Augustine*, 51.

8. To say Augustine took a prolonged and convoluted route to becoming a Christian disciple and subsequent minister of the gospel is an understatement. Along the way, he

Not only was Augustine's route to the bishopric uncannily circuitous, but he also lived during an extraordinary period in Roman history in which the empire experienced an inordinate amount of rapid and intense fluctuations. Brown writes that the Roman Empire of the fourth century was facing the external and internal "strain[s] of perpetual warfare." He describes the empire that Augustine knew in a manner that even the most casual observers of US foreign policy would recognize some congruencies between the two:

> [The Roman Empire] was the prey of barbarian warbands in the North, challenged by the well-organized and militaristic kingdom of Persia in the East . . . [The Emperors] were acclaimed, with an enthusiasm that mounted with every disaster, as "the Ever-Victorious," "the Restorers of the World." Taxation had doubled, even trebled, within living memory. The poor were victimized by an insane inflation. The rich defended themselves by unparalleled accumulations of property . . . Yet, as so often happens, this world on the edge of dissolution, had settled down to believe it would last forever.[9]

The battles were waged on many fronts yet the most ubiquitous and acrimonious were those that were fought within the empire among fellow Romans. Henry Chadwick furnishes a unique context for interpreting Augustine given that the whole of Augustine's life transpired just in the foreground of the all-encompassing backdrop of the unremittingly existential tension and conflict between "a confident and conquering Christianity capturing Roman society and a fierce pagan counterattack."[10]

Controversies had a way of regularly finding Augustine, or perhaps it is more appropriately intimated that he was remarkably uninterested in taking pains to avoid the polemical. As bishop, Augustine defended the Catholic Church against denigrations levelled at it from all sides—against Donatist Christians within the church no less vigorously than against Roman pagans

---

was ensconced in Manichaeism for nine years. Peter Brown describes the Manichees as "the 'Bolsheviks' of the fourth century: a 'fifth column' of foreign origin bent on infiltrating the Christian church, the bearers of a uniquely radical solution to the religious problems of their age." Brown, *Augustine*, 35. Augustine also indulged in a fifteen-year relationship with a concubine with whom he had a son. Their son died at the age of 18 prompting Augustine to write "I had no part in that boy but the sin." *Confessions*, IX/vi/14. In 385, at Monica's urging Augustine abandoned his concubine whose name is lost to history not because he had developed moral scruples but due to his personal ambition. Brown, *Augustine*, 51. Instead, he was betrothed to a young heiress around the age of ten whom Monica had chosen for him. Chadwick, *Augustine*, 20.

9. Brown, *Augustine*, 13–14.
10. Chadwick, *Augustine*, 2.

outside the church. Unfortunately, disputes with both contingents eventually degenerated from metaphysical discourse to physical coercion.

Augustine's rebuttal against the pagans repurposed the writings of their own historians and philosophers to question the authenticity of their collective memories regarding their Republic and its virtues. Given the multitude of demands concurrently vying for the bishop's discerning deliberation, it is unsurprising that he took fourteen years for his meticulous counterargument against the pagans' objections to migrate from his mind to a manuscript. These "migrating ideas" were given the title *The City of God against the Pagans*, a book widely regarded as his paramount legacy inherited by the Church and subsequent Christian thinkers. For as many as believe that *The City of God* represents the pinnacle of the bishop's considerable acumen, his *magnum opus*, there is an equally large and vocal contingent of scholars who consider Augustine's rejoinder to the Donatist controversy to be his *malum opus*, a repugnant liability also inherited by the Church and its future disciples.

The pagans found the Church's adherence to monotheism far too restrictive and even blamed the empire's decline on the atrophy of classical Roman religions. The Donatists' grievances lay at the opposite end of the gamut. If the pagans believed that Catholic teaching was too narrow and demanding, the Donatists accused Catholics of being too theologically permissive and morally compromised by their propinquity to Roman power. As a Roman Christian, Augustine was inexorably susceptible to the accusation he was excessively inhabiting one aspect of his identity while insufficiently cultivating or castigating the other. The Donatists would always view Augustine as inadequately Christian because he was *too* Roman, whereas the Pagans believed the converse, that Augustine's excessive devotion to Christianity would always *impede* him from becoming fully Roman.

These disputes were more than mere rhetorically belligerent sophistry. Rather, these were the seeds of animosity that had been developing since Christianity was incorporated into the empire a century earlier, and when the seeds had finally blossomed they would yield the fruit of violence and death. For the pagans, it was the sack of Rome in 410 that provided the decisive impetus for them to openly accuse their Christian neighbors of orchestrating the deterioration of the empire.[11] Augustine's comprehensive rebuttal to them, *The City of God*, will be discussed more extensively below.

11. Had the Romans been abreast of their recent history, they may have recognized that the beginning of the end of the empire likely occurred much earlier than the Gothic invasion of Rome in 410. Instead, it can be traced to 375 AD with the mismanagement of a refugee crisis. Augustine was just twenty-one years old, when the first wave of some 200,000 Goths began migrating south from their homes in what is now modern-day Ukraine to frontiers of the Roman Empire in order to distance themselves from the

For the Donatists, the final straw that vanquished any genuine hope of restorative fellowship with the Catholics came in the form of an imperial decree posted in June of 405 ironically entitled the "Edict of Unity." By this time, the Donatists were well accustomed to finding themselves on the punitive side of imperial decrees. However, this pronouncement was more austere and pervasive than the others.[12] The edict of 405 had a curious methodology for affecting "unity." Though no Donatist was forced to join the Catholic Church, the edict had the aim of funneling the Donatist clergy and the rank and file into the Catholic Church.[13] The Donatists were branded heretics, and their church was formally disbanded. Afterwards, the Donatist bishop was removed and his church was taken over by Catholics. As Peter Brown explains it, this sequence of events meant that "Augustine would be faced with the unpleasant and arduous task of absorbing a leaderless congregation."[14] Augustine's theological defense for this religious coercion will be addressed in its own section below.

Huns, whom the Roman historian Marcellinus described as a "race savage beyond all parallel." The Goths requested permission from Emperor Valens to cross the Danube and settle in Thrace to which he agreed. The typical and clever Roman approach to "barbarian" immigration was to allow them in and make them Roman. However, the military officials in charge of overseeing the provisions for the Goths were corrupt and saw a grand opportunity to enrich themselves. These profiteering generals purposely mismanaged food stocks in order to inflate prices and profits. Some Goths even traded their children into slavery in exchange for dog meat. The cold Roman reception did not improve over time. In fact, it deteriorated further due to a lengthy famine and a botched kidnapping and assassination attempt of two Gothic leaders. The Goths began raiding the country sides in order to stave off starvation. Valens led an army against the Goths to chastise them for these illicit excursions. When they met in Adrianople in 376, Valens was struck down and his army routed by the superior Gothic cavalry. This battle, not the sack of Rome in 410 by descendants of these same Goths, proved to be the initial sign that the empire was terminally ill. The Goths proved that the Roman army was vulnerable even when fighting within the borders of its own empire. The "barbarians'" impetus to infiltrate the empire significantly outpaced the Romans' capacity to dissuade them from doing so. What was good for the Goths was also good for the Vandals who made themselves at home in the Roman provinces of Gaul and Spain. They were content there until 429 when 80,000 of them crossed the Straits of Gibraltar to occupy the western provinces of Roman North Africa and establish a pirate kingdom at Carthage. The Vandals arrived and began to ravish Hippo in the spring of 430. A few short months later, the elderly and infirmed Augustine passed away while the city where he ministered was under siege.

12. Only a year earlier, the Catholic council of bishops had requested police protection from the Donatists, but they also asked the Emperors to refrain from applying heresy laws to the Donatists that would deprive them of their legal rights and, the bishops feared, produce feigned conversions among prospective litigants en masse. Brown, *Augustine*, 230.

13. Brown, "Religious Coercion," 283–305.

14. Brown, *Augustine*, 230.

It is fitting to revisit the question that initially animated these brief glimpses into Augustine's biography. What makes Augustine a fitting interlocutor in the contemporary American Christian discourse? He was a prolific writer and polemicist fully engaged as both faithful disciple of Christ and subject of the Roman Empire[15]—an exemplar from whom American Christians can learn a great deal. Since he did not write systematically but rather pastorally and polemically, as called for by each unique situation, it is difficult to trace Augustine's fully developed thought on any subject across forty years of his sermons, commentaries, letters, and books. As Peter Brown has expressed in his foreword to Henry Chadwick's biography of Augustine, "To follow the thought of Augustine ... is to follow the grain of a very complex piece of wood."[16] This intricate-thinking Bishop was also no stranger to controversial and theological debates about the Christian deployment of coercive force—a topic he revisits several times throughout his corpus. There is no more fitting point of departure than Augustine for a twenty-first-century American account of the theological ethics of empire and a "just war against terror."

This thesis is acutely wary of anachronistically filtering Augustine through America, rather than the proper way around. Eric Gregory's observation nicely encapsulates my worry: "No doubt Augustine's texts, in all their unsystematic glory, can be pressed into service of all sorts of projects, *including my own*. Part of Augustine's genius lies in the fact that by reading him we often come to read ourselves and wish for another Augustine."[17] While this book does not "wish for another Augustine," it has attempted to measure interlocutors' exegesis against Augustine's own texts, and the viewpoint and priority of values they present. The principal question this chapter seeks to answer is, what does it mean to read and take seriously that Augustine was not a citizen of a liberal democracy but a self-consciously imperial subject?[18]

---

15. Henri de Lubac wrote, "In that thin slice of history that Providence gave Augustine to live, regardless of the emperor in power—pagan, Christian, or apostate, hostile or favorable to his views—he remained 'a faithful subject of the great Roman Empire.'" De Lubac, *Theological Fragments*, 255.

16. Chadwick, *Augustine*, xi.

17. Gregory, *Politics & the Order of Love*, 6. Emphasis mine. Cognizant of this temptation, my aim is to contemplate *with* Augustine the tangible political realities of empires and just wars in a manner that would invite even those who disagree with my conclusions to appraise them as Augustine did Macedonius's letters: "we who know you do not doubt that you wrote this for the sake of raising a question, not for the sake of pronouncing judgement ... " in Augustine, *Letters*, 153/2.

18. This question is timely since Augustine is most often used as a cypher for liberal democratic participation. See Gregory, *Politics & the Order of Love* and Mathewes,

Augustine wrote less than a century after Emperor Constantine's conversion to Christianity, the watershed moment that began the religion's metamorphosis from marginal, oft persecuted, and peculiar religious sect within the Roman Empire to a position of political and personal advantage as the only *religio licita*[19] within the empire it had inherited.[20]

The question before the Church was no longer how to subsist on the edges of empire's shadow but rather how to capitalize on its newly inherited place of power. Peter Brown describes the fourth-century Church in this strange new world as a "group no longer committed to defend itself against the society; but rather, poised, ready to fulfil what it considered to its historic mission, to dominate, to absorb, to lead a whole Empire."[21] Many believed, as did Eusebius, that the Christianization of the empire was the culmination of history and that God was ruling on earth through Constantine. Though initially intrigued by the idea of a radically Christianized empire, Augustine ultimately refused to baptize the empire as wholly Christian.[22] He was quick to remind his congregation that "the Emperor has become a Christian—the devil has not."[23] Augustine was navigating uncharted ecclesial and political waters in which the Church was still trying to reconcile its unexpectedly newfound favor within Rome, which had incongruent epistemological foundations from its own.

Integrating Christianity into Rome or, as some have argued, Rome into Christianity has been both lauded and loathed by contemporary Christian thinkers. John Howard Yoder was famously critical of what he called the "Constantinian shift" that saw the early Church move from rejecting to defending imperialism. Rome's shift from oppressing Christians to repressing the Church's heretics within a few generations by "ruling on what constitutes orthodox belief and punishing dissent"[24] was not without its own ethical implications. Among these serious repercussions was that being a Christian

---

Theology of Public Life. The following chapter contains my interaction with these authors and similar material.

19. Permissible religion.

20. According to Louis J. Swift, "It is a truism that the reign of Constantine (A.D. 306–337) represents a watershed in the development of Christian attitudes concerning war and military service inasmuch as the question is no longer whether participation in war is justified but what conditions should govern the right to declare war (*ius belli*) and what rules should be observed in waging it (*ius in bello*)." Swift, *Early Fathers on War and Military Service*, 80.

21. Brown, *Augustine*, 209.

22. O'Daly, *Augustine's City of God*, 47.

23. Augustine, *Expositions on the Psalms*, 93:19.

24. Yoder, *Priestly Kingdom*, 136.

became "the rule rather than the exception," which meant where it formerly took great courage to confess Christ, it now took greater conviction to deny him.[25] For Yoder, the true church became invisible because nearly everyone became "part" of it for social and/or political reasons.

Peter Leithart interprets the same events more charitably than Yoder did. In *Defending Constantine*, Leithart portrays Constantine as a sincere, though flawed Christian who "baptized Rome"[26] by blunting the fundamental role public sacrifice played in the polity. Through Constantine's actions, the political order had been "desacrificed" in a manner reminiscent of the gospel's end of sacrifice.[27] Yoder would have likely agreed with Leithart's assessment that Rome had been baptized.

However, Yoder would interpret the nature of the "baptism" in more derisive terms, more comparable to the whitewashing of a tomb, whereas Leithart holds it to be a positive sort of "infant baptism," one that marked the beginning of the empire's transformation rather than the culmination of it. Hence Leithart concedes there might have been a "Constantinian moment" but not the tectonic shift that Yoder describes. The claims that sovereign political entities make on the lives of their citizens are poignant, nonetheless. Whether a citizen obliges or rejects her sovereign's demand for sacrifice chiefly orients how she inhabits the empire. Augustine serves as an exemplar of this claim.

Whether the Church is more appropriately portrayed as Rome's evangelist, as Leithart argues, or its convert, as Yoder and Hauerwas contend, Augustine seemed comfortable to live within the tensions that enveloped the growing influence the two polities had on each other. He rejected the conflation of the two but not their interactions. He did not sympathize with Eusebius's inclination to view the Christianization of the empire as the providential culmination of "God's will done on earth as it is in heaven."[28]

Like Yoder, Augustine thought that one effect of Constantine's conversion was that genuine believers became more difficult to discern from the pseudo-faithful. However, Augustine was not as disheartened by this as Yoder would become:

---

25. Yoder, *Priestly Kingdom*, 136.
26. Leithart, *Defending Constantine*, 301–3.
27. Leithart, *Defending Constantine*, 326. See Hebrews 10.
28. "Outside dissenting or schismatic circles Augustine was the only thinker of any stature who was deeply disturbed by the developments of the fourth century towards a sacral conception of the Empire. He rejected the identification of the Church's destiny with that of the Empire, implied in this conception." Markus, *Saeculum*, 157.

[B]ecause that which will not remain with [the Lord] forever in eternity is not really the body of the Lord; but it should have been called "about the true and mixed body of the Lord," or "the true and pretended body," or something else like that; because it is not only in eternity but even now that hypocrites should not be said to be with him, even though they appear to be in his Church. Hence this rule could also have been given the name and title such as "about the Church as a mixture."[29]

For Augustine, this "church as mixture" was the natural result of the church lowering its Gospel nets into the sea of the world. Inevitably it gathered together both clean and unclean animals, but the catch would not be separated until the end time when it was brought ashore. Likewise, if the Lord was pleased to let the wheat and tares grow side by side until the harvest, Augustine was content to do the same with pagans, Donatists, and Catholics in his church who had less than authentic conversions. In his exposition of Psalm 61, Augustine describes the mixed nature of the church by noting that, "The people who throng our churches at the festivals of Jerusalem fill the theatres on Babylon's high days; yet they serve, honor and pay homage to Christ."[30] Whether the assimilation of Christianity and Rome originated as a blessing or curse, it indelibly shaped a great deal of political and theological discourse in the West.

In Augustine's time, the ideas of church and state were not yet the strange bedfellows they would become after the enlightenment. Bishops held ecclesial and limited civil authority. They could hear court cases and issue judgements including administering penalties. These "bishop's tribunals" found their imperial origins in constitutions issued by Constantine in 318 and 333.

For biblical support of the practice, bishops pointed to Paul's teaching in 1 Corinthians 6:1–6 against Christians dragging one another to court in front of the unrighteous rather than settling disputes among themselves before the saints. Augustine held such tribunals, mediating disputes over property ownership, slavery, contracts, and inheritances.[31] Leithart points to these ecclesial courts as evidence of Constantine's "Christianization of the empire" since Roman courts were tilted heavily in favour of the wealthy who could afford to bribe judges to rule more favourably and appeal their cases *ad nauseum*. As the bishop's courts were free and the

---

29. Augustine, *Teaching Christianity*, III/45.
30. Augustine, *Expositions of the Psalms*, 61/10.
31. Augustine, *Political Writings*, 251n4.

bishops were thought to be above the sway of bribery, they were a more equitable administration of justice.

Augustine also put his thumb on the scales of justice, pastorally tilting them toward mercy, by writing 252 letters that have survived to imperial courts and magistrates, believers and non-believers alike. While he did not confuse the roles of pastoring with governing, he did not hesitate to use his influence in both arenas.

Consider, for example, "Letter 133" to the imperial commissioner Marcellinus and 134 to African proconsul Apringius, Marcellinus's brother. In his correspondence, Augustine is supporting a merciful sentence against Circumcellion and Donatist clerics guilty of violent crimes against two Catholic priests. Augustine addresses the men as lords as well as sons—the first an address befitting a citizen subordinate to judges, the latter a bishop counselling his Christian parishioners. The bishop is reminding the brothers that he and they had authority over each other in unique ways. He cites Romans 13:4 as a direct address to Apringius from Paul, "you do not wield the sword without reason, and you are ministers of God, and avengers on the evildoer."[32] Augustine declares this with the caveat that the jurisdictions of the province and Church are distinct and that "The government of the former should be managed by deterrence; the gentleness of the latter should commend itself by its mercy."[33] Augustine argues:

> If you do not listen to a friend begging you, listen to a bishop giving you advice. And yet, since I speak to a Christian, I would not be arrogant in saying, especially in such a case, that *it is proper that you hear a bishop giving you an order*, my excellent and rightly noble lord and dearest son.[34]

Augustine elsewhere confesses that if the brothers were pagans, he would have appealed to them differently, in a subtler manner. However, to Christians, Augustine could be more forthcoming with Marcellinus and Apringius about the natures of true justice and authority.

As part bishop and statesman,[35] Augustine's distinctive voice continues to resonate in political conversations, but this was not the occasion for the *City of God*'s commission. After the sack of Rome in 410, Augustine set

---

32. Augustine, *Letters*, 134:3.

33. Augustine, *Letters*, 134:3.

34. Augustine, *Letters*, 133:3. Emphasis mine. Augustine uses a similar construct in *Letters*, 134/2: "I as a Christian beg the judge and as a bishop warn a Christian."

35. Both "state" and "statesman" are crude anachronisms, but they are also the best metaphors for the prevailing political paradigm of the day and a citizen actively involved in it.

out to defend Christianity from the charge that its rise within the empire was responsible for the empire's decline. In this tome, we have the most extensive single work of the mature and prolific bishop's thoughts on the juxtaposition of the Church and empire.

Augustine brilliantly addressed Roman grumblings by appealing to their own accounts of history as told by their poets, historians, and philosophers. Cicero serves as Augustine's primary interlocutor in *The City of God* through an analysis of Cicero's *Republic,* which provided a readymade, thoroughly Roman perspective that was also a "widely esteemed account of civic virtue, one grounded in a conventionally accepted political vocabulary, along with a critical, historical perspective on Rome's failure to live up to its social ethical ideals."[36]

If the only thing Augustine achieved in writing the *City of God* was to wield Cicero's *Republic* to cleverly defend the church against pagan charges, it would likely still be considered a literary classic. However, he also used the *Republic* to juxtapose pagan and Christian accounts of civic virtue demonstrating with painstaking detail the reason even the most virtuous of Rome's citizens were found morally deficient when measured against Christ. John Milbank summarizes: "what Augustine achieves is a kind of immanent critique, or deconstruction of antique political society . . . He tries to show that, by its own standards, its virtue is not virtue, its community is not community, its justice not justice."[37]

In the *City of God* I/19, Augustine offers up Lucretia as the quintessential exemplar of Roman vice swathed in virtue. The Romans esteemed Lucretia as the epitome of purity for her decision to take her own life after the king's son raped her. Augustine was baffled by the honor bestowed upon her since the Roman law would not permit the execution of even the wicked who were un-condemned, yet it praised the murder of innocent Lucretia by her own hand.

The lauding of Lucretia's suicide, an act usually disdained by the Romans,[38] was more egregious since she slew herself though she was purportedly chaste and innocent. Rather than extol her deed, Augustine reasons she must have been guilty of either adultery or, more likely, murder: "For if she is acquitted of murder, she is convicted of adultery; and if she is acquitted of

---

36. Dodaro, *Christ and the Just Society,* 10.

37. Milbank, *Theology & Social Theory,* 392. This was also the aim in highlighting the incongruities in the US self-perception in the previous chapter.

38. Virgil said that those who committed suicide "threw away their souls" and were prohibited from a return to the overworld. *Aeneid* 6/434 and 6/438 quoted in the *City of God,* I/19.

adultery, then she is convicted of murder ... One can only ask: If she was an adulteress, why is she praised? If she was pure, why was she slain?"[39]

He concludes that Lucretia was chaste and that, "there were two people, but only one of them committed adultery."[40] However, her subsequent suicide was prompted not by a "love of purity, but [by] weakness arising from shame."[41] As the epitome of a Roman citizen disproportionately desirous of praise, Lucretia took her life to exonerate herself from any suspicion of complicity in her violation.

Augustine distinguishes Lucretia's response from those of Christian women abused in the same manner. The latter refused to compound the sin by straying "from the authority of the divine law by doing wrong to avoid the scandal of human suspicion."[42] Not beholden to the court of public opinion, Christian victims take solace in the reality that their chastity remains unmarred before God even if unduly sullied before people. This glory before God cannot be as easily undone as laurels contingent on tenuous public opinions.

Augustine further underscores the incestuous fusing of Roman virtue and vice by discussing another one of its famous suicides, that of Cato the Younger. As a defender of the republic and collaborator with Pompey, Cato took his own life when Caesar's rise to power signaled the death knell of the republic. Although Cato was esteemed as "a man of the greatest discretion [who] yielded to no Roman indignity of purpose,"[43] he refused to be convinced that it was "neither shameful nor dreadful for [him], when he has no other way of salvation, to await salvation at the hands of his enemy."[44] Cato begrudged Caesar the glory of pardoning an enemy. Augustine challenged Cato's logic and wondered why, if Cato found death more honorable than living under a victorious Caesar, he did not spare his own son from the shame that Cato supposedly escaped through suicide.[45]

Rather than encourage others to follow his lead into vain-glorious suicide, Cato kept the gates of Utica shut, allowing his supporters to flee by sea and waited until the last ship departed to take his own life. According to Augustine, Cato's act of valor attempted to limit Caesar's glory while increasing his own. To this end, he succeeded since Plutarch wrote that,

---

39. Augustine, *City of God*, I/19.
40. The source of this quote that Augustine uses in I/19 is unknown.
41. Augustine, *City of God*, I/19.
42. Augustine, *City of God*, I/19.
43. Plutarch, "Cato the Younger," I.
44. Plutarch, "Cato the Younger," LXIX.
45. Augustine, *City of God*, I/23.

upon learning of Cato's suicide, the people of Utica, "with one voice . . . called Cato their savior and benefactor, the only one who was free, the only one unvanquished."[46]

Rhetorical moves like these are not the ones that have made the *City of God* the most enduring among and endearing to subsequent generations of Christians. Few contemporary Christian clergy or laity lose sleep over whether their faith led to the collapse of an empire 1600 years ago. Of far greater import to subsequent readers of the *City of God* is how to orientate themselves within their polities while remaining faithful to the gospel of Christ. For questions of this nature, Augustine's powerful metaphors of the coinciding cities—the cities of man and God—are most illuminating. This is the quintessential paradigm through which Christians have reconciled their "dual citizenships" in ecclesial and political kingdoms for centuries. It is also the lens through which we will explore Augustine's expositions of empire and the "just wars" that are invariably fought for imperial survival.

Augustine's Two Cities

Births, done properly at least, are preceded by love. So, it was with the cities of man and God. It is unsurprising that markedly different loves laid the foundations of cities as disparate as these. In what is the most succinct synopsis of the *City of God*, Augustine describes the conception of the two cities in this manner:

> Two loves, then, have made two cities. Love of self, even to the point of contempt for God, made the earthly city, and love of God, even to the point of contempt for self, made the heavenly city. Thus, the former glories in itself, and the latter glories in the Lord. The former seeks its glory from men, but the latter finds its highest glory in God, the witness of our conscience. The former lifts up its head in its own glory; the latter says to its God, *My glory, and the one who lifts up my head* (Ps 3:3). In the former the lust for domination dominates both its princes and the nations that it subjugates; in the latter, both leaders and followers serve one another in love, the leaders by their counsel, the followers by their obedience. The former loves its own strength; the latter says to its God, *I love you, O Lord, my strength* (Ps 18:1).[47]

By its own strength, the earthly city brings forth new citizens in the conventional manner with a nature vitiated by sin. The heavenly city increases its

---

46. Plutarch, "Cato the Younger," LXXI.
47. Augustine, *City of God*, XIV/28.

census when grace liberates a former slave from the bondages of sin. Both Ishmael and Isaac were born of Abraham, but one according to the flesh and one according to the promise; "In the one case, human practice is displayed; in the other, divine beneficence is acclaimed."[48]

Labors are also notoriously bloody and painful affairs. What distinguishes the two nativities is to whom the blood belongs and the manner in which it was shed. The city of man is characterized by two infamous fratricides—the first by Cain's hand and the second by Romulus. Cain, motivated by his envy of Abel's offering, and Romulus, driven by his refusal to share the glory and power of founding Rome with Remus, used their brothers' blood as mortar to raise their cities' walls. The heavenly city was also brought forth in blood lifted up. However, it was that of Jesus and his martyrs drawn in humility, witness, and worship of God. The blood of these witnesses adorned doorframes as signposts to the God whose judgment passes over His people.

Although it covets immortality, the city of man is painfully aware of its temporal nature. Man seeks to secure a kingdom, "not in eternal life but in a life where the dying pass away and are succeeded by those who are going to die in turn."[49] For this reason, the earthly kingdom must continue to employ Cain and Romulus's *modus operandi* to stave off its death. When the last resident of the earthly city dies, the city perishes with him. It is no surprise Romans cherished glory so dearly as their only hope for immortality was the, "glory by which they yearned to find a life after death, as it were, on the lips of those who praised them."[50] This is why Romans esteemed Lucretia and Cato because they had done what so few can—fabricate a transient veneer of immortality by condensing the whole of their lives into one final, memorable act. Hannah Arendt concurs with Augustine's assessment of the Roman struggle for permanence after death, explaining that

> Immortality means endurance in time, deathless life on this earth and in this world as it was given, according to Greek understanding, to nature and the Olympian gods. Against this background of nature's ever-recurring life and the gods' deathless and ageless beings stood mortal men, the only mortals in an immortal but not eternal universe, confronted with the immortal lives of their gods but not under the rule of an infinite God.[51]

---

48. Augustine, *City of God*, XIV/2.
49. Augustine, *City of God*, V/14.
50. Augustine, *City of God*, V/14.
51. Arendt, *Human Condition*, 18.

The best those who know only the earthly city can hope for is to leave unforgettable deeds behind and attain a type of pseudo-eternalness. Arendt argues that whoever strives after this manner of "immortal fame" must inevitably suffer a short life and premature death.[52] The only way to control one's own narrative is to encapsulate it in a single deed, "forgoing the continuity of living in which we disclose ourselves piecemeal . . . so that the story of the act comes to its end together with life itself."[53] She uses Achilles as the prototype for this heroic, yet tragic immortality, but she could just as fittingly have used Lucretia or Cato.

That even the great Trojan War would have faded from memory if not for the work of Homer several centuries later exhibits what little hope for permanence human greatness has if left to the plaudits of poets. According to Arendt, the fall of the Roman Empire lays bare the claim that "no work of mortal hands can be immortal." This, coupled with Christianity's rise as the imperial religion, made the human striving for earthly immortality as futile as it was vain.[54]

Contrary to the ways of the earthly city, Christian disciples seek a conspicuously different genus of immortality. Rather than live forever in honors bestowed by human memories, which Augustine called mere smoke since it is easily seen but has no weight,[55] the citizen of the heavenly city seeks an eternal communion with God. By seeking fame through their virtue, the Roman heroes have "received their reward in full" in their historians' prose or poets' ballads. Jesus, conversely, admonishes his disciples to "practice their righteousness" discreetly so they will not squander their reward in the public praises of people but receive the secret gift of God the Father.[56] To the extent that Christians' lives exhibit virtue, it is to garner glory for their Father in heaven rather than to cause their hearts to swell with the love of praise.[57]

These living worshipers are but a small part of the eternal city of God. The heavenly city consists of the "whole family of the living and supreme

---

52. Arendt, *Human Condition*, 193.

53. Arendt, *Human Condition*, 194. This Roman idea has also permeated Islam and motivates suicide attacks in *jihad* as one of the few "golden tickets" to paradise.

54. Arendt, *Human Condition*, 21.

55. Augustine, *City of God*, V/1, 7.

56. Matt 6:1–4, quoted in Augustine, *City of God*, V/15.

57. Matt 5:16: "In the same way, let your light shine before others, so that they may see your good works and give glory to your Father who is in heaven." John the Baptist is the epitome of this in his ministry that magnified Christ and minimized his importance: "He must become greater; I must become less." John 3:30.

God."⁵⁸ Augustine calls the part of God's family that still resides in the earthly city "pilgrims" to highlight their transient status and the ephemeral nature of their earthly home. He also admonishes them that "even the temporal life that the faithful have in this world is not to be regretted. In this life, they are schooled for eternity and, like pilgrims, make use of earthly goods without being taken captive by them, while they are either proved or corrected by evils."⁵⁹ Rather than call the heavenly city to withdraw from the earthly city, leaving the latter to pursue its interests even at the expense of the former, Augustine insists that the barrier between the two is permeable. Those born in the city of Cain are not destined to perish there.

In his seminal work *Saeculum*, R. A. Markus argues that the defining distinction between the two cities is eschatological rather than sociological. The heavenly city need not withdraw from the earthly to form some morally superior society nor should the earthly be shut out of the heavenly. Markus adds, "What prevented the Christian from being at home in his world was not that he had an alternative home in the Church, but his faith in the transformation of the world through Christ's victory over sin and death and his hope in the final sharing of this victory in His kingdom."⁶⁰ Similarly, Augustine is convinced that human governance is an institution created by God to benefit his creation. As such the church should support governing authorities, though neither uncritically nor unconditionally. This is true even though Augustine maintains that,

> [God] did not want a rational creature, made in his own image, to have dominion except over irrational creatures—not man over man but man over beasts. That is why the first righteous men were established as shepherds of flocks rather than as kings of men, so that in this way too, God might indicate what the order of created beings requires and what the fault of sinners demands.⁶¹

This excerpt is taken from two chapters in the *City of God* where Augustine is discussing slavery. There are allusions to governing here as well but not strong enough language to conclude, as John Milbank does, that "Certain phrasings in *Civitas Dei* show that Augustine regards the institution of slavery after the fall, and the institution of political power, as virtually the same event."⁶² Perhaps 1 Samuel 8 is a clearer illustration of Milbank's supposition

58. Augustine, *City of God*, I/29.
59. Augustine, *City of God*, I/29.
60. Markus, *Saeculum*, 167.
61. Augustine, *City of God*, XIX/15.
62. Milbank, *Theology and Social Theory*, 411. Here Milbank references the same chapters in Augustine that are quoted here. Rather than paint Milbank as a Christian

that earthly rule by any authority other than God is a divine concession that results from sin—both Adam's and his heirs.[63]

Whether Augustine believed there would have been "government" even without the fall or what form it may have taken is open to speculation. However, Augustine left no such ambiguity when articulating the origins of individual and kingdom authority:

> We should not ascribe the power of granting kingdoms and empires to any but the true God. It is he who gives happiness in the kingdom of heaven to the godly alone, and it is he who gives earthly kingdoms to the godly and ungodly alike according to his pleasure, which never takes pleasure in anything unjust . . . The same is true of individual men. The same God who gave power to Marius also gave it to Gaius Caesar; the same God who gave power to Augustus also gave it to Nero; the same God who gave it to the Vespasian, father and son, the most temperate emperors, also gave it to Domitian, the cruelest; and—there is no need to mention each emperor individually—the same God who gave power to Constantine the Christian also gave it to Julian the Apostate . . . Clearly, the one true God rules and governs all these things as he pleases. And, if his reasons are hidden, does that mean that they are unjust?[64]

---

anarchist, here are some of the lines that follow that offer a fuller context, "Political rule, for Augustine, is only 'natural' in a twofold manner. First of all, the intellectually and morally inferior should naturally be guided by their superiors . . . In this sense, there would have been 'government' even before the fall . . . Secondly, coercive political rule, like slavery, is 'natural' for the period after the fall, because providentially ordained by God to curb human sin." For Milbank, this is the most problematic area of Augustine's social theory because it is tantamount to curbing sin with more serious sin marked by the pride and self-sufficiency of governance.

63. Oliver O'Donovan argues along Augustinian lines that the political theology of Israel was resistant to the idea of the monarchy since the right of government belonged exclusively to *Yahweh*. He adds that if the throne of David was a concession to Israel's weakness, Jeroboam's reign certainly was not. The people chose Jeroboam for themselves as an image of God to sit in God's rightful throne. This act, according to O'Donovan, was as idolatrous as it was rebellious. He argues that the early church adopted a similar stance that political representation was fundamentally rebellious. The cross of Christ stands over the "powers and principalities" embodied by governments. Concerning Romans 13, he says, "the whole question of the representative status of government is passed by in silence, and its rationale is found exclusively in the tasks of justice. Government is to enact God's word of judgement; that and nothing else. The desire to have a government in one's image is like the desire to have God in one's image." O'Donovan, *Common Objects of Love*, 53–54.

64. Augustine, *City of God*, V/21.

For one who would become so influential in political theology, Augustine does not seem particularly bothered by what form political institutions took or those who were in charge of them. In the *City of God*, he purposefully constructs the political metaphors of the heavenly and earthly cities as each was only partially embodied by the concrete political lives of Rome and the church. Both cities preceded and would outlive their contemporary representatives. Neither the fall of Rome nor the church would decimate their respective cities. From this perspective Augustine made claims that those who covet power will find inexplicable:

> For, as far as this mortal life is concerned, which passes and is over in a few days, what difference does it make under whose rule a person lives who is soon to die, just so long as those who rule do not compel him into anything ungodly and wicked? . . . But with regard to security and good morals, the true notes of human dignity, I utterly fail to see what difference it makes that some are conquerors and others conquered, apart from the utterly empty arrogance of human glory.[65]

This passage suggests that Augustine had no political preference for the form of authority in power over him. It also intimates that, had he survived the Vandal invasion, he would have preferred his role as an infirmed seventy-five year old slave to that of his conquerors:

> It is a happier lot to be enslaved to a man than enslaved to lust; in fact, it is the very lust for domination itself, to mention no others, that ravages the hearts of mortals by exercising the most savage kind of domination over them. And, within that order of peace by which some men are subject to others, while humility is beneficial to those who serve, pride is harmful to those who rule.[66]

Rather than alluding to a politically aloof Augustine, these statements indicate that he was open to objectively evaluating the dominant form inhabited by political power in his day no matter how and by whom it was wielded. He refused the temptation, to which Eusebius had succumbed, to sacralize Rome as the new "city on a hill."

Neither did he make the converse error by preemptively demonizing all earthly authority. Augustine examined empire, the political structure under which he was born, through a keenly theological lens. Whether one believes that providence or fortunate accidents of history determined the

---

65. Augustine, *City of God*, V/17. The Church would be well served to heed Augustine's advice here.

66. Augustine, *City of God*, XIX:15.

particulars of Augustine's birth, his assessment of the Roman empire under whose sign he was born is profoundly helpful to American Christians who live under the imperial auspices of the stars and stripes.

Empires: Outsized Cohorts of Thieves with Impunity

> Remove justice, then, and what are kingdoms but large gangs of robbers? And what are gangs of robbers but small kingdoms? The gang, too, is a group of men ruled by a leader's command. It is bound together by a pact of association, and its loot is divided according to an agreed law. If, by constantly adding desperate men, this scourge grows to such an extent that it acquires territory, establishes a home base, occupies cities, and subjugates peoples, it more openly assumes the name of kingdom, a name now publicly conferred on it due not to any reduction in greed but rather to the addition of impunity. For it was a witty and true response that a certain captured pirate made to the famous Alexander the Great. When the king asked the man what he meant by infesting the sea, he defiantly replied, "Just what you mean when you infest the whole world! But because I do it with one tiny ship, I am called a robber; and because you do it with a great fleet, you are called emperor."[67]

Oliver O'Donovan writes that it was Augustine's theological perspective that endowed this quip with the dignity of a political principle. Augustine could dismiss the Roman political culture of antiquity without turning his back on society because he simultaneously pointed to a divine authority and a permanent social order.[68] Augustine pointed out that the Roman empire's establishment of world order was actually based upon a lust for conquest and proposed a reform of empire that would entail a decentralized relational linking of many dispersed local centers.

More drastically, Augustine questioned the fundamental nature of the Roman polity to understand what was inherent in its self-understanding as a *res publica*.[69] He expanded upon Cicero's definition of a people as a "mul-

---

67. Cicero, *The Republic*, 3/14, 24, quoted in Augustine, *City of God*, IV/4.
68. O'Donovan, *Desire of the Nations*, 7. See *City of God*, IV/3,4.
69. This word, as Augustine uses it, has proven somewhat slippery for interpreters. The translator's note in *Augustine: Political Writings* frames the problem this way: "*Res publica* means literally 'public thing'. In *Letter* 138:10 Augustine refers to Cicero's well-known definition, which may be translated: 'the "public thing" is a thing of (belonging

titude joined together by a common sense of what is right and a community of interest."[70] Augustine argued a republic cannot exist where a tyrant has taken over or if the people are unjust. Far from being undermined by Christianity, as some Romans had asserted, the Roman republic had long been deceased and Cicero had delivered the eulogy for it 40 years before the birth of Christ writing, "For it is due to our own vices, not to any mere chance or accident, that we now retain the republic in name only, having long ago lost it in reality."[71] How did a society that placed such a premium on virtue and worship fall into such a depraved state?

The deficiency of the Roman liturgy as Augustine framed it was not that people cared too little about the worship of gods, but that they were concerned too much with the profane devotion to so many gods to the neglect of the worship of the one, holy, and true God. He surmised that, "One was not enough for men who so loved a multitude of gods that each wretched soul, scorning the chaste embrace of the one true God, prostituted himself to a horde of demons."[72] Rebutting those who held Christianity culpable for the sack of Rome in 410, Augustine wondered where the Roman gods had been when it had been ravished before Christ? In an ironic twist of fate, the Romans were deserted to defend the temples of the very gods that were supposed to be protecting them. Based on this evidence, it was disingenuous to fault Christ for Rome's latest stumble yet allow the Roman pantheon to recuse itself from culpability in Rome's past misfortunes.

In Augustine's assessment, so numerous were their gods that Rome should have never been assailed. For as the empire grew so did the number of its deities as the existing gods were deemed insufficient to defend Rome's greatness.[73] Augustine cites as evidence that there were at least eleven gods and goddesses responsible for overseeing corn production from the planting of the seed to harvesting of the crop. He found it laughable that the growth and protection of the empire should be attributed to any deity other than the Christian God since none of the Roman deities was powerful enough to grow mere corn on their own! Even if Rome could attribute the expansion

---

to) the people.' Concretely the phrase can refer to public affairs or to the organs that administer public affairs (roughly what we would call 'the state'), or to a political society as a whole. Sometimes, therefore, it has been natural to translate as 'public life,' sometimes as 'government' or 'empire.' In *Letter* 138 in particular, where Augustine plays upon Cicero's definition, the word "commonwealth" has proved to be the most convenient translation." Dodaro and Atkins, *Augustine: Political Writings*, xxviii.

70. Augustine, *City of God*, II/21.
71. Cicero, *Annals*, fragments, V/1 quoted in Augustine, *City of God*, II/21.
72. Augustine, *City of God*, IV/8.
73. Augustine, *City of God*, III/12.

of their empire to their gods, he wondered which deity would get the glory since "[the Romans] did not think it proper to entrust their love to any one god."[74] This led Augustine to conclude that "Rome had lived more happily when she had fewer gods."[75]

Rome had fewer gods when the empire was smaller, and Augustine argued that the more diminutive the empire, the more felicitous it was. He writes that it is unfitting for good people to rejoice in the breadth of their empire. The Romans had the iniquity of their neighbors, more so than the aid of their gods, against whom Rome waged wars to thank for its expansion since, "that empire would undoubtedly have remained small had their neighbors been peaceful and just, and so never provoked them into war by doing them harm."[76] If all peoples were peaceful and just then all kingdoms would be small and live in concord with one another. Since this is not the case, wars are waged and kingdoms are subdued.

While the wicked take pleasure in this, the good lament it as a necessary evil since though it would be far worse for the "unrighteous to lord over the just" it would be far better to have concord with a good neighbor than to control the wicked neighbor through warfare.[77] Certainly, it is a sign of vice to pray for "someone to hate or to fear in order to have to have someone to conquer."[78] Therefore, if Rome acquired so vast an empire by just means it should have rightly added the goddess of "Foreign Iniquity" to its pantheon and given her a share of the tribute for the empire's expansion as she who caused wars that the goddess Victory brought to a successful conclusion.

History is rife with examples that show that, whether empires spread through subjugation or incorporation, their demise is frequently facilitated by their often getting too large and unwieldy to manage. The enemy of empire is size. This prompted Augustine to ask, "Why must an empire be unquiet in order to be great?"[79] With another apt metaphor, Augustine compares the empire to the human body. Is not a moderate stature with good health preferable to a grossly oversized frame plagued by illness in proportion to its size?[80] Inevitably, as the empire expands so do its concerns. A political sort of "elephantiasis" is an unavoidable symptom of imperialism

---

74. Augustine, *City of God*, IV/8.
75. Augustine, *City of God*, IV/5.
76. Augustine, *City of God*, IV/15.
77. Augustine, *City of God*, IV/15.
78. Augustine, *City of God*, IV/15.
79. Augustine, *City of God*, III/10.
80. Augustine, *City of God*, III/10.

since "the greatest glory belongs to the greatest empire."[81] While pride and avarice lead to the empire's overextension, anything short of expansion is viewed as atrophy and weakness. Here lies the instability inherent within imperialism, there is conflict whether the empire is expanding or contracting; the only difference is the location of the quarrel.

As the boundaries of the empire grow, so do the number of those identified as "allies" and "enemies." However, even this distinction can be difficult to discern, as Augustine notes: "In the miserable conditions of this life, we often believe that someone who is an enemy is a friend, or that someone who is a friend is an enemy."[82] This is yet another mechanism by which fear infiltrates an empire. As the number of alliances increases, there is greater trepidation that misfortune may befall them and require intervention on their behalf. This is not limited to the commonplace concerns like natural disasters or wars but also includes the greatest apprehension they who the empire once considered friends may become enemies.[83] Hence imperial peace must remain narrowly defined as "peace for us," since today's allies are potentially tomorrow's adversaries. This leads Augustine to conclude that even peace is an uncertain good because,

> [W]e do not know the hearts of those with whom we wish to maintain peace. Moreover, even if we could know them today, we should not know what they might be like in the future . . . Even when the city is at peace and free from actual sedition and civil war, it is never free from the danger of such disturbance or, more often, bloodshed.[84]

Even self-interested peace—Augustine would say especially this peace when measured against neighbor-loving peace—is impossibly elusive since it is so precarious. The means of its procurement—war, expansion, the chore of discerning allies from enemies—are also its undoing.

For Augustine, the growth of the empire was simply another gift of God that was worshipped instead of the giver. The glory that rightly belonged to the one, true God was divided and doled out to deities who could not protect the empire but needed its protection. Though not credited with the expansion of the empire, Christianity was faulted for its atrophy. Augustine pushed back against this assertion, arguing that the Christian God oversees the rise and fall of all empires, good and bad. As Rome's chroniclers had noticed, the understanding of imperial virtue changed as

---

81. Sallust, *Cait.*, 2:2 quoted in Augustine, *City of God*, III/14.
82. Augustine, *City of God*, XIX/8.
83. Augustine, *City of God*, XIX/8.
84. Augustine, *City of God*, XIX/5.

the empire's boundaries widened. The love of praise that came to characterize Roman virtue was contrary to the Christian gospel whose adherents confessed along with John the Baptist that Jesus must be magnified, even at the cost of diminishing their own glory.[85]

Augustine asserts that had Rome worshipped its true founder with earnest faith and virtue rather than Romulus in a self-aggrandizing fashion, then it would have been a better earthly kingdom. Even were that not the case, the Romans would have been rewarded with a more secure, magnificent, and eternal kingdom. A better or worse empire is an important distinction. Augustine's qualification turns on his definition of what constitutes a "people,"

> [L]et us say that a "people" is an assembled multitude of rational creatures bound together by a common agreement as to the objects of their love. In this case, if we are to discover the character of any people, we only have to examine what it loves . . . However, the better the objects of this agreement, the better the people; and the worse the objects, the worse the people.[86]

Augustine's nuance of Cicero's definition of a "people" that changes "common agreement to what is right (*jus*)" to "common objects of love" is shrewd as it anticipates people's propensity to readily assent to what is right yet live quite contrarily, thus revealing their loves. Jesus explained that our treasures reveal our hearts, rather than the opposite. In the same way, love is the antecedent of justice instead of its fruit.

Though the Romans commonly espoused justice as the foundation for their endeavors, the "common objects" that revealed the united heart of Roman society were its affections for freedom, glory, and dominion. These appetites were not satiated by Rome's liberty, which it secured relatively quickly, so it sought to rule over its neighbors.[87] Consequently, their desire for freedom mutated into a lust for mastery.

Augustine argued that earthly glory is always insecure. It is always provisional and fleeting. It wanes both with passing time and the rise of

---

85. John 3:30.

86. Augustine, *City of God*, XIX/24. Oliver O'Donovan emphasizes the shared and loving aspects of Augustine's "common objects of love." Love is necessarily a communal act, not something people merely do but a relationship in which they participate. This is not love in the idealistic sense that leaps prematurely to "bear all things, believe all things" and "never fails" while ignoring the sting of sin. Rather it enables, "a people capable of common action, susceptible to common suffering, participating in a common identity," to emerge from among a multitude. O'Donovan, *Common Objects of Love*, 21–22.

87. Augustine, *City of God*, XIX/4.

others whose magnificence threatens to undermine and surpass our own. It was this affinity for honor and fear of its loss that led Rome to achieve many great deeds yet also led to the empire's exhaustion. In contrast, the most glorious eternal city is not founded upon, "the plaudits of vanity, but on the judgement of truth."[88] The heavenly city grows through humbling of people at the foot of the cross not at the end of the sword.

If Augustine was correct in his belief that the loves of freedom and mastery drove the imperial machine, fear undoubtedly fueled it. An empire cannot exist with a fearless citizenry. It was the fear of being mastered more than love of liberty that compelled the empire to subjugate others. Even if their fears subtly subsided, it was not because peace had been won but because the sense of war's grievous burdens had been lost.[89] This variety of fears prompted imperial conquest yet made the same domination curiously unsatisfying.

The Romans, though free, "always lived in dark fear and cruel lust, surrounded by the disasters of war and the shedding of blood, which, whether that of fellow citizens or enemies, was human nonetheless. The joy of such men may be compared to the fragile splendor of glass: they are horribly afraid lest it be suddenly shattered."[90] The love of its glorious and tenuous liberty may have united the empire, but this liberty also held the empire hostage. Even when there was peace the specter of war loomed heavily over Rome. So, the empire found misery in both wars waged for peace and peace riddled with the fear that its liberty could quickly rekindle war.

This fear diverges with scripture's teaching that only God is to be feared and that even this kind of fear is of a qualitatively different ilk that imparts wisdom[91] rather than bondage. For this reason, Jesus told his disciples, "do not fear those who kill the body but cannot kill the soul. Rather fear him who can destroy both soul and body in hell."[92] Even while mourning his friend Marcellinus's death,[93] Augustine reiterates that death is no great fear in the city of God:

> But God's judgement has often permitted the present life even of good men to be taken by the bad so that we do not think

---

88. Augustine, *City of God*, II/19.
89. Augustine, *City of God*, III/17.
90. Augustine, *City of God*, IV/3.
91. Prov 9:10
92. Matt 10:28

93. The imperial commissioner mentioned above whom the *City of God* was addressed was killed by Rome when accused by the Donatists of rebellion against the emperor after Marcellinus had ruled against them at the council of Carthage.

it is evil to suffer such things. What harm, in fact, can dying in the flesh do to those who are destined to die? Or what do they achieve who fear to die but that they can die a little later? Whatever harms the dying comes from life, not from death. If in death they have the sort of souls that the grace of Christ rescues, their death is certainly not the end of a good life but the occasion of a better one.[94]

Robert Dodaro frames the contradictory attitudes towards fear in this manner:

Because he believes that happiness is predicated upon the knowledge and love of God as the supreme good, [Augustine] concludes that fear of death epitomizes the fundamental threat to the formation of a just society. Justice is not found wherever fear of death impedes action aimed at the attainment of lasting happiness. Virtue is, therefore, necessary to overcome the fear of death, all the more so because it leads human beings to choose permanent over temporal goods.[95]

By these criteria, it is impossible for an imperial society to be just. Imperial societies cannot justify their expansion and subjugation of others without fomenting a thick sense of fear among its citizenry. Without fear, the empire would wither because its subjects would have too little incentive to risk their lives. Whether the justification is bringing civility (and often religion) to the "savage" other, preserving "our way of life," or preemptively protecting its borders from attack, the empire benefits by portraying itself as the altruistically noble opposition to some encroaching evil. This is an expediently charitable way of framing conflict since any dubious means the protagonists utilize are considered relative goods given the greater evil they purportedly scuttle.[96]

---

94. Augustine, *Letters*, 151/7.
95. Dodaro, *Christ and the Just Society*, 35–36.
96. See the discussion of the permanent state of exception in the previous chapter. The United States loves an "-ism" with which to galvanize the populace: socialism, communism, and now terrorism are portrayed as unadulterated evils to be resisted and defeated by any means necessary. In contemporary American parlance, resist is a euphemism for war and that war is usually preventative rather than responsive though it will always be couched as a defensive war since that is more palatable. Even the US initiative to limit illicit drug use among its citizens was deemed the "War on Drugs", though a compelling argument can be made that it would have been more appropriately called a war on the poor and minorities who were disproportionately incarcerated during the initiative.

J. Warren Smith differentiates between preemptive (inevitably immanent) war and preventative (fought for freedom from all fear of attack rather than immediate security). Smith maintains that preemptive war is a justifiable reflex of a people under inexorable duress, but preventative war is a morally dubious impulse animated by fear. He elaborates,

> There is a sense that living with fear is living with the reality of death and the threat of our judgment by God. Living with such knowledge cultivates humility. By contrast, the quest for security and freedom from fear is a quest for autonomy that refuses to live with the reality of our ultimate mortality and impending judgment before God. Augustine, by condemning Rome's third war with Carthage, rejects a policy of preventive military action that falsely promises peace and the freedom from fear through eliminating points of geopolitical vulnerability. Such a policy rests upon the faulty assumption that peace and security can be achieved by guarding one's frontiers against external threat.[97]

Augustine knew that such an attempt to live free of fear is a vain chasing after the wind. One cannot manage her own household without fear of sedition, how much less so a city or empire? Augustine develops this line of reasoning further:

> And, if not even the home is safe, our common refuge amid the evils of mankind, what of the city? The larger the city, the more its forum teems with lawsuits, both civil and criminal, and this is true even when a city is not disturbed by the turbulence, or more often the bloodshed, of sedition and civil war. For cities may sometimes be free from such events, but they are never free from the risk of them.[98]

Only the children of God can live fearlessly in a world that would convince them they have every reason to be terrified. However, if death cannot be lorded over us as some horrendous final trepidation, there is nothing to fear but the author of life and peace himself. The refusal to cling to life as an ultimate good and an end in itself produces a people with different loves. These people may pursue genuine peace, not the mere absence of conflict that the earthly city is content to pawn off as peace, but the peace that is *shalom*—wholeness. It is to these divergent pursuits of peace that we now turn.

---

97. Smith, "Augustine and the Limits of Preemptive and Preventative War," 141–62.
98. Augustine, *City of God*, XIX/5.

Just Wars, Part I—Principal Sources and the Common Narrative

There is no shortage of writing on Augustine and the just-war tradition.[99] Rather than inadequately recreate in a few lines what others have done in volumes, I will summarize a few foundational passages common to many accounts not mentioned elsewhere in this book before offering my reading.

Answer to Faustus, a Manichean, ca 397—Here Augustine delves into many topics to defend the congruity of the two testaments. On violence he writes, "The ministers of the Old Testament, who also foretold the New Testament, served God by killing sinners; the ministers of the New Testament, who also explained the Old Testament, served God by dying at the hands of sinners."[100]

Augustine lays the groundwork for the just-war criteria later formalized as "just cause" and "right authority" when he wrote, "For it makes a difference for which causes and under what authority people undertake the waging of war."[101] Deeds done in obedience to God or some legitimate authority are just, where the same deed done apart from such a command would be sin. To deny that a fallen world might necessitate that some people die subduing others in order to live in peace is, "the mark of the cowardly and not of religious people."[102]

War is not incompatible with Christian discipleship. He cites John the Baptist's exchange with soldiers and Jesus's with the centurion in Luke 7. Neither called for the men to lay down their weapons or desert their posts. Augustine surmises that it is not war or military service that Christians should eschew but rather "the desire to do harm, cruelty in taking vengeance, a mind that is without peace and incapable of peace, fierceness in rebellion, [and] the lust for domination."

Sermon 397—On the Sack of the City of Rome, 410/411. It is difficult to overstate how profoundly the Visigoth sack of Rome in 410 affected the empire. Christianity made an easy target for pagan accusations as the root cause of the decline of the empire. As tragedy often does, the sack also caused believers and non-believers to question God's justice. *City of God* is

---

99. See Mattox, *Saint Augustine and the Theory of Just War* and Wynn, *Augustine on War and Military Service* for two recent contributions to the discourse.
100. Augustine, *Answer to Faustus*, 22/79.
101. Augustine, *Answer to Faustus*, 22/75.
102. Augustine, *Answer to Faustus*, 22/74.

Augustine's lengthy rebuttal to the first charge, and Sermon 397 is his more concise reply to the latter issue.

Augustine reminded his parishioners that God's standard of justice is much more stringent than any human conception. There is nothing more grievous or unjust in war than what the Lord suffered on behalf of humanity. Augustine also asked that Romans take the longer view of history and that enduring trials and tribulations better calibrate the sufferer for eternity. He preached, "Whatever people may suffer here, if they let themselves be corrected by it, it means their improvement; if they are not corrected by it, it means a double condemnation. I mean, they pay the temporal penalty here, and there they will experience the eternal one."[103]

Augustine claims it was God's mercy rather than his wrath prominently on display in the sack of Rome. Neither the city nor its citizens were annihilated like Sodom. Anticipating the question of why a "Christian empire" would suffer such a loss, Augustine quotes scripture, "For the Lord disciplines the one he loves, while he whips every son whom he receives."[104] Rather than grumble against God as to why he allows his children to suffer, Augustine admonishes Christians to remember:

> There's only one flail, though, experienced by the threshing floor, both to cut up the straw and to cleanse the grain; there's only one fire experienced by the goldsmith's furnace, both to reduce the straw to ashes and to eliminate the dross from the gold. In the same way Rome endured just one tribulation, in which the godly were either delivered or corrected; while the ungodly were condemned, whether they were snatched from this life to pay even more the justest of penalties, or whether they remained here to go on blaspheming more damnably than ever, or even, out of the unimaginable clemency of God, who knows who are to be saved, to be kept by him for repentance.[105]

The great scourge of the sack of Rome was not that it brought death, which was a blessing to the redeemed and justice to the unrepentant, but that it did not produce more fruit of repentance and sanctification among the empire's citizens.

Letter 138: To Marcellinus, ca 412. Here Augustine replies to the charge that the meekness taught by Christ is incompatible with the practices of the

---

103. Augustine, *Sermons*, 397/4.
104. Heb 12:6, Augustine's translation.
105. Augustine, *Sermons*, 397/9.

state[106] by arguing that Jesus's teaching on retaliation in the Sermon on the Mount referred to "dispositions of the heart"[107] rather than literal, physical prohibitions against violence. While Christians must practice patience and restraint, they also have to do many things including physical coercion, "against the will of people who need to be punished with a certain kind of harshness, for we have to consider their benefit rather than their will."[108] That is the reason war is not anathema for Christian soldiers who can wage merciful wars to suppress or eliminate profligate vices. Augustine also creates the space for mercy and grace to pardon injuries rather than avenge them developing and strengthening a more just empire.[109]

Augustine argues that if all war was contrary to Christian doctrine, John the Baptist would have advised the soldiers who came to him to lay down their weapons and desert their posts rather than telling them to "Do violence to no one; slander no one; let your wages suffice for you."[110] Augustine challenged those who think Christ opposed the state to produce an army of such soldiers that were obedient to this gospel command. Emboldened, he elaborated,

> Let them give us such people of the provinces, such husbands, such wives, such parents, such children, such masters, such slaves, such kings, such judges, and finally such taxpayers and tax collectors as Christian teaching prescribes, and let them dare to say that this teaching is opposed to the state; in fact, let them not hesitate to admit that it would be a great boon for the state if this were observed.[111]

Augustine argues that the imperial subject obedient to the gospel is the citizen *par excellence* in a flourishing and peaceful state.

Letter 189: To Boniface, ca 417. Boniface was the Christian tribune in Africa, who later became a count also in charge of implementing the punishments imposed upon the Donatists.[112] In the fourth paragraph of the letter, Augustine rebuts that being a soldier makes it impossible to please

---

106. Augustine, *Letters*, 138/9.
107. Augustine, *Letters*, 138/13.
108. Augustine, *Letters*, 138/13.
109. Augustine, *Letters*, 138/10.
110. Luke 3:14, Augustine's translation. There is a real sense in which, by telling them to do no violence, John had in fact hamstrung the soldiers from doing their duty.
111. Augustine, *Letters*, 138/15.
112. Augustine wrote to him at length concerning this situation in *Letter* 185, which Augustine referred to as *Correction of the Donatists* in *Revisions*, 2/48.

God. Augustine reminds the general that David was both a man of war and "a man after God's own heart."[113]

Similarly, Jesus was pleased with the centurion who understood authority so well that he knew Jesus could heal his ill servant with the power of his command alone.[114] There was also Cornelius, the centurion whom scripture describes as "a devout man who feared God with all his household, gave alms generously to the people, and prayed continually to God," and to whom God sent the Apostle Peter to preach the gospel so Cornelius and his household were among the first fruits among the Gentiles to receive the baptism of the Holy Spirit.[115]

Augustine unequivocally reminds the general that as he struggles against visible barbarians on behalf of the citizens, the Christians among them are fighting too against invisible enemies on Boniface's behalf by praying for him.[116] Augustine writes that the bodily strength with which Boniface takes up his military weapons is a gift from God and that he should be mindful not to use that gift to act against God. He develops this idea further by writing that, "Your will ought to aim at peace; only necessity requires war in order that God set us free from necessity and preserve us in peace. For we do not seek peace in order to stir up war, but we wage war in order to acquire peace."[117] Augustine also says that mercy is *owed*[118] to the captive about whom there is no fear of the disturbance of the peace.

Letter 229: To Count Darius, ca 428. This relatively brief letter was written by Augustine to praise Darius's peaceful negotiations with a rebellious Roman general. The key remarks from this letter are centered around Augustine's esteem of peace won by words over peace secured through violence. He praises soldiers for their courage, particularly Christian soldiers who are deserving of a "more genuine praise." Although soldiers still conquer and win peace by killing, "it is a mark of greater glory to slay wars themselves by word rather than by human beings by the sword, and to win and obtain peace by peace, not by war. After all, even those who fight, if they are good, undoubtedly seek peace, but they still do so by bloodshed."

---

113. 1 Sam 13:14.
114. Matt 8:8–10, Luke 7:6–9.
115. Acts 10.
116. Augustine, *Letters*, 189/5.
117. Augustine, *Letters*, 189/6.
118. Emphasis mine.

Just Wars, Part II—"Live Free or Die Bravely"

Augustine identified Roman yearnings for glory as the appetite that animated much bloodshed. This longing for glory created fertile ground in which domination, glory's corollary desire, naturally took root. These two complimentary principles were so esteemed that Romans readily embraced the kill or be killed binary in their defense. Augustine explains,

> This glory [Romans] loved with a passion. It was for this sake that they wanted to live and for its sake that they did not hesitate to die. Their boundless desire for this one thing kept all their other desires in check. In short, since they considered it shameful for their country to serve, but glorious for it to dominate and rule, what they desired with all their hearts was first for it to be free and then for it to be dominant.[119]

It is reasonable to concede that Romans justified their willingness to kill and die for glory and dominion as necessary underwriters for peace. Peace lacks the inherently selfish connotations that saddle vainglory and mastery of others. However, not even peace is immune from being imbued by self-interest. Much the opposite, peace is so frequently and narrowly framed by selfishness as to render the word sterile without the addition of thick, descriptive qualifiers. Augustine describes the ingrown nature of peace in this way:

> For, just as no one does not wish to have joy, neither is there anyone who does not wish to have peace. In fact, even those who want war want nothing other than victory; what they desire, then, in waging war is peace with glory . . . It is with the aim of peace, therefore, that wars are waged . . . Even those who want to disrupt the state of peace that they currently have do not despise peace; rather they want that peace to be changed to one they like better. What they want, therefore, is not no peace but rather the peace they wish to have.[120]

It is too simplistic to say that peace is a "common object of love" for a commonwealth without asking the essential questions of how and for whom peace will be secured. Even though war is viewed as a means to peace, it is peace whose terms are dictated by the victorious—those most skilled at coercion through violence. Augustine was not only permissive of the state's exercise of coercive force to secure peace but also commended it. Lawful

---

119. Augustine, *City of God*, V/12.
120. Augustine, *City of God*, XIX/12.

and just punishment rightfully corrected those within the empire who, through their misdeeds, had become enemies of domestic peace. Augustine noted this is advantageous for both the offender and the community against which he or she has transgressed.

For Augustine, mercy has little value if it does not lead to repentance of the wrongdoer. The parable of the unforgiving servant in Matthew's gospel lends credence to his position. If the king's leniency is not a transformative act that fosters some emulation by the debtor, the king will exact a harsher, more just punishment.[121] Augustine develops this idea further adding that

> Just as it is not an act of kindness to help someone if he thereby loses a greater good, so it is not a blameless act to spare someone if he thereby falls into graver sin. If we are to be blameless, therefore, our duty includes not only doing no harm to anyone, but also restraining him from sin or punishing his sin, so that either he who is chastised may be corrected by his experience, or others may be warned by his example.[122]

This seeking of peace through correction should be mutually beneficent. However, for earthly kingdoms, whose survival is often the greatest (if not only) good, this peace-seeking is often skewed heavily in favor of the governing authority, so rather than seeking the peace of all, it seeks its own peace even at the cost of the other.[123]

Hence Augustine notes that the Gates of Janus, which remained open during wartime and closed during times of peace, were rarely shut.[124] He does not offer a blanket condemnation of war, instead condemning its excessive use when other more just alternatives were available. Augustine maintains that, initially, Rome had justly defended itself from the onslaught of its neighbors. These defensive wars were not driven by Rome's "greed for human praise, but by the necessity of defending life and

---

121. Matt 18:21–35; see also Augustine, *City of God*, XV/7: "It is in this way that the citizens of the City of God are healed while they are pilgrims on this earth, as they sigh for the peace of their heavenly country."

122. Augustine, *City of God*, XIX/16.

123. "Other" here can be understood most readily as those outside the empire, but it can also include those within the empire whose conduct is deemed detrimental to the empire's peace and has made them "outsiders within" the empire's borders. The Nazi use of *Untermensch*, literally sub-human, to describe Jews, ethnic minorities, and the disabled the Reich wished to eliminate captures this sense. For a powerful treatment of the "other" and how societies distinguish between "grievable" and "ungrievable" lives, see Judith Butler's *Frames of War*.

124. Augustine, *City of God*, III/9.

liberty."[125] Indeed, Augustine views this as the only justification for war. His notion of defensive war (not thinly defined as self-defense, which he views as beyond the pale) is the cornerstone upon which the Christian just-war tradition was built. This war that protects life and liberty privileges neighbor-love over and against love of self.

Though the empire may have increased honorably by these means, Augustine wonders if there were no other measures short of force by which Rome could have kept its enemies at bay and perhaps permanently shut Janus's gates. Augustine praises Romulus's successor Numa Pompilius, as Numa was renowned for his devotion to the gods and peace. Roman historian Livy wrote that it was Numa's emphasis on refocusing Roman religious practice that drew the people's attention away from violence and arms.[126] However, Augustine is quick to note that the peace that Rome enjoyed under Numa was not due to the will of the gods it venerated but by the restraint of its neighbors who did not provoke bellicose Rome to war.[127] Augustine calls this earthly variety of peace achieved by eliminating all of one's enemies through war the "lowest kind of good."[128]

Even a more favorable view of earthly peace as "an ordered concord of civic obedience and rule to secure a cooperation of men's wills for attaining the things which belong to this mortal life"[129] is viewed by Augustine as inferior to the eternal peace that belongs exclusively to the heavenly city. However, he reminds those who are citizens of both cities neither to repudiate earthly peace nor be captivated by it but rather to "make use" (*uti*) of it since they live simultaneously as captives and pilgrims in this mortal life.[130] Instrumentalizing the temporal peace of the earthly city, pilgrims are to seek the "Supreme

---

125. Augustine, *City of God*, III/10.

126. Livy, *The History of Rome*. See also Plutarch's account: "[Janus's] temple at Rome has two gates, which they call the gates of war, because they stand open in the time of war, and shut in the times of peace; of which latter there was very seldom an example, for, as the Roman empire enlarged and extended, it was so encompassed with barbarous nations and enemies to be resisted, that it was seldom or never at peace. Only in the time of Augustus Caesar, after he had overcome Antony, this temple was shut; as likewise once before, when Marcus Atilius and Titus Manlius were consuls; but then it was not long before, wars breaking out, the gates were again opened. But, during the reign of Numa, those gates were never seen open a single day but continued constantly shut for a space of forty-three years together; such an entire and universal cessation of war existed." Plutarch, *Lives of the Noble Grecians and Romans*, 90.

127. Augustine, *City of God*, III/10.

128. Augustine, *City of God*, XV/4.

129. Augustine, *City of God*, XIX/17.

130. Augustine, *City of God*, XIX/17.

Good" that is "peace in eternal life" or "life in eternal peace."[131] In so doing, the city of God refuses to be held hostage by a peace that can be manufactured only by denying the lives and liberty of others.[132]

The city of God also distinguishes itself from the city of man by the way it seeks and uses earthly peace. The unfaithful household pursues peace "based on the goods and advantages of this temporal life."[133] Alternatively, the heavenly city "makes use of earthly and temporal things like a pilgrim. It is not captivated by them, nor is it deflected by them from the path that leads toward God, but it is sustained by them."[134] Just as God causes the sun to rise on both the righteous and wicked, each will use the same light of peace to achieve vastly different ends.

Here Augustine is employing his *uti/frui* dialectic where things that are *uti*, like earthly peace, are not to be pursued, used, or enjoyed as ends in themselves. Things that are *frui* are pursued for their own enjoyment as ends in and of their selves like eternal peace.[135] R. A. Markus elaborates,

> Augustine's dichotomy between the two cities in these terms—loving God or loving something else—is oversimplified if taken to mean that the citizens of the heavenly city do not "love" the objects "loved" by the citizens of the earthly city. They do; the temporal goods on which the latter set supreme value are good in themselves, and proper objects of "love". It is the way in which such objects are loved that is in question: whether they are "used" [*uti*], and thus valued conditionally, in reference to something else of more ultimate value, or loved to be "enjoyed" [*frui*], that is unconditionally, for their own sake. The heavenly city, then, is constituted by those who set supreme value only on

---

131. Augustine, *City of God*, XIX/11.

132. ". . . the Roman empire itself, which had already grown great by subjugating many people, and which was an object of terror to the rest, was itself bitterly injured, gravely alarmed, and with no small effort avoided a disastrous reversal. . ." Augustine, *City of God*, IV/5.

133. Augustine, *City of God*, XIX/17.

134. Augustine, *City of God*, XIX/17.

135. Augustine writes, "A person becomes wicked, however, when he loves things for their own sakes that should be used for some other purpose and seeks for some other purpose things that should be loved for themselves. In that way he upsets, as much as in him is, the natural order in himself, which the eternal law commands him to preserve. But he becomes righteous when he does not seek to use things for another purpose than that for which they were established by God but enjoys God for his own sake and himself and his friends in God for the sake of the same God. For one who loves the love of God in his friend loves his friend for God's sake." Augustine, *Against Faustus*, 22/78.

God, and subordinate all other loves to this one love; the earthly city sets up some other objective as its ultimate goal.[136]

Rome was not blessed for its sake alone but also to benefit the citizens of the heavenly city during their pilgrimage through the earthly city.[137] Christians should obey laws that do not violate their religion since they share a common mortality while they overlap. The pilgrim's use of peace has a peculiarly centripetal quality that the earthly "use" of peace lacks. Augustine explains,

> So long as this heavenly city is a pilgrim on earth, then, it calls forth citizens from all peoples and gathers together a pilgrim society of all languages. It cares nothing about any difference in the manners, laws, and institutions by which earthly peace is achieved or maintained . . . for they all aim at one and the same thing—earthly peace. Thus, even the heavenly city makes use of earthly peace during its pilgrimage, and, so far as sound piety and religion allow, *it defends and seeks accommodation among human wills with regard to the things that pertain to humanity's mortal nature*.[138]

Augustine called upon Christians to not only "make use" of the peace but to also proactively work to bring it about. He echoes *Yahweh*'s admonishment to the exiles in Babylon to "seek the welfare of the city where I have sent you into exile, and pray to the LORD on its behalf, for in its welfare you will find your welfare."[139] Augustine is quick to differentiate between the peace that is the church's "peculiar possession" and that which it shares in common with the earthly city. The former is the "joy of blessedness" that is shared eternally with God while the latter is "only a solace for our wretchedness," that leads pilgrims to pray for the forgiveness of trespasses committed and suffered.[140]

Prayer was not the only way Christians could bring about the peace of the empire. Augustine also encouraged Christian to participate in civic leadership. Rather than forbid Christians from holding political offices, he asserted that, "when those who are gifted with true godliness and live good lives also know the art of governing peoples, nothing could be more fortunate for human affairs than that, by the mercy of God, they should also have the

---

136. Markus, *Saeculum*, 68.
137. Augustine, *City of God*, V/16.
138. Augustine, *City of God*, XIX/17, emphasis mine.
139. Jeremiah 29:7, see Augustine, *City of God*, XIX/26.
140. Augustine, *City of God*, XIX/27; Matt 6:12.

power to do so."[141] Far from a political power play, Augustine saw Christian governance as a blessing attributable solely to the grace of God.

While he thought Christians with the skills to govern were best suited for leadership, he rebuked those who would become Christian merely to gain political advantage. He surmises, "No emperor, however, should be a Christian merely in the hope of securing the felicity which Constantine enjoyed; for every man should be a Christian only for the sake of eternal life."[142] Even with proper motives for seeking governing roles, the Christian emperor should "rejoice more in being a member of the Church than in being the ruler of the world."[143] Thus the Christian civil servant should not be driven by the "lust for mastery" or insatiable desire for glory that characterized the offices of many of their pagan counterparts. Rather, Christian emperors as pilgrims are moved by compassion to act on behalf of those who are outside the gates of the heavenly city whom they "desire to see redeemed and fear to see perish. They feel pain if these do perish, and gladness if they are redeemed."[144]

It seemed apparent to Augustine that Christians from judges to emperors would have to rule differently than those who were concerned only with the earthly city. He warned Christian rulers not to become drunk with their authority, because "The more exalted you become in your power, the lowlier may you become in your piety."[145] He presumes that both Christian and pagan governors would seek peace and rebuff injustice, employing the law for those under their authority. Augustine shares the general assumption of his society that force is a legitimate way to protect his community both materially and religiously.[146] His blessing of force to uphold law sowed the seed that would grow into the Christian just-war tradition.

What is unique in his articulation of the Christian use of force to mediate justice is how it is bridled by an appeal to a higher authority than the one who judges. Augustine refused to allow the emperor the final word for authorizing violence. In discussing one's moral culpability for violence, Augustine differentiates between the act, the agent, and the authority.[147] Acts clearly against the teaching of scripture, such as murder, can be morally upright when the agent is acting in obedience to the proper authority. He

141. Augustine, *City of God*, V/19.
142. Augustine, *City of God*, V/25.
143. Augustine, *City of God*, V/26.
144. Augustine, *City of God*, XIV/9.
145. Augustine, *Letters*, 153/10.
146. Augustine, *Political Writings*, xix.
147. Augustine, *Answer to Faustus*, XXII/73.

cites as an example Abraham's intended sacrifice of Isaac, which would have been detestable had God not commanded it.[148]

For Augustine, proper authority is not limited to divine command but also resides in the civil authorities, which, by God's providence, should restrain evil—through institutionalized coercion when necessary. Augustine saw "the might of the emperor, the judge's power of the sword, the executioner's hooks, the soldier's weapons, the correction a master gives his slave, and even the strictness of a good father" as having "their own limits, causes, explanations and uses."[149] The common thread that justifies the use of each type of discipline is that, "they inspire fear and thus put a check on the bad, so that the good may live peacefully among the bad."[150]

In the opening book of the *City of God*, Augustine reiterates that not all killing is murder and therefore a violation of God's law. He expounds upon this by saying that one who acts under general law or divine fiat is no more culpable for murder than a sword in the hand of a slayer.[151] It logically follows that,

> [T]hey who have waged war in obedience to the divine command, or in conformity with His laws, have represented in their persons the public justice or the wisdom of government, and in this capacity have put to death wicked men; such persons have by no means violated the commandment, "You shall not kill."[152]

He again references Abraham whose obedience to the command of God was fidelity and not wickedness even had the deed been carried out.

What Augustine is quick to remind the agent, even one acting under the right authority, is those who judge should know continually their sinful nature and the reality they too will be judged by God, since they are merely "judging [their] own equal[s], a human judging a human, a mortal judging a mortal, a sinner judging a sinner."[153] Augustine illustrates this restraint by appealing to Jesus's response to the mob that brought the adulteress before him in John 8. Jesus turned the tables by questioning the woman's interrogators rather than her and pronouncing his judgment on the judges rather than the defendant. Jesus's statement about who was worthy to carry out her death sentence did not circumvent the law but was an assessment that

---

148. Augustine, *Answer to Faustus*, XXII/73.
149. Augustine, *Letters*, 153/16.
150. Augustine, *Letters*, 153/16.
151. Augustine, *City of God*, I/21.
152. Augustine, *City of God*, I/21.
153. Augustine, "Sermon 13," in *Political Writings*, 122.

there was no one present fit to dole out the prescribed punishment. Hence the climax of the story is not when the crowd disperses but when Jesus says, "Neither do I condemn you." Augustine imagines Jesus at this point posing the question, "If hatred was able to spare you, why should you fear innocence?"[154] The only one who could properly administer the judgment refused to do so to create ample space for repentance in the woman's life: "Go, and from now on do not sin anymore."

The just judge must examine his or her heart before levelling punishment, and even then, it can only correctly be administered in love. Only those who have quenched the desire for hate-fueled vengeance with the greatness of love are fit for administering punishment. His apt metaphor for this loving judgment is how a father disciplines his son whom he loves. Where any father would prefer his son's disobedience was brought into line with mere verbal reprimands or praise, the same father should not hesitate to inflict punishment upon the son he loves with the child's well-being and security in mind. In a paradox, to strike the child out of love is a harsh kindness for his benefit while the refusal to do so would be the cruel ruining of him. Augustine contends that one does not fear being accused of hatred for a child whom he disciplines when his goal is preventing even greater offences (whether in quantity or quality). Failure to love the recipient of punishment destroys not only justice but also the person under judgment. Augustine neither denied nor forbade punishment, rather he insisted that it be administered in a "spirit of love, in the spirit of concern, [and] in the spirit of reform."[155]

The Roman practice of torture tested Augustine's idea of loving discipline to extract confessions. According to fourth-century Roman law, only those confessions secured by application of torture were considered valid.[156] Augustine was profoundly uncomfortable with torture, calling it, "abhorrent to [the Christian] way of thinking,"[157] though he never categorically prohibits its use. Instead, he petitioned leaders to exercise mercy and create the most significant possible margin for repentance.

Despite lobbying magistrates to prevent torture, Augustine never describes it as anathema for Christians. The reason for Augustine's hesitancy to do so is found in *City of God* XIX/6, his fullest treatment of torture. He

---

154. Augustine, *Letters*, 153/15.

155. Augustine, "Sermon 13," in *Political Writings*, 125. Unfortunately, later inquisitors would invoke Augustine's moral arguments for coercion without the crucial caveat that correction should be implemented as a loving familial chastisement exercising minimal force.

156. Augustine, *Political Writings*, 253, FN 20.

157. Augustine, *Letters*, 104/14.

writes that torture, though miserable and deplorable, cannot fail to be present in every city, no matter how peaceful they are. The role of the judge is lamentable for he must apply torture to the guilty and innocent in an attempt to discern culpability. The pitiful situation is that even when torture produces a confession, the judge cannot know with any measure of certainty that justice has been done. Though the judge has applied the rod to prevent the slaying of the innocent, the innocent may still perish either by confessing so they may escape affliction or death while being tortured. Consequently, the same judge who sought justice through torture has tormented and killed an innocent person—all without knowing it.

Augustine writes that both the judge's duty and ignorance are inescapable. For these reasons the judge is not guilty if he tortures and condemns the innocent, but neither is he pleased by the demands of his office that require him to do so. Augustine fittingly concludes the discussion by appealing to divine help:

> Surely, it would be more compassionate, and more worthy of the dignity of man, if [the judge] were to acknowledge that the necessity of acting in this way is a miserable one: if he hated his own part in it, and if, with the knowledge of godliness, he cried out to God, "From my necessities deliver Thou me."[158]

Despite these concessions for justified Christian violence and killing, Augustine seems to suggest that the church, when most genuinely inhabiting its calling as pilgrim, would rather die than to fight:

> No fear—not fear of some mere mild offense to Roman minds, not even fear of vast and varied punishments, and not even fear of death itself, which is feared more than anything else—could keep a whole multitude of martyrs among all peoples of the world from not only worshipping Christ as God but openly professing him as God. And the city of Christ, even though it has taken in whole hosts of people while still on its pilgrimage here on earth, never once fought back against its ungodly persecutors for the sake of securing its temporal well-being. Instead, it did not fight back for the sake of securing its eternal wellbeing. Its people were manacled, imprisoned, beaten, tortured, burned, maimed, slaughtered—and they multiplied. It was not for them to fight for safety's sake, except by disdaining safety for their savior's sake.[159]

---

158. Ps 25:17. Augustine, *City of God*, XIX/6.
159. Augustine, *City of God*, XXII/6.

Compelle Intrare

If there is a potential blemish on Augustine's otherwise impeccable record of public and parochial service, it is his advocacy of imperial coercion to settle a century-old schism between Catholics and Donatists.[160] The rift developed over whether sacraments performed by *traditors*, those who handed over sacred books or vessels during the Decius persecution to avoid martyrdom, were valid. At the center of the dispute was Caecilian, Catholic bishop of Carthage when the Donatist schism began. The Donatists said his ordination was invalid because it was performed by Felix of Aptungi, an alleged *traditor*.

Early in the conflict Augustine sought to be a peacemaker, appealing to scripture and history as he wrote to the Donatists assuming they were men ready to be corrected rather than as heretics.[161] In Letter 51, Augustine writes that schisms among God's people are calamitous. He references Korah's opposition to Moses in Numbers 16. The ground opened up and swallowed alive the sewers of dissension, and fire poured down from heaven and consumed those who had had been persuaded by them. Augustine notes that division among God's children was punished more harshly than idolatry[162] and the burning of scripture.[163]

Augustine noted in several letters that it was the Donatists who first appealed to Rome, though they showed contempt for the resulting imperial orders.[164] After being rebuffed twice at episcopal councils in Rome and Arles, the Donatists continued to appeal to Constantine until he also ruled against them in his verdict at Milan in the fall of 316. Augustine did not hesitate to underscore this by writing,

> And now what but the judgement of Constantine the Great remains valid against your sect, the judgement that your predecessors chose, that they forced by their constant appeals, and that they preferred to the judgement of bishops? If you are dissatisfied with the imperial judgements, who first forced the emperors to issue them against you?[165]

---

160. The account that follows is Augustine's own as detailed in *Letters* 105.

161. Augustine, *Letters*, 43/1–2.

162. Exod 32:1, 6.

163. Jer 36:23.

164. The most detailed account of which can be found in *Letters* 43, though Augustine revisits the point in *Letters* 105/10 and 185/6.

165. Augustine, *Letters*, 88/5.

Augustine confesses that initially, he did not want to use coercion against the Donatists because it is preferable to have people restored to worship through instruction instead of fear of punishment and pain. However, the latter is preferable to losing unified worship. Failure to take coercive means to keep one from harming himself is analogous to allowing an enemy to run headlong off a cliff and making no effort to catch and bind him. Augustine knew that he who interceded against the will of his enemy would "seem most troublesome and hostile to him at the very time when he was most beneficial and merciful."[166]

He uses the parable of the wedding feast in Luke 14[167] to draw analogies between the Donatists and the initial guests who were invited but those who did not heed the invitation were coerced to attend (*compelle intrare*).[168] Augustine was acutely aware of the problematic potential of compulsion, but he would concur with C. S. Lewis's later assessment that,

> The words *compelle intrare*, compel them to come in, have been so abused by wicked men that we shudder at them; but, properly understood, they plumb the depth of the Divine mercy. The hardness of God is kinder than the softness of men, and His compulsion is our liberation.[169]

By the early years of the fifth century, increased Donatist violence and the exhaustion of all of his rhetorical options led the Bishop of Hippo to employ his last option: openly appeal to their Roman governors to maintain peace. Augustine believed he was acting in the best interests of Donatist and Catholic alike: "For a person whose freedom for wickedness is taken away is conquered to his own benefit, because nothing is more unhappy than the happiness of sinners that nourishes their penal impunity and strengthens their evil will like an internal enemy."[170]

Unsurprisingly, the Donatists vehemently baulked against Augustine's appeal to Rome, which they viewed as nothing short of Catholic-sanctioned imperial persecution; but Augustine faulted Donatists for begging the question of who was persecuting whom:

> [A]ll of you, who say that you suffer persecution under the supposedly terrifying laws of the Catholic emperors, remain secure in your possessions and those of others, while we suffer from

---

166. Augustine, *Letters*, 93/2.

167. And the master said to the servant, "Go out to the highways and hedges and compel people to come in, that my house may be filled. For I tell you, none of those men who were invited shall taste my banquet." Luke 14:23–24.

168. Augustine, *Letters*, 185/25.

169. Lewis, *Surprised by Joy*, 229.

170. Augustine, *Letters*, 138/14.

> your people such unheard-of evils. You say that you are suffering persecution, and we are being killed by your people armed with clubs and swords. You say that you are suffering persecution, and our homes are destroyed by the pillaging of your armed people. You say that you are suffering persecution, and our eyes are put out by your people armed with lime and acid.[171]

In Letter 87 to Emeritus, the Donatist Bishop of Caesarea, Augustine wrote that the Catholic appeals to the established authority were not an attempt to persecute the Donatists but were defensive in posture as the Catholics sought protection from illicit and private acts of violence.

In Letter 185/26–28, the Bishop of Hippo goes into more graphic detail when he describes the assault on Maximian, the Catholic Bishop of Bagai. After Maximian had won a judgement against the Donatists, they overcame him in his basilica, beat him with clubs and shards of the altar, and stabbed him in the groin with a dagger. In Augustine's estimation, Maximian would have bled out from his wound if he had not been dragged on the ground allowing the earth to form a makeshift clot around the hemorrhaging vein. After he was left for dead, Catholics ministered to him and attempted to carry him away singing Psalms. This enraged his attackers all the more, and they overcame the Catholics, took Maximian's seemingly lifeless body to a tower, and threw him from its highest point. Miraculously, Maximian survived and sought the help of the Christian emperor—not to avenge himself but for the protection of his church flock. Augustine argues this was analogous to Paul's alerting of the tribune in Acts 23 of the forty men who conspired not to eat or drink anything until they had killed Paul.

Paul's conversion also features prominently in Augustine's defense of religious coercion. He notes that Christ did not restrain Saul, the great tormentor of God's Church, with words alone but also, "laid him low by his power."[172] When those who object to coercive restoration ask, "With whom did Christ use force? Whom does he compel?" Augustine replies, "See, they have Paul the Apostle; let them acknowledge in him Christ first using force and afterwards teaching, first striking and afterwards consoling."[173] In anticipation of questions regarding a damaged faith or fellowship, Augustine remarks, "It is amazing, however, how that man [Paul] who came to the gospel, forced by bodily punishment, labored more for the gospel than all

---

171. Augustine, *Letters*, 88/8.
172. Augustine, *Letters*, 185/22.
173. Augustine, *Letters*, 185/22.

those who were called only by words. And though greater fear drove him to love, his *perfect love cast out fear* (1 John 4:18)."[174]

Though Augustine advocated for imperial intervention to bring about peace between the two factions of the church, he did so mercifully. This is apparent in Letter 100 to Donatus, a Catholic layman and proconsul of Africa, about his treatment of the Donatist heretics.

> We desire that, by making use of judges and laws that cause fear, they be corrected, not killed, so that they do not fall into the punishments of eternal condemnation. We do not want discipline to be neglected in their regard or the punishment they deserve to be applied. Repress their sins, therefore, in such a way that those who repent having sinned may still exist . . . Hence, if you think that human beings should be put to death for these crimes, you will make us afraid that something of the sort may come to your court by means of our effort. And once this has been discovered, those people will roam about seeking our destruction with greater audacity since we will be compelled to choose even to be killed by them rather than to denounce them to your courts to be put to death.[175]

Even among those most violently resistant to maintaining fellowship, Augustine never abandoned hope for the repentant restoration of a unified body of Christ.

Conclusion

Psalm 25:17 seems to be a fitting prayer not only for the Christian judge but also for each imperial pilgrim. This cry for deliverance resonates so clearly within the church since being a citizen of an empire entails that certain "necessities" (war, torture, murder, and nefarious economic policies) are ostensibly committed for the sake of the commonwealth in which the citizens of heaven pass through as pilgrims.[176]

Augustine cannot be easily caricatured as either an unabashed patriot or antagonistic revolutionary. He was born a citizen of Rome and became a citizen of heaven. He neither baptized imperial practices nor called for the total withdrawal of the church from the empire. Instead, he held these competing allegiances in patent tension and called the church to do the

---

174. Augustine, *Letters*, 185/22, emphasis in the original.

175. Augustine, *Letters*, 100/1.

176. A more thorough examination of Christian complicity with these "imperial necessities" will be treated in its own chapter at the culmination of this book.

same. His acumen to theologically scrutinize his distinct political milieu shaped an exceptionally rare account of the inexorable friction among the fault lines created by the juxtaposition of the two cities.

For Augustine, Rome, like all governments, found its true origin in God's providence and its proper purposes in restraining wickedness so its citizens might enjoy both life and liberty. These aims were perverted when the empire became discontent with its domestic peace and security and sought to grow through its lust for mastery. Augustine called upon Christians as imperial pilgrims to "make use" (*uti*) of the peace (albeit a lesser one) of Rome even as they sought the higher peace of the eternal city. More than merely utilizing Rome's peace, he called Christians to actively pursue it through their prayers and participation in governance when they were equipped to do so. He questioned and critiqued (but stops short of forbidding) Rome's less savory means of securing peace like war and torture. Instead, he clarified how Christian involvement in these activities should be strikingly different from that of their non-Christian counterparts. Punishment should be administered lovingly with the aim of repentance and restoration rather than in domineering fashion with the intention of division and execution.

Augustine's reluctance to embrace or reject imperialism has opened him up to criticism from both sides. There are those who thought he was not radical enough in distancing the church from Rome and still others who thought the call to sacrificial neighbor-love was an unrealistic and untenable expectation of non-Christian polities. The diversity of criticism points to the very complexity of the issues he was trying to resolve. Perhaps the fact that he is unequivocally embraced by neither secularists nor separatists is a sign of the measure of success he had in navigating the intricate relationship between the two cities.

Peter Brown laments that "Augustine lived to see violence destroy his life's work in Africa."[177] Possidius describes Augustine's final days during the Vandal invasion of North Africa in lurid detail:

> The man of God saw whole cities sacked, country villas razed, their owners killed or scattered as refugees, the churches deprived of their bishops and clergy, and the holy virgins and ascetics dispersed; some tortured to death, some killed outright, others, as prisoners, reduced to losing their integrity, in soul and body, to serve an evil and brutal enemy. The hymns of God and praises in the churches had come to a stop; in many places, the church-buildings were burnt to the ground; the sacrifices of

---

177. Brown, *Augustine*, 429.

> God could no longer be celebrated in their proper place, and the divine sacraments were either not sought, or, when sought, no one could be found to give them.[178]

Although these were the last and perhaps most enduring images of the earthly city to which Augustine bore witness, I must respectfully disagree with Peter Brown's conclusion concerning Augustine's life work. No degree of violence could deprive Augustine's flock of the riches with which his pastoral edification had established an eternal endowment beyond the reach of moth, rust, or Vandal.

Augustine's life work was certainly not embodied by perishable and limited goods such as a basilica, book, or even his life—all of which were only fruitful to the extent that they helped prepare the catechumen for eternal communion with the Holy Trinity. Even in the midst of coming to terms with his realization that he had little time remaining in the earthly city, Augustine was acutely aware of the scope of his influence.

In light of this authority, Augustine had the foresight to spend the majority of his final three years of life in his library. He did so not as an old man pining to relive his former glory but rather as one with his steely gaze fixed unwaveringly on the future.[179] He refused to let his voluminous theologically pastoral labor evaporate into the ether. Augustine diligently worked around the clock until his death to catalogue and preserve his vast literary legacy.[180] Even in the midst of the siege of his homeland, each night was devoted to re-reading, revising, and clarifying his earlier works.[181] Mean-

---

178. Possidius, *Life of Saint Augustine*, XXVIII, 6–8.

179. Brown, *Augustine*, 434.

180. Brown, *Augustine*, 433.

181. Augustine's "night shift" would produce his *Revisions* (*Retractiones*) that organized and criticized his writings (at least in part, as he died prior to revisiting his letters and sermons) in chronological rather than topical order. This is an important feature for Augustine scholars, as several of the occasions for his compositions overlapped and were spread out over many years. For example, Augustine began writing *Teaching Christianity* in the mid-390s, over two decades prior to beginning work on *City of God*, yet both books were completed around 426. Upon learning that Augustine took thirty years to finish writing *Teaching Christianity* and fourteen years to complete *City of God*, I felt slightly less self-conscious that this book has taken seven years to complete. In the prologue to *Revisions*, Augustine clearly demarcates the aim of his project was to, "reconsider my works from an uncompromisingly critical perspective, whether they be books or letters or sermons, and in these pages to single out for censure what I disapprove of... I wanted to write this in order to put it into the hands of the people from whom I cannot ask back what I have already published and needs correction... Hence those who are going to read these works should not imitate me in my errors but in my progress towards the better. For whoever reads my works in the order in which they were written will perhaps discover how I have made progress over the course of my writing." Augustine, *Revisions*, prologue 1, 3.

while, each day would find him in the same library working on manifold new problems that required his wisdom and voice. He was concurrently dictating a response to eight new books published by the importunate Pelagian heretic Julian of Eclanum[182] while writing a catalogue of all heresies against the Christian faith since the time of Christ that would explain each heresy's belief and how it was to be defeated. The former project was hastened by the request of Augustine's childhood friend Alypius even though Augustine had already responded to four of Julian's books. The latter project on heresy was Augustine's capitulation to the persistent pleadings of the deacon Quodvultdeus.[183] Augustine's daytime projects hindered his progress on the work that he longed to complete more than any other, his *Revisions*. Regrettably, Augustine was only able to complete about half of each book's manuscript before his death in August 430.

Augustine was neither the first nor the last "political theologian." However, his unique place in history is that of the most prominent and prolific Christian thinker in what was arguably the watershed moment of the church's self-understanding of its identity in relationship to the government that ruled over it. This is why his evaluation of the imperial dilemma continues to carry such gravitas over a millennium and a half later. Henry Chadwick astutely surmises that the weightiness of Augustinian thought can become a millstone around the neck of those who haphazardly wield it without first critically appraising it. This is the kind of idolatry that Augustine would never have invited. Chadwick expresses it in this manner; "[Augustine's] misfortune was to be treated as a towering authority in the history of western Christianity in a way that he himself would have strongly deplored . . . At least it can be said that Augustine had a deep abhorrence of being treated as a person whom people wanted to follow without pondering his reasons."[184]

Each subsequent theologian has had to evaluate the ramifications of her citizenship in markedly different governing paradigms. This is an arduous calling since political landscapes are never static, even over the brief period of one's life. The remaining chapters represent my endeavor to deconstruct the American political situation since September 11 in a cogently Augustinian manner with a particular focus on how the US has waged the "war on terror" and to offer a theological appraisal of the American church's complicity with it.

---

182. Augustine, *Letters*, 224/2, 10*:1.
183. Augustine, *Letters* 221–224, 25*.
184. Chadwick, *Augustine*, xiv.

III

A "Just War on Terror?"

A long and very respectable tradition of thinking about the morality of warfare has accustomed us to looking at Augustine's views on the "just war" through the wrong end of the telescope.[1]

—R. A. Markus

Augustine biographer Henry Chadwick has written that Augustine's political attitudes have received "diametrically opposed interpretations."[2] Some paint him as a dedicated patriot who has too readily embraced the imperial idea while others find him too detached from the world showing little interest in its welfare or prosperity. Chadwick surmises, "since both interpretations can cite texts of Augustine in their support, it is worth looking about for any alleviation of the contradiction."[3] The seeming contradictions that Chadwick mentions are real, but it is important to note that they are more firmly rooted in the various interpretations of Augustine's work rather than the work itself.[4]

Whether one understands war to be *the* inevitable political act or merely an unfortunate byproduct of the political, Phillip Wynn offers a markedly less charitable view of Augustinian scholarship in this arena, "Much of what has been written on Augustine's views on war and military

1. Markus, "Augustine's Views on the 'Just War,'" 1.
2. Chadwick, *Augustine*, 139.
3. Chadwick, *Augustine*, 139.
4. I am not suggesting that Augustine was rhetorically immutable, rather that Augustine's writings on certain issues evolved the longer he considered them.

service in especially twentieth-century scholarship is at best misconceived, and at worst simply wrong."[5]

Augustinians of the last century have emphasized Augustine's exhortations on the administration of justice. They lament along with the church father the need for violence to restrain evil as they outline cases for state-sanctioned coercion through "just wars." Historically, these arguments have only seemed capable of compelling states to wage war but have been impotent in restraining any state from engaging in combat. The same arguments remain in vogue among contemporary scholars as they consider the US "war on terror." However, none take seriously that imperially sanctioned coercion is the undercurrent that overwhelms their arguments for an Augustinian "just war on terror."

These scholars have rightly picked up on the bishop's zealousness for justice. However, what is often glossed over in their exegesis of Augustine's writing is that he always held justice in palpable tension with mercy, and whenever the two seemed perilously incompatible, he favored forgiveness over retribution. To be clear, I am not advancing a non-violent reading of Augustine—although that would be more accurate than those who have turned him into the patron saint of *realpolitik*. I concur with John Milbank's assessment that,

> It is, in fact, the ontological priority of peace over conflict (which is arguably the key theme of his entire thought) that is the principle undergirding Augustine's critique. However, this principle is firmly anchored in a narrative, a practice, and a dogmatic faith, not in an abstracted universal reason.[6]

However, there are undeniable realist tendencies in Augustine's writings that subsequent generations have come to emphasize and embellish. Hence the violent exception to the ontological priority of peace has become the rule that, though meant to limit the scope of violence, has come to justify all manner of it.

The contemporary Augustinians may rightly portray him as a political realist, but they do so without the crucial caveat that he was always a *reluctant* realist admonishing his readers that violence was always the last recourse. Augustine reasoned that killing vanquished any space for repentance and preempted the judgment of God, who alone could justly separate the wheat from the tares at the ultimate harvest. Subsequent generations of theologians preserved Augustine's justifications for violence

---

5. Wynn, *Augustine on War and Military Service*, 148.
6. Milbank, *Theology and Social Theory*, 392.

but discarded his nuanced and compassionate cautions against allowing violence to metastasize unfettered.

Augustine's *City of God* was a theological reevaluation of citizenship that might never have been written were it not for an enemy's attack. Similarly, 9/11 has produced many theological responses, but none with the sophistication of Augustine's to place the tragedy within in its proper historical and cultural contexts. This chapter will consider those who have echoed Augustine's call for justice without nuancing justice as a supernatural work of messianic mercy.

This chapter's title is partially derived from of a section in Charles Mathewes's *Republic of Grace*.[7] It has been repurposed to reflect my wariness of Mathewes's and others claims who have used Augustine to defend the US response to 9/11. The quotation marks around "war on terror" and question mark are my addendums, as I am skeptical of framing the US's response to 9/11 as a war—"just" or otherwise. However, to get bogged down in such semantic quibbling is to miss the more important questions of whether Augustine would have been an apologist for the aims and methods employed by the authorities or whether he would have lamented them and called the Christians among the empire to repent of such exercises of power.

Mathewes is one of the new Augustinian theologians—so named because they seek to use Augustine to lay the groundwork for responsible political participation. They do so under the assumption that Augustine is a useful guide for teaching the church how to engage in the political processes of a liberal democratic society. Their utilization of Augustine presupposes that America is a liberal democracy, and their arguments search for material in his corpus that supports their aim to encourage participation within that democracy.

These Augustinians are united by their resistance to the suggestion that their writing from privileged positions within an imperial milieu is of theological relevance. The principal question raised in this chapter is, what does it mean to read and take seriously the fact that Augustine was not a citizen of a liberal democracy but a self-consciously imperial subject?

In the previous chapter, I concurred with those who consider Augustine's work a contemporarily relevant and constructive framework within which to think about the church as a political entity in the overlapping kingdoms of heaven and earth. However, I must diverge with treatments of Augustine that blunt the force of his critique of the city of man and its edifying potential for American Christianity by reading him as the patron saint of the liberal democratic nation-state instead of the unmistakably

---

7 Mathewes, *Republic of Grace*, 47–52.

imperial citizen, reproving voice to power, and Christian bishop. This vantage point opens a richer space for engagement with the American political landscape—one that, among other vexing problems, forces citizens to reconcile their faith with their complicity in the "war on terror" that the empire wages on their behalf.

As chapter 1 detailed, most US Christians do not recognize their nation's conspicuous resemblance to its imperial predecessors. The most glaring difference between contemporary congregations and Augustine's own is that we think we *should* participate in the political space, an idea that most of Augustine's parishioners would have found quite strange. Even if the church can and should be motivated in the manner that Mathewes and others advocate, it would be prudent to ask whether its peculiarly imperial context problematizes Christian complicity with the American project.

This chapter will approach these questions by looking at the work of Christian ethicists who have employed Augustine in an attempt to reconcile the US's response to 9/11 with the Christian just-war tradition. It will begin with Reinhold Niebuhr. Though he died a full thirty years before the "war on terror" began, his reading of Augustine is highly influential among many of the moral theologians that would follow.

Following Niebuhr, we will examine Jean Bethke Elshtain's work seeking to resolve her meticulous reading of Augustine with her role as theological apologist for the George W. Bush administration, the "war on terror," and American hegemony as a necessary prophylactic against global chaos. Next, we will engage the British complement to many of Elshtain's premises—Nigel Biggar's defense of just war, which is tantamount to an assault on pacifism, both the Christian and secular varieties. Like Elshtain, he is also in favor of the United States's assumption of a more imperial posture from which it could oversee international law and order.

Charles Mathewes argues that the US fills the role described by Biggar due to other nations' abdication of their moral and political responsibilities. He describes the US as an "inadvertent empire," a necessary hegemon in a world where most nations lack the will and the strength to maintain proper world order. Mathewes compares Augustine's struggles with the Donatists to the "war on terror," and finds Augustine's course of action prescriptive.

The final three authors whose works this chapter will explore—Daniel Bell, Lisa Sowle Cahill, and R. A. Markus—read Augustine differently as they interpret the just-war tradition through the respective lenses of discipleship, justice, and history.

Reinhold Niebuhr—Augustine as Excessive Realist

Reinhold Niebuhr, himself a "Christian realist," called Augustine the first great realist in the West.[8] Christian realists are acutely vigilant for the persistent effects of sin in humanity, particularly instances of self-interest and power as factors in social and political situations. Niebuhr uses the words of Machiavelli, himself a notorious realist, to identify the purpose behind the realist's approach, which is "to follow the truth of the matter rather than the imagination of it; for many have pictures of republics and principalities which have never been seen."[9]

Niebuhr pins Augustine's conception of evil on excessive self-love, pride or *superbia*, that is the result of making one's self the ultimate end in place of God.[10] The *civitas terrena* (earthly city) is dominated by this self-love to the contempt of God. Niebuhr notes that the *civitas terrena* for Augustine was not the city-state or even the empire but the "whole human community on its three levels of the family, the commonwealth, and the world."[11] Every level of community has friction, tension, and even overt conflicts, thus they "could not maintain themselves without the imposition of power."[12] Niebuhr comments that this power-play is at work in every empire and nation-state, even democratic ones that he describes as social integrations, in which a small group "holding the dominant form of social power, achieves oligarchic rule, no matter how much modern democracy may bring such power under social control."[13]

Augustine's critiques of government led Niebuhr to claim that Augustine's realism was "excessive."[14] Niebuhr bases his conclusion on two

---

8. Niebuhr, "Augustine's Political Realism," 124.

9. Niebuhr, "Augustine's Political Realism," 123.

10. Niebuhr, "Augustine's Political Realism," 125. This is more rightly understood as the Augustinian source of sin rather than evil. For Augustine, as Elshtain will explain below, evil is vacuous and only defined by the absence of good.

11. Niebuhr, "Augustine's Political Realism," 127.

12. Niebuhr, "Augustine's Political Realism," 127–28. This seems to be an interpolation on Niebuhr's part, though he cites *City of God* XIX/21 in support of his attribution of the necessity of power to Augustine: "Without injustice the republic would neither increase nor subsist. The imperial city to which the republic belongs could not rule over provinces without recourse to injustice. For it is unjust for some men to rule over others." This move is tenuous and does not resonate with Augustine's work overall.

13. Niebuhr, "Augustine's Political Realism," 128.

14. In contrast to my assertion last chapter that Augustine was a "reluctant realist," authorizing power to rein in lawlessness with the least amount of force necessary, Niebuhr insinuates that Augustine is too skeptical of government and should be as just as leery of anarchy as he is of tyranny.

comparisons that Augustine made without, at least for Niebuhr, significant distinctions. The first was between government and slavery, since Augustine suggested that man was never intended to rule over other men. It seemed incongruous to Niebuhr that the consequence of sin should also be its remedy. He continues that Augustine did well to avoid the absolute sanctification of government but failed to recognize the difference between legitimate and illegitimate subordination (ordinate and inordinate subordination) without which the "institutions of civilization could not exist."[15] Recall from chapter 2 that Augustine was not heavily vested in the power structures of the institutions of civilization that ruled over him as long as Christians could worship their God freely.

The second shortcoming in Augustine's critique of ruling authority according to Niebuhr was Augustine's comparison of the commonwealth to a band of robbers as both collectives are bound together by common interests. Niebuhr thought Augustine's assessment failed to acknowledge the sense of justice in the Roman Empire's constitution.[16] Though both the thief and the emperor are vulnerable to the corrupting influence of self-interest, the latter is charged with maintaining the social peace of society and therefore is a necessary curb to sin. Augustine was underscoring the former point while acknowledging the latter.

Augustine avoids what Niebuhr calls morally cynical or "nihilistic realism" by refusing to make the universal corruption of human freedom normative. Instead, Augustine makes love into the norm for the community. Niebuhr applauds the move of making love rather than justice the ultimate norm as shrewd as long as one is careful to distinguish it from the "modern forms of sentimental perfectionism."[17] Augustine passes Niebuhr's litmus test for normative love because Augustine "takes account of the power and persistence of egotism, both individual and collective, and seeks to establish the most tolerable form of peace and justice under conditions set by human sin."[18]

Lastly, Niebuhr critiques Augustine's realism because Niebuhr feels that the New Testament's *agape* (neighborly love) is misrepresented by Augustine's conceptions of *caritas* (love/charity) and *amor dei* (love of God).[19] Niebuhr accuses Augustine of obscuring the self-sacrificial nature of *agape*

---

15. Niebuhr, "Augustine's Political Realism," 129–30. Again, this seems to be an overextension of Augustine's writing.

16. Niebuhr, "Augustine's Political Realism," 128.

17. Niebuhr, "Augustine's Political Realism," 131.

18. Niebuhr, "Augustine's Political Realism," 131.

19. Niebuhr, "Augustine's Political Realism," 136.

and of subordinating neighbor love to love for God since Augustine writes that we are to love our neighbor for God's sake.

The first portion of Niebuhr's criticism seems unjust, because Augustine emphasized it quite regularly. However, the second charge Niebuhr levels is true but with good cause. Augustine subordinates *caritas* to *amor dei* as a safeguard against idolatry and as a buffer for the grief one feel's when the ones whom they loved for God's sake are lost to the "rivers of Babylon."

Jean Bethke Elshtain—Jingo Unchained

My reading of Elshtain's works began with her post 9/11 offering *Just War Against Terror: The Burden of American Power in a Violent World*. In it she was asking many of the same questions as I am here. Only after pondering this book and her methodology at great length, did I read her books written prior to 9/11 with a particular interest in her construction of Augustine and how it had come to inform her conclusions in *Just War Against Terror*. Rather than finding a reading of Augustine that provided a sturdy foundation for her later application of the same, her pre and post 9/11 works seem to be written by different authors or at least one person with two drastically incongruent perspectives. The third act, as it were, of my exploration of Elshtain's use of Augustine, just war thinking, and the "war on terror" was to read every journal entry and book chapter that I could find released after the publication of *Just War Against Terror* to see if she applied her knowledge of Augustine to the revelations of American injustices committed during the "war on terror" and whether such work had tempered her enthusiasm for it at all.

Augustine and the Limit of Politics, originally published in 1995, is a very meticulous reading of Augustine that is second to none, whereas *Just War Against Terror* seems to be a poor misappropriation of her earlier, impeccable reading. To what can we attribute the profound difference? The most conceivable shift, at least the only one of tectonic proportions to be found between 1995 and 2003, is September 11, 2001. The trauma of 9/11 seems to have indelibly colored Elshtain's perception, as it did for so many other Americans as well, of Augustine moving forward.

In her foreword to *The Impact of 9/11 on Religion and Philosophy: The Day That Changed Everything?* she confirms this hypothesis in part by writing, "September 11 invited reflection on one's own heritage and backdrop, on the excesses of one's tradition over time and on strong theological arguments countering those excesses as illegitimate and not authentically

Christian at all."[20] She continues by calling 9/11 an extraordinary moment for "teaching and learning," but laments that so many were ill-equipped to do either. I concur with her assessment, but I would add that the most pronounced repercussion of this lack of preparedness for such a teachable moment was the subsequent coopting of the Augustinian just-war tradition by Elshtain and other theologians to construct a moral narrative that would provide plausible ethical cover for the "war on terror."

As a widely respected Augustine scholar, Elshtain was invited to the Bush White House along with other academics and clergy in the weeks following September 11 to help the administration formulate a morally coherent response to the terrorist attacks. Undoubtedly, Elshtain's most significant contribution was her knowledge of Augustinian just-war tradition. She would later prove to be an ardent defender of the United States's second war in Iraq on humanitarian grounds even after the primary objective of the war (finding and destroying weapons of mass destruction) proved to be a red herring.

Early in *Just War Against Terror*, Elshtain claims that, "If we get our descriptions wrong, our analysis and our ethics will be wrong too."[21] If my reading of Elshtain is correct, it seems that she has gotten her descriptions spot on but fumbled through the analysis and ethics portions. We shall compare competing claims in her work in search for moral cohesion.

My reading of Augustine in chapter 2 is commensurate with a great deal of Elshtain's *Augustine and the Limits of Politics*. She readily admits that Augustine was "no liberal democrat,"[22] but rather a subversive, "working with analogies, trying to find a thread through the no-man's-land of war and empire."[23] His subversion shifted "the center of earthly gravity away from the political order to the 'solid rock' of the *civitas Dei* on pilgrimage."[24]

She concurs with John Milbank that Augustine begins with the presumption of peace and its priority over war, however she devotes great effort to communicate that "peace is attained fitfully in the *altera civitas* in its earthly pilgrimage; haphazardly, at best, in all earthly cities; and in its full richness only in the city of God."[25] She is leery of earthly peace and its illusory nature because peace is often the pseudonym for the human desire to impose one's will to subject others. It is a great irony that most prominent

20. Elshtain, *The Impact of 9/11*, xiv.
21. Elshtain, *Just War Against Terror*, 9.
22. Elshtain, *Augustine and the Limits of Politics*, 5.
23. Elshtain, *Augustine and the Limits of Politics*, 98.
24. Elshtain, *Augustine and the Limits of Politics*, 26.
25. Elshtain, *Augustine and the Limits of Politics*, 94.

disturbers of peace are "often those who claim to be upholding it—the great empires and great men—overtaken by a lust of sovereign dominion which disturbs and consumes the human race with frightful ills."[26] She quotes Augustine in support of her apprehension of peace:

> Peace vied with war in cruelty, and peace won! War struck down the armed, but peace the unarmed. War allows those who were being struck to strike back if they could, but peace did not allow those who survived to live but only to die without fighting back at all.[27]

This is an unusual passage for Augustine, not because he highlights the earthly city's perverted conception of peace, which he is keen to do in several places througout his work, but that he does not categorize the butchery of civilians after the war has ended as murder rather than an excessive or unjust war. Elshtain echoes Augustine in saying that earthly peace should be cherished nonetheless, but surely this peace described in *City of God* III/28 that culminates in the massacre of innocents is not what either had in mind.[28]

For Elshtain, this is precisely the point where the just-war tradition does its heaviest lifting since just war reproves domestic and international order, providing ethical standards for the purposeful uses of power and order and acts as "a lens through which to look at the heart of what constitutes what is called peace."[29] Equipped with the moral tools to do so, Christians should confront false peace wherever they encounter it. Though unable to affect the perfect peace of the Heavenly City, there is still earthly work to be done in the name of peace.[30] As Elshtain frames the discussion, a great part of that work is to resist, in the name of love, the narrative that violence is the only way to affect social change.

While I am more optimistic about the efficacy of non-violent Christian witness than Elshtain is, her hesitancy to unqualifiedly embrace earthly peace is well-founded and Augustinian at its root. Elshtain includes an excellent chapter comparing Hannah Arendt's "banality of evil" with Augustine's metaphysical conception of evil as the diminution of the good until none remains.[31]

26. Elshtain, *Augustine and the Limits of Politics*, 26.
27. Augustine, *City of God*, III/28. Quoted in Elshtain, *Augustine and the Limits of Politics*,105–6.
28. Elshtain, *Augustine and the Limits of Politics*, 26.
29. Elshtain, *Augustine and the Limits of Politics*, 111.
30. Elshtain, *Augustine and the Limits of Politics*, 105.
31. Elshtain, *Augustine and the Limits of Politics*, 69–87.

As it certainly does in most Augustinian political projects, the allegory of the two cities features prominently in Elshtain's work on Augustine. She reasons that humans are not inherently political but are social by nature.[32] According to Elshtain, the distinctive sin of the *civitas terrena* is the exercise of "arbitrary power."[33] Rome like all earthly cities held a false conception of "justice" because they were dominated by the interest of the stronger.[34] For this reason, Augustine rejects Cicero's definition of a people who agree upon certain rules and the pursuit of justice. Elshtain comments that Cicero's definition is "inadequate, [because it is] simply not up to the task of recognizing and deepening the work of *caritas*."[35] This can only be done by a people bound together by common objects of love, Augustine's more refined characterization of the commonwealth.

Within Augustine's allegory of the two cities Elshtain notes that "Augustine creates a complex moral map that offers space for loyalty and love and care, as well as for a chastened form of civic virtue."[36] Augustine equally reproves those who put too much hope in the success of the earthly city and those who disdain any hope for it. The pilgrim will "make use" of the earthly city's imperfect peace while she helps contribute to the peace by "calling out citizens from all nations and so collects a society of aliens, speaking all languages."[37]

Elshtain underscores the twofold pilgrim ethic—do not harm anyone and help everyone whenever possible. The pilgrim would rather serve than ignore her neighbor because she knows that "in loving God, we also love our neighbor."[38] Elshtain offers a beautiful assessment of the manner in which the pilgrim loves her neighbor:

> Authentic compassion (*com*, together; *pati*, to suffer) eradicates contempt and distance. The Christian is not afraid that he or she will lose something by offering him or herself. That is what the ethic of *caritas* is about—not moralistic self-abnegation but an abundant overflowing of the fullness of life.[39]

---

32. Elshtain, *Augustine and the Limits of Politics*, 26.
33. Elshtain, *Augustine and the Limits of Politics*, 42.
34. Elshtain, *Augustine and the Limits of Politics*, 97.
35. Elshtain, *Augustine and the Limits of Politics*, 39.
36. Elshtain, *Augustine and the Limits of Politics*, 91.
37. Elshtain, *Augustine and the Limits of Politics*, 96.
38. Elshtain, *Augustine and the Limits of Politics*, 59.
39. Elshtain, *Augustine and the Limits of Politics*, 36.

This last section of *Limits of Politics* is particularly insightful given the argument Elshtain will advance in *Just War on Terror*. Despite our compassion and *caritas* for our neighbor that draws us nearer to them, there are times in which the pilgrim must purposefully distinguish between her earthly home and herself. This is due to the reality that "if one brings the city of God into too tight a relationship to the city of man, then the latter begins to make claims that take on the character of the ultimate."[40] This is the sacralizing of the state that Augustine ardently resisted.

Elshtain specifically contextualizes what is at stake here for US Christians: "Clearly Augustine would have a thing or two to say to those folks who equate America with a sacral order. This is not 'God's country,' Augustine would surely say, but yet another nation 'under God's judgement.'"[41] This is true of all governments since none possess absolute value and thus cannot be defended by unacceptable means.[42] "Defended" is the operative word here, because Rome, like most empires, proclaimed all their wars were defensive. This prompted Augustine to suggest that they build a monument to the goddess of foreign iniquity, as she was used to "conjure up an implacable foreign foe to justify these ravages."[43]

So bellicose was Rome, flushed through and through with the *libido dominandi*, that in the absence of an external enemy upon whom to galvanize its violent focus, they would turn upon fellow neighbors as though they were strangers.[44] Elshtain's insight in 1995 was that the US, in between wars as it was, was treading the same Roman path towards another civil war. She elaborates:

> Is this not what we are up to in American society? Are we not busy building barriers between ourselves, bustling away, proclaiming that we cannot speak to one another, cannot understand one another, and must not have anything to do with one another?[45]

---

40. Elshtain, *Augustine and the Limits of Politics*, 98.
41. Elshtain, *Augustine and the Limits of Politics*, 94–95.
42. Elshtain, *Augustine and the Limits of Politics*, 107. Interestingly Elshtain does not mention which forms of defense are unacceptable, a glaring omission in her writing that she never fully addresses.
43. Elshtain, *Augustine and the Limits of Politics*, 106.
44. Elshtain, *Augustine and the Limits of Politics*, 107.
45. Elshtain, *Augustine and the Limits of Politics*, 107. I would argue that the situation is even more dire now than in 1995, in part because most Americans feel as though the "war on terror" has been won and forget that the US military is *still* fighting openly in Afghanistan and covertly throughout the Middle East.

In summary of Elshtain's final section, pilgrims should be leery of sacralizing the state for it will begin to make ultimate claims of them. She believes Augustine would rebuke anyone who equated America (or any nation) with sacral order, and thus the means of defending governments are limited to "acceptable" means, as ambiguous as the term may be. Lastly, Rome coveted a foreign adversary with whom it could make war, and in the absence of one infighting would begin. Elshtain diagnosed America with the same Roman volatility in 1995.

In her previous work on war published in 1987, *Women and War*, Elshtain placed some conditions on just-war thinking as a civic virtue. She asserts that just-war thinking presupposes a particular kind of self, "one attuned to moral reasoning and capable of it; one strong enough to resist the lure of seductive, violent enthusiasms; one bounded by and laced through with a sense of responsibility and accountability."[46] In other words, Elshtain is arguing that a morally formed civic character is a necessary prerequisite for just-war thinking. She also writes that the just-war tradition shares with pacifism the capacity to refrain from violence when one has been victimized. She can write such a provocative statement because both in pacifism and just-war thinking violence, not nonviolence, must bear the burden of proof.[47] With these criteria in mind, let us now turn to her post-9/11 response in *Just War Against Terror* to see how Elshtain used her expertise, impeccable reading of Augustine, and morally formed civic character to apply the just-war tradition to the fledgling "war on terror."

Like Stanley Hauerwas and Bill Cavanaugh, Elshtain rightly describes the September 11 hijackers as "mass murderers" rather than "soldiers" or "martyrs." However, her analysis leads her to diverge from Hauerwas's and Cavanaugh's moral judgment that, as murderers, they and their co-conspirators should have been pursued as criminals and brought to justice by a coordinated international police action rather than through military operations.[48] Instead, she echoes the Bush administration's characterization of the attacks as "acts of war" that compelled a comparable response.[49]

46. Elshtain, *Women and War*, 152.

47. Elshtain, *Women and War*, 151.

48. See Hauerwas, "September 11, 2001: A Pacifist Response," 425–33 and Cavanaugh, "Terrorist Enemies and Just War," 27–35. Also for biting critique of Elshtain's book and her equally stinging response, see Hauerwas, Griffiths, and Elshtain, "War, Peace & Jean Bethke Elshtain."

49. Before the first tower had fallen, Vice President Dick Cheney told President Bush, "Sounds like we have a minor war going on here, I heard about the Pentagon. We're at war . . . somebody's going to pay." The National Commission on Terrorist Attacks Upon the United States, "The 9-11 Commission Report," 39.

As a vigilant reader of Augustine, Elshtain purposefully does not describe the wars in Afghanistan and Iraq in terms of self-defense like the Bush administration and its sympathizers have. She knows that for Augustine self-defense is beyond the pale for Christian pilgrims who cleave to their eternal rather than earthly lives. However, in the modern, sterile, and secularized version of just war, self-defense is the most easily justifiable reason for war as evidenced by the oft-quoted Article 51 from the United Nation's charter:

> Nothing in the present Charter shall impair the inherent right of individual or collective self-defense if an armed attack occurs against a Member of the United Nations until the Security Council has taken measures necessary to maintain international peace and security.[50]

In Elshtain's assessment, it is indisputable that the US met the criterion of "just cause" before its response to September 11. This is apparent to her since it was acting not merely in the defense of its own citizens but also, through proxy, all inhabitants of the globe that currently enjoy or desire the freedoms inherent in the American way of life. Elshtain proposes that the "war on terror" is an act of neighbor-love but does little to account for the remarkable coincidence that the US only chose to love its neighbors immediately after it had suffered an attack. Although she seems cognizant that self-defense has been made to do a disproportionally large amount of the heavy lifting in post-Enlightenment just-war thinking, her Augustinian account of what it means to love one's neighbor seems to misconstrue the second greatest commandment as, "Love yourself, as your neighbor."

Elshtain goes to great lengths to justify the invasion of Afghanistan not merely on the grounds of self-defense but also as an act of beatific benevolence by the United States. She notes that many expatriates returned to Afghanistan following the expulsion of the Taliban and that the plight of Afghani women also significantly improved as the severe restrictions placed on them by the Taliban's regime were lightened.

It was similar compassion for its innocent neighbors in Iraq rather than the presence of weapons of mass destruction (WMD) that Elshtain asserts should have been foregrounded as the just cause for the United States's invasion of Iraq in the spring of 2003. Saddam's attempted genocide of the Kurds, his retaliatory draining of the marshes that displaced

---

50. UN, "Charter of the United Nations." This is perhaps the only positive thing Elshtain attributes to the UN. It is only since genocides in Bosnia and Rwanda that the idea of a "Responsibility to Protect," which authorizes nations to intervene within other nations without first being attacked, has been incorporated into the charter.

nearly 200,000 *Madan* (Marsh Arabs), and his mass murder of Shiites after the first Gulf War in 1991 provided ample and legitimate grounds for war. Even so, the timing of the invasion remains suspect as the US was aware of these atrocities well before 2003.

For Elshtain, the suspicion of WMD only served to concretize these injustices. She neatly accounts for the absence of any of these weapons, a cause of great embarrassment[51] for the United States and the "Coalition of the Willing,"[52] by stating that they were most likely smuggled across Iraq's northwestern border and hidden in Syria. She cites chief weapons inspector David Kay's preliminary address to Congress in October of 2003 as support for her claim.[53]

Initially, Kay testified before Congress that "There is ample evidence of movement to Syria before the war—satellite photographs, reports on the ground of a constant stream of trucks, cars, rail traffic across the border. We simply don't know what was moved, [and] the Syrian government there has shown absolutely no interest in helping us resolve this issue."[54] Yet in his Senate hearing only three months later Kay would confess, "It turns out that we were all wrong, probably in my judgment, and that is most disturbing."[55] Again for Elshtain, this revelation even when coupled with the fact that Iraq was not involved in the 9/11 attacks is inconsequential in light of the other injustices perpetrated by Saddam Hussein's regime.

According to Elshtain, what makes this particular set of circumstances exceptional is what the United States is defending itself against. A sovereign nation-state did not attack the US with a specific list of political grievances against the US that could have been negotiated through diplomacy. Instead, it was assaulted by a conglomerate of ideologues whose indictments were against ideals intrinsic to the American way of life, not mere policies.

However, she fails to acknowledge that the same issues that obfuscated diplomacy also problematized a just-war response. Though fifteen of the

---

51. The Bush administration was so eager to invade Iraq that they did so on the word of a single informant who just so happened to be lying. Elshtain never mentions, and perhaps did not know at the time of publication, that the administration was confident that Iraq had chemical and biological weapons because Iraq had used them in the war against Iran, a fact that the US knew and never protested. Harris and Aid, "CIA Files Prove America Helped Saddam as He Gassed Iran."

52. "Coalition of the Willing" was the name given by President Bush to the forty-nine countries who supported the US-led invasion of Iraq although only a few were willing to support the invasion directly with troops and some did not have a military at all (making it seem more like an "Army of One").

53. See the full text of the address: Kay, "Text of David Kay's Unclassified Statement."

54. Kay, "No Evidence Iraq Stockpiled WMDs."

55. Kay, "David Kay at Senate Hearing."

nineteen September 11 hijackers were Saudi Arabian, the first military target was the *al Qaeda* stronghold of Afghanistan. Even if one accepts at face value that invading Afghanistan was the logical first response, the subsequent war in Iraq, a country with no ties to *al Qaeda* or 9/11, was a much less morally justifiable second act of the "war on terror."

It is difficult to imagine Augustine advocating fighting for the city of man's "way of life" as does Elshtain. He made clear that the earthly city, founded as it was in murder, was never meant to live eternally. Even if one cedes what is by no means self-evident, that the US is the best moral exemplar of the city of man among few good options, the US is destined to end as it was conceived—in death. As mentioned above, he instructed his parishioners to pray for the peace of Babylon. He advised them to use (*uti*) the peace of the earthly city and even made an argument for responsible Christian military participation so that the good may live peaceful lives among the wicked. Still, it seems that a clarion call for Christians to "lay down your life for the empire's way of life" is an unambiguously un-Augustinian appeal.

Augustine experienced Alaric's sack of Rome in 410 the same way many Americans experienced 9/11—from within the empire, yet strangely removed from the attack.[56] I have yet to find evidence in his work of a response that mirrors Elshtain's, which is a more sophisticated version of what many Americans felt after 9/11. After the sack of Rome, he did not grieve as one whose metaphysical inviolability had been torn from within him. Neither did he call, as Elshtain has, for swift and retributive justice against those who assaulted the city and their sympathizers. Furthermore, there seems to be no plausible claim that Augustine would have approved of a preventative war that would ferret out and eliminate *potential* enemies, real or imagined, before they could attack so that his imperial republic could live perpetually free of fear. Instead, Augustine would seemingly be a proponent of a rightly ordered fear—one of God, rather than of men—that led to repentance rather than revenge.

Despite this, Elshtain writes that war was not only the last resort, but it was also the *only* possible recourse. Capitulation to the demands of *al Qaeda* (even if it were possible and she adamantly argues that it was not) would not appease it. The issues are more significant than American foreign policy in the Arab world or its perceived global flaunting of its liberties that are opposed to the Muslim way of life. To be more precise, the Islamists[57] oppose

---

56. I write this fully aware of the manner in which the continuous media loop enabled the world to be peculiarly estranged eyewitnesses to the horrific sights of the day in a way that Augustine could not have been. Atrocity, though, is still provocative whether imagined or seen.

57. This is the name Elshtain uses for those who practice an aberrant and violent

the very values that are inextricably part of the moral fiber of America. Elshtain summarizes these ideals in five universal truths:

1. All human beings are born free and equal in dignity and rights.

2. The primary subject of society is the human person, and the legitimate role of government is to protect and help to foster the conditions for human flourishing.

3. Human beings naturally desire to seek the truth about life's purposes and ultimate ends.

4. Freedom of conscience and religious freedom are inviolable rights of the human person.

5. Killing in the name of God is contrary to faith in God and the greatest betrayal of the universality of religious faith.[58]

The list is agreeable enough, yet one may reasonably wonder what makes killing in the name of the state whose only God is mammon morally superior to killing in the name of God? This is particularly vexing for a people who worship a God who chose to inaugurate his kingdom with nails rather than swords in his hands.

It has not always been so peculiar for disciples of Jesus to imagine a people that practice peace and refuse to accept the "kill or be killed" binary. However, it is always disorienting to murder a people who refuse to defend themselves in kind. In the absence of such a moral imagination, Elshtain surmises that the only way to appease those who attacked the US on September 11 is to renounce these five truths and effectively cease to exist as America, which is a non sequitur for consequential diplomacy.

Neither she, nor any proponent of the "war on terror" whom I have read has explained the rationale behind killing an enemy for whom death is not a deterrent but is rather embraced as the rare guarantee of eternal life. They propagandize their deaths as a tool to recruit and radicalize more jihadists since it justifies their false "clash of civilizations" narrative. Elshtain would do well to listen to the insight of Tony Campolo, whom she criticizes for advocating for repentance post 9/11. Campolo has proposed an approach to terrorism that is radically different from war. He asserts that "We are not going to get rid of terrorism by killing terrorists any more than we can get rid of malaria by killing mosquitoes. We have to get rid of the swamps that breed mosquitoes. So it is that we don't get rid of terrorists by

---

form of Islam as opposed to those who are moderate and peaceful adherents to that "Great World Religion."

58. Elshtain, *Just War Against Terror*, 74–75.

killing terrorists, but by getting rid of the swamps that breed terrorists (i.e. The oppressive social conditions under which they live)."[59]

Elshtain seems unwilling to accept that there was once, and will be again, a time when America did not exist and that the rise and fall of the cities of men does not impede the flourishing of the city of God. Augustine was less concerned with the temporary sovereign provided the church was free to pursue and enjoy God as its ultimate end—something that the attacks on September 11 could not threaten.[60] Augustine also knew that even when the church was made invisible and forced underground as it was under certain Roman emperors, the kingdom of God grew more rapidly.

While Elshtain was concerned that capitulation to the terrorists would cause America to cease to exist, I am more concerned with whether the unjust ways it has prosecuted the "war on terror" might produce the same result that Elshtain feared. The Christian citizen must remain mindful that part of pursuing God as the highest common good is the willingness to renounce the evil with which we are told we must resist evil.

In response to 9/11, Elshtain helped author "What We're Fighting For," an open letter to Islamists justifying the US response to the 9/11 murders.[61] Nearly two decades later, the US is still entangled in Afghanistan, which has now become the longest war in American history. Moreover, most Americans would be hard pressed to formulate a plausible rationale for their country's continued presence in Afghanistan even if you make the generous assumption that most Americans are still aware that war effort in Afghanistan is still underway. Had I the good fortune of being able to meet Professor Elshtain for a coffee or something stronger, I would have asked her, "What are we *still* fighting the 'war on terror' for and how will we know if we have won?" Augustine would not have advocated for war in perpetuity, but this is the only kind of war that can be waged against the shadows of terror. It is difficult to contest that the US has surpassed any reasonable limit of proportionality some time ago.

Her book is more than the misappropriation of Augustine to bless the US response to 9/11, of which he would have likely been much more critical and skeptical than she was. If her only error was advocating for an action of

---

59. Campolo, "Undoing the Mess that America Made."

60. I imagine that many may retort that a Christian in an Islamic state is not free to pursue her God. I anticipate Augustine would respond by saying the courage to pursue Christ in a land that worships foreign gods is a crucible that purifies rather than prohibits worship. Such refining is preferable to a permanently mixed body of Christ that produces benign disciples in a society that worships Christ in word only.

61. The letter was published as an appendix in Elshtain, *Just War Against Terror*, 193–218.

which should be repented, the book would not have been as provocative nor muddled the line between jingoism and justice in the manner that it did.

Her second objective is revealed by the book's subtitle: *The Burden of American Political Power in a Violent World*. She contends that not only was the US response to 9/11 just, but also that anything less than the US continued role as world police would be less just still. Both the subtitle and claim reflect American hubris. To the extent that a violent world burdens American power, it is a violent world that the United States uninhibitedly fashioned in its own image. The US is the only nation to have used nuclear weapons on noncombatants to terrorize an enemy into submission. If vaporizing 120,000 citizens instantly, in addition to watching tens of thousands more dying from radiation exposure, does not qualify as terrorism, then the word is utterly void of meaning. The only nation to unleash such an abominable weapon on non-combatants is curiously also the principal judge that discriminates between countries that can legally possess the same weapons that only it has used and those who cannot lest their nation draw the ire of the judge that is eager to suffocate insubordinate nations under international economic sanctions and military subterfuge.[62]

Conceivably, Elshtain would answer my earlier questions by saying that the US is still in Afghanistan because Afghanistan and the Middle

---

62. The US has done a poor job in this respect. The US policy has been to incentivize nuclear disarmament for those countries that already have nuclear arsenals and to offer protection to states without nuclear weapons so that they will have no need to pursue their own nuclear programs. While this seems like a reasonable suggestion, its implementation has proven far less promising. Ukraine is an apt example. After the collapse of the Soviet Union, newly independent Ukraine found itself as the sole proprietor of the world's third largest nuclear arsenal. In 1994, the Ukraine, the United States, Russia, and the United Kingdom signed the Budapest Memorandums on Security Assurances promising Ukraine that, in return for its complete nuclear disarmament, the other parties would respect its independence, sovereignty, and existing borders while also refraining from the threat or use of force against the territorial integrity and political independence of Ukraine. Ukraine held up its end of the agreement. By 1996, it had transferred all of its nuclear warheads to Russia. With the assistance of the United States, all remaining elements of the intercontinental ballistic missiles were dismantled or transferred to Russia by 2002. The United States and Russia, however, have been less than faithful to the treaty. In February 2014, the United States supported the coup against Ukraine's democratically elected, pro-Russian president Viktor Yanukovych. Russia in response, annexed Crimea and refused to recognize the results of the presidential election the following May that saw pro-European businessman Petro Poroshenko become the head of state. Appeals to the UN's Security Council proved ineffectual since the political and territorial sovereignty of Ukraine was being violated from both directions by two of the Security Council's permanent members. Instances like this one cast serious doubts on whether current nuclear powers can oversee peaceful disarmament and non-proliferation.

East[63] need the United States' stabilizing influence as the world's "sole remaining super-power." She makes no mention of the fact that the United States is the sole remaining superpower because it bankrupted the Soviet Union with a nuclear arms race during the Cold War. The continued US presence in the region undermines its stability by underwriting Israel's nuclear weapons program while sanctioning any of the apartheid state's neighbors who seek the same weapons.[64]

How does Elshtain think that the US should respond to global injustices, inequities, and terrorism? She suggests that imperialism is the solution because "Sometimes the most effective new frameworks are old ones resituated in a new reality."[65] Perhaps she is right, but more often the old frameworks have been retired precisely because they have proved untenable or unconscionable as the political landscape has changed, and to return to them would be a remarkable regression rather than progress. It is surprising that she begins the conversation with the word imperialism given its problematic history and that it is typically a pejorative charge levelled against the United States.

This move is reminiscent of President George W. Bush and Secretary of State Colin Powell's incendiary use of the term crusade[66] to describe the US "war on terror." The critical difference is that both Powell and Bush acknowledged they had misspoken when using a word that has such a complicated history and evokes strong, negative connotations that they did not intend and subsequently removed it from their public lexicon.

Rather than rescind the word, Elshtain doubles down on its use by trying to distinguish what she is proposing from the "bad old imperialism" that sought political and territorial aggrandizement. Rather, what she intends to articulate through the use of the word imperialism is the idea of altruistic "nation-building." In doing so, she further develops arguments initiated by commentators like Sebastian Mallaby and Michael Ignatieff to assert that

---

63. Like Mitri Raheb, I find the term "Middle East" somewhat pejorative. Middle of where and east of what? It might more appropriately be called the center or origin of civilization. See Raheb, *Faith in the Face of Empire*.

64. Though, as we discussed above, the US will gladly arm Arabs with inferior weapons to kill other Arabs, Iranians, and Russians.

65. Elshtain, *Just War Against Terror*, 166.

66. Another galling line of reasoning taken by Elshtain in the book is her defense of the Crusades, and her criticism of those like Tony Campolo who she claims would attempt to make Christians feel culpable for the actions of others in the eleventh and twelfth centuries. She remarks that Christians who make apologies for the Crusades rarely mention the violent expansion of Islam that removed Christians from lands in the Middle East where they had lived for centuries. To this I would reply that Christians should repent of the sins of the church and leave Muslims to do the same for Islam.

this new model of nation-building imperialism is a form of deterrence that safeguards against the "failed state, within which hapless citizens are victimized by the ruthless and terrorists are given carte blanche to operate." However, some words cannot be so easily divorced from the cumbersome burden of their vitriolic past. When one is discussing Western foreign policy, particularly in nations that are predominantly Muslim, imperialism is surely one word that is certain to reinvigorate animus.

Elshtain's new imperialism is opposed to isolationism, which she writes is an immoral abdication of the US responsibility to its weaker neighbors—which is presumably everyone since it is the "sole remaining superpower." It is an uniquely American responsibility since it alone has the power to be the new "guarantor of human dignity."[67] This phrase, as well as this entire line of reasoning, is problematic at best and jingoistic at worst.[68] Perhaps China, Russia, and the United Kingdom (when it fully ironed out the final terms of its awkward divorce from the EU) for instance, might take umbrage with Elshtain's claim that the US is the world's only remaining superpower. Absent any coherent criteria, the most arduous burden would be determining which states are failing or have indeed already failed. Even if the criteria could be established through international consensus, presumably the number of failed or failing states would be too numerous for even the mighty US to intervene in each one. What moral calculus will the US employ to choose in which states it will magnanimously nation-build and from which others the US will wickedly abscond from its duty as the world's stabilizing police force?

Even the descriptor "failed state" is far too ambiguous to be useful. Does Elshtain mean a state without a functioning government, one that abuses its citizens, or simply one whose policies conflict with US interests? Depending on the standards one uses to identify which states are failing or indeed have already failed, there could be two to three dozen nations in need of the US's philanthropic intervention, some of whom the US considers allies. Having read Augustine's admonition against imperial overstretch in the *City of God*, Elshtain must not agree with the bishop's conclusions that empires work better when they are smaller since the rule of too many people by too few is the recipe for revolt and imperial collapse.

To Elshtain's credit, she truly comprehends what is at stake in the "war on terror." It is the fleeting grasp of an empire for control of its own destiny. For America to fight a "just war on terror," according to Elshtain, it must

---

67. Elshtain, *Just War Against Terror*, 167.

68. Nationalism, for most, carries the same historical baggage as imperialism, as the former usually leads to the latter. For a compelling argument for ethical nationalism, see Gay, *Honey from the Lion*.

continue to extend its influence into every crevice of the globe, particularly to places with weaker governments whose political agendas are in conflict with America's own (which based on recent history seems to be the most accurate descriptor of a failed state I can find). She has failed to realize that what she calls munificent nation-building many others call manipulative racketeering or, to borrow her phrase, the "bad old kind of imperialism." She seems tone deaf to the reality that much of the world resents the manner in which the US guarantees human dignity.

Elshtain's pilgrimage in the earthly city ended in 2013, but not before she saw the photographs from *Abu Ghraib* prison, heard that there were no weapons of mass destruction, read the CIA's torture report of innocent detainees, and learned of our country's morally dubious drone policy. She lived to discover some of the more sordid details of the "war on terror" yet never wavered in her certitude that US's response to 9/11 was a just one. She was in the midst of writing the follow up to *Just War on Terror* with the working title of *Torture and Terror in a Time of Troubles* when she passed away.[69] Of her unpublished work, Elshtain wrote, "The basic position hasn't changed: the need to confront systematic terroristic violence against civilians, because that's what terrorism is. The question is not, 'Do you?' but, 'How does one do it?'"[70]

In searching through her post–*Just War on Terror* articles, lectures, and book excerpts, there are a few recurring themes. The most prominent is what Elshtain calls an "ethic of responsibility," which she says the just-war tradition concretizes the responsibilities of "statesmen and stateswomen for their polities; the responsibility of one polity for another; the shared responsibility of all states to a system that helps sustain a world of diverse bodies politic."[71] This is reflected in the United Nations' "Responsibility to Protect" (R2P) clause that only materialized in the late twentieth century after international indifference allowed the attempted genocides in Rwanda and Bosnia. Elshtain has little faith in any power besides the US fulfilling this responsibility, saying, "it is always a good bet that the UN will be paralyzed" and that European powers merely pay lip service to humanitarian intervention even in situations in which they are historically implicated.[72]

Under the more recently developed arm of just-war thinking known as *jus post bellum* (justice after war) Elshtain argues against the "premature"

---

69. Trainer, "Elshtain Considers the Moral Necessities of War."
70. Trainer, "Elshtain Considers the Moral Necessities of War."
71. Elshtain, "Just War and an Ethics of Responsibility," 124.
72. Elshtain, "Just War and an Ethics of Responsibility," 124.

US withdrawal from Iraq.[73] Whether one thinks the initial invasion was just or not,[74] Elshtain contends, has now been rendered moot and the international focus should be on the *jus post bellum* criteria that oblige the United States to "leave Iraq with something better, or at least not worse, than what went before."[75] For Elshtain the ethics of responsibility for *just post bellum* requires what she calls a "just occupation" and "eventual withdrawal" that leaves behind a "minimally decent state."[76] All three terms are fraught with peril, particularly the way Elshtain wields them.

She boasts of how the US remains in Europe seventy years after the conclusion of World War II and in the Korean Peninsula sixty years from the truce that ended that conflict. If this is what she is prescribing for Iraq, it seems like *just*[77] occupation without pretension of withdrawal. What she would like to see happen is a modern-day Marshall Plan for the entire region but laments the US occupation of Iraq is "made doubly difficult because we are no longer in an era when the United States can muster the will and resources to reorder and garrison entire societies."[78] It is clear that Elshtain's solution to global stability remains American imperialism.

As for what counts as a "minimally decent state," she explains that it is not necessarily a democratic replica of the US or any other regime, "save to say that no one is born to be a slave, to be tormented, to be slaughtered because of who he or she is—whether American or Israeli or Palestinian, whether Jew or Christian or Muslim, whether male or female."[79] By her definition, I am not certain that many states including the United States meet the "minimally decent" standard.[80]

I can write such a provocative statement due to the US policies of torture and targeted killing. Elshtain only briefly addresses the latter but places them in the same category of "executive powers *in extremis*."[81] She admits

---

73. Elshtain, "The Ethics of Fleeing," 91–98.

74. Elshtain, "The Ethics of Fleeing," 94. Elshtain, for her part, sticks by her earlier thesis that the second US invasion of Iraq was a just war but she now adds the caveat, "The tragedy of the Iraq War is that this cluster of concerns [*just post bellum*] was not thought through rigorously, if at all."

75. Elshtain, "The Ethics of Fleeing," 94.

76. Elshtain, "The Ethics of Fleeing," 95.

77. As in *only*, not as in *justified*.

78. Elshtain, "The Ethics of Fleeing," 95.

79. Elshtain, "A Response," 504–5.

80. The murdered bodies of George Floyd, Breonna Taylor, Botham Jean, Philando Castille, and many of the other one hundred sixty-four African Americans killed by police officers in the first eight months of 2020 testify to this fact.

81. Elshtain, "A Response," 503. Also described in her fullest account of torture in "Reflection on the Problem of 'Dirty Hands,'" 77–89.

what some of her detractors have been saying from the beginning, that "much of the time the war against terrorism is a police matter."[82] She limits these times to when terrorism occurs in the domestic space or "zone of peace." Elshtain contrasts this to the "zone of war" created by government-sponsored terrorism of the ilk of the Taliban in Afghanistan that invited legitimate self-defense from the United States post 9/11. She admits there are legal and moral problems created by what she calls "the in-between space . . . where there is no declared war, but the writ of the state does not run effectively either."[83] She raises the issue of targeted killing as the exemplar of the in-between place without ever really addressing the practice itself as anathema or necessary. She finally comes to rest on the quite elastic principle that extreme measures should be *resisted* "for as long as we can [because] [i]t is vital that we not normalize the extreme exceptions."[84] Elshtain resists normalizing the exceptions but by leaving ample room for the *in extremis* to be legitimate practice she has created enough moral wiggle room for the exception to become (all but) the rule.[85]

Elshtain offers a fuller treatment of torture post 9/11 but essentially arrives at the same conclusion, "Torture remains a horror and, in general, a tactic that is forbidden. But there are moments when this rule may be overridden."[86] The overriding should be *in extremis* (or as *close* to it as possible, she adds) and she includes the qualification that "one overrides the rule in recognition that a moral wrong does not make a 'right' but it might bring about a 'less bad' or 'more just' outcome."[87] This is the limit of Niebuhrian realism—how one loves her God and neighbor is reduced to an obscure moral calculus of relatively consequentialist goods and evils.

Elshtain's torture essay begins with the tired dilemma between two morally dubious and unimaginative options. The hypothetical scenario plays out as follows: a bomb has been planted in an elementary school in a city with several hundred such schools and the police are *certain* they have captured the person who knows which school contains the bomb, but he refuses to talk.[88] The classic options considered are the utilitarian

82. Elshtain, "A Response," 503.
83. Elshtain, "A Response," 503.
84. Elshtain, "A Response," 503. See the discussion of Lincoln's Lieber Code above, which like Elshtain's move here was meant to curb unjust war practices but ended up justifying all manner of atrocity under the guise of "military necessity."
85. See the discussion of Giorgio Agamben's "permanent state of exception" discussed above.
86. Elshtain, "Dirty Hands," 83.
87. Elshtain, "Dirty Hands," 82.
88. Elshtain admits that swallowing this scenario "as is" takes *at least* a modicum

approach that will torture the criminal until he confesses the location of the bomb thus allowing the police to save the children and the deontologist approach that refuses to treat "another human being as a means rather than end in himself,"[89] forgoes the torture, and allows the innocent school children to be slaughtered. Elshtain is burdened by the fact that "deontology makes something called 'torture' impossible, [while] utilitarianism makes it too easy and too tempting."[90] She admits that prior to 9/11 she was among the deontologists who thought torture could never be morally permitted by the United States as that was (and remains) something that only reprehensible regimes did. After America was attacked on 9/11, Elshtain had a change of heart.

Elshtain's solution to the moral morass is to retread the largely discredited tradition of moral casuistry. She writes that under the Geneva Conventions the category of torture is too indiscriminate to be useful. She adopts Mark Bowden's use of the term "torture lite" for acceptable forms of coercion that *should* not be housed under the banner torture proper because "although excruciating for the victim, these tactics generally leave no permanent marks and do no lasting physical harm."[91] Bowden's list of "lightly" coercive measures includes:

> Sleep deprivation, exposure to heat or cold, the use of drugs to cause confusion, rough treatment (slapping, shoving or shaking), forcing a prisoner to stand for days at a time or sit in uncomfortable positions, and playing on his fears for himself and his family.[92]

Even if one concedes that these belong under the heading of "coercion" rather than "torture," which is no small concession, Elshtain remained silent about many other dubious practices of which she was undoubtedly aware were employed by the US that leave "no permanent marks and do no lasting physical harm." The following actions are described in General Antonio Taguba's Investigative Report on abuses at *Abu Ghraib* prison.[93]

- videotaping and photographing nude male and female detainees

---

of suspension of belief. 1) There is the certainty that you have the right criminal who will 2) tell the truth when tortured rather than lie to stall and allow enough time for the bomb to go off and 3) that you have the time to torture him *and* evacuate the school in time *but* 4) you do not have time to evacuate every school?

89. Elshtain, "Dirty Hands," 78.
90. Elshtain, "Dirty Hands," 79.
91. Bowden, "The Dark Art of Interrogation."
92. Bowden, "The Dark Art of Interrogation."
93. Taguba, "Investigation of the 800th Military Police Brigade."

- forcibly arranging detainees in various sexually explicit positions for photographing
- forcing detainees to remove their clothing and keeping them naked for several days at a time
- forcing groups of male detainees to masturbate themselves while being photographed and videotaped
- arranging naked male detainees in a pile and then jumping on them
- positioning a naked detainee on an MRE Box, with a sandbag on his head, and attaching wires to his fingers, toes, and penis to simulate electric torture
- taking photographs of dead Iraqi detainees
- breaking chemical lights and pouring the phosphoric liquid on detainees
- threatening detainees with a charged nine mm pistol
- threatening male detainees with rape
- sodomizing a detainee with a chemical light and perhaps a broom stick.

These detainees did not know the location of any elementary school bombs, but they ostensibly *could* have.[94] Presumably, this fact would not have changed whether or not Elshtain thought that these questionable actions were torture but just whether or not the questionable actions were *justified*.

It is practically un-American not to make the possible terrorist masturbate and film it if doing so would certainly save 500 adolescents from their untimely deaths. Casuistry forces a nation, a soldier, or a citizen to give specific and sordid names to the evil she is willing to do in order to do "good" or "marginally less evil." It is highly doubtful that any children were saved by the above tactics, but I cannot say that with any measure of certainty. However, I am quite certain that many children were endangered by dehumanization of inmates at *Abu Ghraib*. *Al Qaeda* could not fabricate more provocative propaganda than those images made by the US soldiers. Dehumanizing the (often unknown) enemy makes it easier for them to dehumanize our non-combatants.

---

94. One of the problems noted in General Taguba's report is that the release process for detainees who offered little or no intelligence value and posed minimal or no security risk was painfully slow and led to overcrowding at the prison and the likely abuse of detainees who posed no national security threat to Iraq or the United States.

Part of Elshtain's arguments for permitting torture lite *in extremis* is that we face war against enemies who "know no limits . . . In warfare, the rules of *just ad bellum* and *jus in bello* have no meaning to them. The whole point of terror is the purposeful, random killing of innocents, defined as those who are no position to defend themselves."[95] What distinguishes the US military, she writes, "those restraints—most importantly non-combatant immunity—are central to the way the United States makes war. Soldiers abide by rules of engagement that limit what they can do, and to whom."[96] Yet her argument is undermined when she tacitly sanctions the loosening of those restraints by American soldiers as they practice in secret what their government deplores in public.

She resists American academic and lawyer Alan Dershowitz's suggestion that court ordered warrants be sought prior to torture on the grounds that Elshtain feels that this "normalizes" torture.[97] Though I cannot see how this would give rise to more precarious actions than individual soldiers being forced to define ad hoc which hyper-coercive measures are permitted in which borderline cases.

What Elshtain desires is an administration with the fortitude that is willing to get its hands "dirty" by doing wrong in the most exceptional of cases to affect a comparatively greater good, but with the moral integrity to "confess" their responsibility for the wrongs done so as not to become anesthetized enough to allow the wrong to become normative rather than an exception. Perhaps this is what George W. Bush meant by "compassionate conservative."[98] Whatever one calls it, it is inconsistent with a just peace.

Elshtain seems to land largely in the same vicinity as Bowden when it comes to torture and coercion (torture *lite*). They agree that torture is a crime against humanity and therefore beyond the pale, but coercion, "is an issue that is rightly handled with a wink, or even a touch of hypocrisy; it should be banned but also quietly practiced."[99] Is this position casuist? Absolutely. Is it Christian? Doubtfully. Is it Augustinian? Unquestionably not.

95. Elshtain, "Dirty Hands," 80.

96. Elshtain, "Dirty Hands," 80. These words were published in the same year the torture reports were released. I would expect her position to evolve on the subject much like Augustine's in many facets of his work, but I find no trace of walking back these statements, or any expression of contrition at US actions in her later writings.

97. This legal sleight of hand is precisely what Attorney General Alberto Gonzalez managed to achieve by classifying the inmates as "detainees" rather than "enemy combatants" or "criminals" providing the detainees the Geneva Convention protections of neither.

98. The late comedian Robin Williams said a "compassionate conservative" is kind of like a "Volvo with a gun rack."

99. Bowden, "The Dark Art of Interrogation."

Nigel Biggar—Love Thy Neighbor (To Death)

Written a dozen years after the beginning of the "war on terror" commenced, Nigel Biggar's *In Defense of War* offers a thicker and more nuanced treatment of just war that includes, but is not limited to, the "war on terror." Where the book overlaps with Elshtain's *Just War Against Terror*, Biggar assumes the position of Tony Blair–apologist adapting more or less the same accommodating posture as Elshtain had for George W. Bush. Biggar's final verdict on the second Iraq war was that "It was good that it happened. It could have been done better. And it isn't over."[100]

Augustine would concur with Biggar's primary premise that "peace is seldom simple."[101] However, Biggar more closely resembles Niebuhr's description of an excessively enthusiastic realist than Augustine does.[102] His rhetorical analysis begins with a facile dismissal of Christian pacifism as wishful thinking. He reasons that those who refuse to commit the "evil" acts of war must readily confess to the "evils" they allow by omission. Accordingly, pacifists are enveloped by the same obscure moral calculus as just-war theorists as neither knows if the sin committed by participating in or refusing to participate in war is greater than the sin prevented. On Biggar's reading, pacifists often find themselves in moral deficits they are loathe to admit—see Rwanda and Bosnia for recent, lamentable examples.

Biggar calls pacifism "parasitic," claiming that the cost of the pacifist's clean conscience is hands stained with the blood-guilt of war.[103] To critics of the "enlightened self-interest" by which more powerful nations intervene in less powerful ones, Biggar retorts, "Surely, it is better to be inconsistently responsible than consistently irresponsible."[104] In this regard, pacifism has proven *at least* as ineffectual as the just-war tradition in preventing unjust

---

100. Biggar, *In Defense of War*, 310.

101. Biggar, *In Defense of War*, 168.

102. The ironic title of his book gives some indication of this as if war is some endangered species that will cease to exist if the academy does not rush to its rescue.

103. Stanley Hauerwas, whom Biggar vigorously takes to task in the pages of *In Defense of War*, has a thoughtful reply to this common realist accusation: "Our task . . . as a people of peace is to make the activities we care about determine rather than be determined by those forces that claim they are ensuring our future. All they are insuring is our survival, not our lives . . . At least for Christians, taking time to be at peace derives from our strong conviction that the 'realities' that claim to rule this world, that give us the security to be at peace, in fact are not capable of such security. Instead, we believe that God has done all that is necessary to give us time to learn to be at peace in a world at war." Hauerwas, "Taking Time for Peace," 99.

104. Biggar, *In Defense of War*, 233.

wars, but the latter can at least lay claim to exercising a particular good by its restraint of evil with love.

Lost in Biggar's discussion of the moral shortcomings of pacifism is any notion of theodicy. If the pacifist is guilty of sins of omission is not God complicit in these non-interventions? God, no less than pacifists, failed to restrain the Hutus from slaughtering the Tutsi in Rwanda. Biggar is also operating under the false assumption that Christians choose non-violence as a moral high ground or an attempt to end all war rather than as Hauerwas, echoing Yoder, has written, because "in a world full of war, as faithful followers of Jesus, we cannot imagine being anything other than nonviolent."[105]

In countries like the US that are anaesthetized from grieving the loss of the "other" by perpetual war, war hardly needs defending. Biggar makes wars that have already become all too palatable to American appetites even more indulgent by invoking love as the proper motivation for war. This is the crux of Augustine's writing on violence, which Biggar's reading follows closely. However, Biggar's reading of the New Testament leads him to argue that love, not nonviolence, is normative. Biggar proposes a narrow understanding of the kind of violence that Jesus resisted, limiting it to that which is not publicly authorized or inspired by religious nationalism.[106] Furthermore, he writes that Jesus used physical violence in the clearing of the temple and rhetorical violence against the Pharisees. In this respect, Biggar's account resonates with Augustine's, which also argues from the Scripture that military participation is not incompatible with faith in Christ.[107]

Curiously, neither Augustine nor Biggar make the case for the cross—the very place where love and violence are starkly juxtaposed in the body of Christ—as Jesus's normative declaration on violence. Surely Jesus's exchange with the Centurion and Pharisees or clearing of the temple does not carry greater weight than Jesus's refusal to violently defend himself in the midst of being falsely accused, tried, tortured, and sentenced to death. Would Biggar argue that Jesus did not resist because he was condemned under a lawful (albeit unjust) authority? The truth is the cross remains a stumbling block for anyone who would argue that violence, even violence "motivated by love," is a normative part of faithful obedience to Christ.

The violence as "kind harshness" motif in Augustine that Biggar often draws from is predicated on a loving relationship analogous to a good father who disciplines his son. While the father would prefer that

---

105. Hauerwas, *War and the American Difference*, 38.

106. However, Biggar does not also seem leery of nationalism elevated to religious status.

107. See the discussion of Augustine's outline of just war in the previous chapter.

words alone would reprove his child, the former will resort to physical coercion rather than allow the latter to ruin himself. What neither Augustine, Elshtain, nor Biggar expressly admit is that for this paradigm to play out on a global scale requires a "paternal" political entity, e.g., an empire. One loving "father state" to judge whether the actions of other subordinate states are permissible or in need of loving discipline. For this reason, Elshtain's argument naturally turns to the necessity of American imperialism. Likewise, Biggar has affirmed that a defense of imperialism would be the logical follow-up volume to his *In Defense of War*.[108]

Though Biggar agrees with Augustine's claim that retributive punishment is an act of "kind harshness," Biggar dispenses with Augustine's loving father metaphor in favor of a "fraternal model of punishment, not a paternal one."[109] He argues that a paternal model is not well suited to the way in which nation-states relate and must be debunked if the just war theory is to remain plausible.[110]

Opting for fraternal justice may suit the modern nation-state, but it does not resonate with Augustine's thought. One can imagine that Augustine considered Biggar's idea of fraternal punishment but found it wanting in light of the manner in which Cain and Abel, Romulus and Remus, Jacob and Esau, and Joseph and his brothers demonstrate that brothers rarely govern together equitably. The lust for domination usually consumes some brothers, and they kill or lord over the others who serve.

The Christian just-war tradition predated the idea of the nation-state by 1,200 years and was born in a particularly imperial context. Just war is a peculiarly imperial phenomenon since "right authority" is one of the first established of the *jus ad bellum* criteria. The fraternal system of "sovereign equals" that Biggar favors can only justify wars of self-defense since any other conflict, even in humanitarian crises like Rwanda and Kosovo both of which Biggar strongly argues for intervention, would be a violation of at least one nation's sovereignty.

Contrary to Biggar's assertion, nation-states function less like a conglomeration of equals and more like a caste system segregated by wealth, military power, and class disparities. This is underscored by the fact that even the most beatific plans of the United Nation's 193 countries, the oldest representation of a functional international fraternal body of authority that exists, can be scuttled by a single member of the five permanent members of the security council (China, France, Russia, the UK, and the US). The inequity

---

108. Biggar, "Give War a Chance? Conference."
109. Biggar, *In Defense of War*, 166.
110. Biggar, *In Defense of War*, 165.

that exists between countries that are world players and those that are pawns is demonstrated by the reality that international economic policy is largely determined by two annual meetings of a handful of prominent countries—the G-7,[111] whose member nations represent 50 percent of global GDP, and the G-20, which accounts for 80 percent of global GDP.

Biggar's notion of a global fraternity is further undermined by the inconsistent manner justice is administered among nations. The US annually gives Israel between three to four billion dollars in foreign aid while the Israelis conspicuously cement an apartheid state by illegally occupying and building settlements on Palestinian land.[112] For a similar violation of international law, Russia was more appropriately given international sanctions rather than aid when it forcefully annexed Crimea.[113] The hypocrisy of the US doling out carrots to some and sticks to others for the same illicit behavior is only magnified by the nation's war crimes committed with impunity during its "war on terror."

Brothers quarrel, they compete, and yes, they can even love one another. The proximity of their age, strength, and wisdom obscures any authority that one would attempt to exert upon the other. In this case, a power struggle ensues, and one sibling is more likely to meet the fate of Abel and Remus than to share authority willingly. Augustine's metaphor of discipline wrought from paternal love is more fitting as there is no ambiguity in authority or purpose. The father wants to form his son whom he loves into a good man, into his own image after God's image. For Augustine, it is only this manner of love that can adequately legitimize yet restrain physical coercion.

The nation-state that does not exercise such compassion in disciplining its citizens seems ill-equipped to extend the same kind of loving restraint to those who are strangers. Even those uninitiated by the crucible of war can imagine how the love of country, neighbor, or life could be the existential reason that helps a soldier overcome humans' natural aversion

---

111. The G-7 consists of Canada, France, Germany, Italy, Japan, the United Kingdom and the United States.

112. "Unfair treatment of Israel" was also the stated motive behind the United States' recent withdrawal from the UN Council on Human Rights. US Ambassador Nikki Haley reasoned that "we take this step because our commitment does not allow us to remain a part of a hypocritical and self-serving organization that makes a mockery of human rights." Dwyer, *U.S. Announces Its Withdrawal From U.N. Human Rights Council.*

113. The irony here is that by annexing Crimea, Russia is paying lip service to the very kind of neighborly love and fraternal dispensation of forceful justice that Biggar espouses. Russia has said the annexation was at the request of the two million Russians (58 percent of the population) that live there.

to killing one another[114]—even another who believes that he is justly fighting to protect the same loves. What seems implausible is the notion that killing the enemy is an act of *agape* on his behalf.

Biggar's retelling of the just-war narrative lacks Augustine's palpable pastoral anguish over the death of the punished. Augustine mourned the dead's lost margin for repentance, whereas Biggar writes in a cold, seemingly detached manner that seems to suggest that such hope for the enemy's repentance is fanciful and indulgent. Despite this under-realized eschatology, Biggar writes that the Christian soldier can love the one he kills. He claims that killing someone is not incompatible with loving them since,

> I might deliberately kill an aggressor, not at all because I hate him, not because I reckon his life worth less than anyone else's, not because I want him dead, but because, tragically, I know of no other way to prevent him from perpetrating a serious injury on an innocent neighbor. My deliberate killing is loving, therefore, in two respects: first, its overriding aim is to protect the innocent from serious harm; and second, it acknowledges the aggressor's equal dignity, it wishes him no evil, and it would gladly spare him if it could.[115]

Biggar's argument inadvertently exposes the gaping blind spot in the just-war tradition—that killing and war are failures of imagination because we, "know of no other way." The church first and foremost are a people called to contemplate "other ways" than exercising the conventional wisdom of their day. Though the just war should be the last resort, frequently alternatives are rushed through and dismissed. It is also quite telling that Biggar can envision himself as having the physical strength to kill a would-be aggressor[116] but not subdue or restrain him until police arrive. Furthermore, distinguishing the innocent neighbor who deserves our protection from the aggressive neighbor whom we should resist even unto death is rarely as simple and obvious as Biggar would have us imagine. Chapter 1 in this book is rife with examples

---

114. For an excellent account of soldiers' instinctive resistance to killing and how modern armies have overcome it with technology and operant conditioning, see Grossman, *On Killing*.

115. Biggar, *In Defense of War*, 49.

116. Be mindful of the fact that because Nigel Biggar lives in the United Kingdom where guns are not ubiquitous as they are in the United States, he would presumably have to kill the attacker with his bare hands or an improvised weapon such as a tea kettle or a hardback copy of his *In Defense of War*.

of the convoluted political reality that often both "neighbors" enmeshed in conflict are unsavory candidates for legitimate defense.[117]

When placed in contexts other than war, Biggar's argument seems even less plausible. A father who disciplines his child to death is neither loving nor just, he is a murderer. A husband[118] that physically coerces his partner to bend her will to his own does not love her as Christ loves the church. Rather than give himself up for her, he sacrifices his wife's body in a way that no one other than the abuser would seek to justify.

Biggar might respond that war is a unique act of judgment[119] in a manner that the covenant of marriage and the discipleship of children is not. While Augustine would agree with this observation, he would be leery of a people that always assumed the judgment seat yet refused to openly acknowledge that they too will be judged by the fruit that they bore while judging. Augustine was mindful that it does not take a great deal of power for the human proclivity for autonomy to metastasize into a lust for domination.

The reader should consider that the Good Shepherd laid *his* life down defending his sheep from the predator in a way that one who did not love the sheep would not. While love is rarely without sacrifice, it is most often the sacrifice of self rather than the beloved. Biggar begs the question of whether or not the shepherd loves the wolf also. Would love lead the good shepherd to reactively restrain the wolf as necessary or proactively seek to cull it from the countryside? The former is a lamentable necessity that Augustine conceded while the latter is an empty grasp for security that finds no sure foothold in the Augustinian corpus.

---

117. The Soviet-Afghan war is a prime example. When Afghani guerilla factions known as *mujahideen* (those engaged in *jihad*) attempted to overthrow the Soviet-supported Communist government of Afghanistan, the US had little trouble choosing sides. The US trained and armed the *mujahideen* for ten years until they successfully expelled the Soviet troops that had come to the aid of the collapsing government. Upon the Soviet Union's exit, a power struggle ensued among the factions, and the Taliban led by Mohammad Omar emerged victorious in 1994. Just seven years after taking control of Afghanistan they accomplished what the Soviet Union had not in forty years of cold war—an attack on US soil.

118. While violence is not the exclusive prerogative of men, it is more pervasive in my gender. I agree with Stan Goff's synopsis of the problem: "War is implicated in masculinity. Masculinity is implicated in war. Masculinity is implicated in the contempt for and domination of women. Together, these are implicated in the greatest sins of the church." Goff, *Borderline*, 1.

119. Biggar could count Oliver O'Donovan as an enthusiastic supporter of this idea. See O'Donovan, *The Ways of Judgement*, 211–41.

Charles Mathewes—An Augustinian War on Terror?

Despite Charles Mathewes's claim that, historically, empire has been a "crude tool used to bludgeon one's way through political life,"[120] he frames empire in a manner that Augustine would certainly recognize:

> [Empire is] not finally a political concept, but a theological one ... "empire" is what happens to human rule when it unmoors itself from proper service to God; empire is what humans do—to themselves, to others, and to the whole of creation—when they decide they will not only be *like* God (which is bad enough) but will instead try to *be* God, to supplant God's sovereignty with their own.[121]

Locating the origins of empire in original sin[122] as he does, it is no surprise that Mathewes seeks to distance the United States from such a qualification. Instead, he calls America an "inadvertent empire," as if governments could accidentally unmoor themselves from proper service to God. He claims that "American hegemony is not an act of naked, or even covert, imperialistic designs; it is crucially dependent on what other nations did not do."[123]

On Mathewes account, the rest of the world has, "ceded the playing field of power politics to the US" because America plays an "inescapably central role in the global order and economy."[124] Even the "traditional allies of the United States are increasingly and inevitably losing both the material and moral energies that enabled them to [previously] help the United States govern the world."[125] This is an apparent misreading of the contemporary landscape where nations that challenge US hegemony are slapped with sanctions or worse. The US does not "accidentally" maintain nearly 700 military bases in 38 countries. Nor does it unintentionally spy on its enemies, allies, and citizens. Neither does it involuntarily torture people in the name of national security nor kill its enemies via remotely controlled drones. The US is no more of an inadvertent empire than the Tower of Babel just happened to be the tallest building in the plain of Shinar. Both were purposefully crafted

---

120. Mathewes, *Republic of Grace*, 41.
121. Mathewes, *Republic of Grace*, 40. Emphasis in the original.
122. See Dietrich Bonhoeffer's account of Adam and Eve's desire to be *Sicut Deus* (like God) as the origin of sin and theological reflection that attempts to know good and evil apart from God, in Bonhoeffer, *Creation and Fall*, 111.
123. Mathewes, *Republic of Grace*, 84.
124. Mathewes, *Republic of Grace*, 84.
125. Mathewes, *Republic of Grace*, 86.

to make a great name for their people and to secure them from "being scattered over the face of the earth."

Mathewes will concede no such point. He unapologetically writes that "the US currently fields the mightiest army in the history of the world for a very modest fraction of gross domestic product."[126] However, his presentation of the facts is a bit misleading. While it is true that according to the Central Intelligence Agency, in 2016 the US spent 3.28% of its GDP on defense—ranking it twenty-fifth in the world in this respect behind such military juggernauts as Namibia (4.4%) and Azerbaijan (3.64%),[127] the statistic Mathewes cites is disingenuous in light of the fact that the US spent $611 billion on defense—outspending China, the next largest spender, by a margin of more than three to one.[128] In fact in 2016, US spending on defense accounted for more than one-third of global military spending.[129]

These realities notwithstanding, Mathewes insists that there is no danger of American "imperial overstretch"[130] since American hegemony is secured by what other countries have failed to do, namely "continue to invest, ideologically and materially, in the ability to make war to achieve their aims."[131] However, many countries invest materially and ideologically in war and can easily be categorized as allies (UK and France) or enemies (North Korea, Russia, and China).

The US does not play world police because no one else wants the job. Instead, it refuses to cede the duties of the position of privileged power that it gained when the previous imperial power collapsed under the burden of its own girth. Undeterred, Mathewes continues, "The United States will remain the indispensable nation, the sheriff of the global commons; it will stand alone, it will stand firmly, it will do so for the foreseeable future, and it will do so on the cheap."[132] His apologia for US hegemony resonates with the American ethos but not with an Augustinian one.

One will not find in Augustine any notion that Rome was indispensable, and, unlike Mathewes, Augustine was unquestionably leery of "imperial overstretch." Augustine thought that it would be a much better

---

126. Mathewes, *Republic of Grace*, 88–89.

127. Central Intelligence Agency, *Military Expenditure*.

128. It is indeed a great irony that China holds such a large proportion of US debt. The world's most massive military power is dependent on the second largest military power to subsidize the former's defense. To this end, North Korea proves a dangerous intersection of both the US and China's commercial and defensive interests.

129. McCarthy, "Military Expenditure in 2016."

130. Mathewes, *Republic of Grace*, 88–89.

131. Mathewes, *Republic of Grace*, 88–89.

132. Mathewes, *Republic of Grace*, 88–89.

situation if all kingdoms were small, rejoicing in concord with their neighbors.[133] This fact prompted him to ask, "Why must an empire be unquiet in order to be great?"[134] Given the texts explored in the previous chapter that showed Augustine was not overly concerned with who ruled over the people, it is hard to imagine Augustine sacrificing his life at the empire's behest or calling upon his parishioners to do the same.

From within this atrophying empire plagued by wars and rumors of war, Augustine was embroiled in a conflict of his own. Mathewes has a peculiar reading of Augustine's struggle against the Donatists, which Mathewes calls Augustine's personal "war on terror." Even if we agree that both campaigns began as responses to violence publicly suffered, Augustine's to the Catholic priests who were blinded and killed and America's to the attacks of September 11th, the similarities beyond that are difficult to find.

Mathewes points out that Augustine's first response was to invite Donatist leaders to a public debate so that they could work out their theological quarrels. Since the US, as a matter of policy, does not negotiate with terrorists, its first response was to invade the *al Qaeda* stronghold of Afghanistan and subsequently Iraq, albeit for less clear reasons.

Augustine's appeal to the empire was to quell the civil unrest among its subjects within its own borders—an appeal to the domestic judicial and police functions of Rome. In contrast, the "war on terror" seeks to secure American safety by preemptively finding and rooting out any potential terrorists wherever it may find them in the world, even if the manner in which it does so creates more enemies than it kills. Mathewes wrongly conflates an issue of domestic lawlessness with the imperial pretension of prosecuting international lawlessness. Where Augustine sought to correct and restrain but not slay the Donatists, the American response to 9/11 makes little distinction between restraining and killing, as it does both without formal charge or legal hearing, presumably because terrorists cannot be rehabilitated. It is difficult to imagine Augustine praising the assassination of an unarmed Osama bin Laden when he could have been captured and imprisoned.

If Augustine experienced a war on terror, it would have been with the Visigoths not the Donatists. However, conspicuously absent from Augustine's writings is the clash-of-incongruous-civilizations language of preserving a way of life (Elshtain), protecting the innocent and defenseless (Biggar), or restoring world order (Mathewes). Instead, Augustine filled the first four chapters of book I of *City of God* with praise for the restraint shown by the

---

133. Augustine, *City of God*, IV/15.
134. Augustine, *City of God*, III/10.

Goths who, as Arian Christians, respected Christian churches as places of sanctuary during the siege.

Daniel Bell—Just War as Christian Discipleship

In stark contrast to those who view the just-war tradition primarily as an implement in the hands of the state, Daniel Bell attempts to reclaim the tradition's ecclesial moorings by recentering it in its rightful origin, the church. The question that Bell has set out to answer is, what are the characteristics that distinguish the just-war tradition embodied by the church as an authentic form of Christian discipleship from the widespread modern use of just war as statecraft? In doing so, he offers up a thoroughly authentic Augustinian recalibration of the tradition.

Bell sees this as a necessary endeavor since just-war theory as it is used by contemporary states and as the foundation for international law has been severed from any of its intrinsically theological foundations. This is a peculiarly modern problem. As the public authority of the church has waned, so have the moral force of its disciplines, including its ethics surrounding war. Bell frames the reconfiguration as follows:

> The problem that just war faced at the outset of modernity, then, was *not* that of how to disarm Christianity and square it away safely in an apolitical box so that it would not disturb an otherwise peaceful society and politics. Rather, the question that thinkers like Grotius sought to answer was how to articulate just war in the wake of the collapse and fragmentation of the Christian vision. How is war restrained in a world where Christian convictions do not seem to hold or where they are not shared? The solution pursued was to deemphasize (and eventually replace) the distinctively or particularly Christian features in favor of what was thought to be a universal norm that, in principle, could be known by and applicable to everyone, regardless of their faith affiliation or lack thereof.[135]

Hence the Dutch lawyer and Christian Hugo Grotius endeavored to codify the laws of war that would hold true even if "we should even grant, what without the greatest wickedness cannot be granted, that there is no God, or that he takes no care of human affairs."[136] While the tradition may have been built on the work of Christian thinkers like Augustine, Aquinas, and others, their arguments were later sterilized of biblical influence so

---

135. Bell, *Just War as Christian Discipleship*, 55. Emphasis in the original.
136. Grotius, *Rights of War and Peace*, I/XI.

that they would be more palatable for burgeoning nation-states. The great modern irony is that the tradition is invoked by both state and church but seemingly employed by neither.

Bell's argument lays bare the dichotomy between what he describes as "Just War as a Public Policy Checklist" and "Just War as Christian Discipleship." At times, the public policy checklist as Bell presents it resembles a straw man, as one would be hard pressed to find any government or politician that uses the criteria in the deliberately mechanical manner he describes. However, his hyperbole is not without merit. Both sides often use the just-war criteria after a war has begun to assuage the national conscience by justifying the war, as Elshtain and Biggar have done, or provoke the national conscience by condemning the war. Nevertheless, Bell does provide a useful framework for Christocentric reflection on the just-war tradition.

Bell begins by denouncing the prevalent idea that war, even a just one, is a kind of "lesser evil." This assertion runs counter to the Niebuhrian realist accent that is perceptibly pervasive in the contemporary just-war discourse. Michael Ignatieff is among those who would grant that "life's toughest choices are not between good and bad, but between bad and worse."[137] A similar line of thought was taken up by Paul Ramsey in his reflection on combating guerrilla warfare in Vietnam,

> Anyone who identifies every sort of "doing evil" with wickedness simply has not faced the facts that most actions—whether they are in the personal or the political or the military realms—have many consequences and not one effect only . . . To choose the least evil that can be done is to choose the good that alone is possible.[138]

Bell challenges this notion that Christians are called to do evil, even evil characterized as either qualitatively or quantitatively "less" than the alternative option. He says that a "lesser evil" conception would not only be quite foreign to the principal figures in just war's development within Christianity but also to the gospel.

Like Biggar, Bell draws upon Augustine to identify war as "a positive act of love directed toward both the innocent or unjustly attacked as well as the aggressor."[139] To plausibly make this shift, one must privilege an understanding of grace over sin, in effect rejecting the Niebuhrian realist paradigm. Bell writes,

137. Ignatieff, *The Lesser Evil*, xiii.
138. Ramsey, "How Shall the Counter-Insurgency War Be Conducted Justly?" 427–464.
139. Bell, *Just War as Christian Discipleship*, 88.

> The Christian tradition at its best has known and proclaimed the good news that Christ came to set us free from the power of sin and that through the sanctifying power of the Spirit manifest in the various means of grace that are available to the church, we are empowered not to settle for lesser evils but to inhabit the good.[140]

In essence, Bell reasons that if one gives priority to humanity's fallenness, a charge that could be levelled at Biggar, war can at best be a lamentable evil that restrains greater wickedness. However, if one gives precedence to the redemption and sanctification of God's people, war can be virtuous. Augustine would be located near the median between these two poles as war was neither the greatest evil nor peace the highest good when won through bloodshed.

For Bell, inhabiting the good means the intentional cultivation of virtues like patience, courage, justice, and temperance within a community of character that is the church. He maintains that it is naïve to believe the virtues necessary to discern proper participation in or abstinence from war will suddenly materialize as they are needed during a war if the church does not collectively cultivate and nurture them in all seasons. More precisely Bell writes, "discipleship is the sum total of our lives as Christians . . . loving and seeking justice for our neighbors in times of war is inextricably connected to how we love and seek justice for our neighbors in our everyday lives in times of peace."[141] Just war as Christian discipleship cannot be relegated to the responsibility of a few select government officials and military personnel on the eve of the next armed conflict. Instead, it is the obligation of all Christians who confess that their paramount consideration in regard to war is no different than the preeminent question in all other areas of their life—what does it mean to follow Jesus Christ faithfully? Here Bell harmonizes well with Augustine as both advocate for mercy, forgiveness, and peace in the smaller deeds of daily life. Bell argues that by doing so, the church becomes filled with people who have already been conditioned to seek justice when the specter of war looms.

I concur with Bell's assessment that those who are not frequently engaged in communities that reflect on issues of justice in the nearer and more trivial things will be ill-equipped to do so with wars from which they are far removed.[142] It is precisely because war is seen as an abstract idea that

---

140. Bell, *Just War as Christian Discipleship*, 35.

141. Bell, *Just War as Christian Discipleship*, 20.

142. One point of contention is that Bell fails to describe how just war principles can be cultivated in times of peace if the earthly city is perpetually at war.

happens in other countries that many American Christians fail to see the urgency in practicing just war as Christian discipleship that Bell advocates. This fact was exposed on 9/11 when the violence manifested itself in the United States, many Christians were ready to fight but few could articulate how doing so could be an act of love for victim and villain alike.

Bell describes three ways the just war tradition has been misused and rendered ineffective. Using dental analogies for each insufficient inhabitation of the just-war tradition, he dubs the first errant application of just war as just war "without teeth." Here, necessity may supersede any or all of the criteria. He cites prominent secular just-war theorist Michael Walzer's claim that a "supreme emergency" would oblige a state to violate the just-war criteria.[143] He clarifies that a supreme emergency is a moment in which a society's way of life is in grave danger. This is reminiscent of Elshtain's account of the threat that terrorism poses to the United States except that she does not believe the US has violated any of the criteria in its response.

Bell writes that another misappropriation of the tradition has "too many teeth." In this account, one or more criteria are made so stringent that no war could ever meet them. For example, if discrimination is couched to mean that absolutely no non-combatant deaths are permissible, there has never been nor could there ever be a just war. Used in this way, those with an aversion to war could systematically condemn every war one by one claiming that they are using "just war" grounds without ever genuinely engaging the tradition.

The third and final exploitation of the tradition is one in which a "few teeth have been pulled." Bell gives two ways in which this could be the case. In the first instance, some criteria are pitted against one another so that one is given greater moral weight and trumps the others. The second way the tradition "loses teeth" is when the criteria are measured as a whole, if more criteria are met than not this supposedly tips the scales toward justice.[144] Bell argues that historically the considerations of *jus ad bellum* have been given preeminence to the extent that once states are convinced that they have the right authority, then the cause, intention, and all other means to achieve success tend to be rubber stamped as relative goods.

What Bell hopes to establish with just war as Christian discipleship is an account of the tradition that considers each criterion individually, acknowledging that if even one element is dismissed the discipline as a whole is undermined and the result is injustice. With this in mind, the lines that

---

143. Walzer, *Just and Unjust Wars*, 251–55. See the discussion of the permanent state of exception in chapter 1. This is reminiscent of Elshtain's *en extremis* argument.

144. Bell, *Just War as Christian Discipleship*, 94.

follow will highlight the distinctive attributes that distinguish "Just War as Christian Discipleship" from "Just War as Public Policy Checklist."

Bell does not dispute the traditional placement of the authority for declaring war in the hands of the government. Where the Christian discipleship model parts ways with the secular model is locating the origin of the right to do so. Bell, like Augustine before him, unequivocally asserts that authority, rather than being intrinsic to governments, is conferred upon them by God; its power is "not natural but theological."[145] To establish the foundation for this, he cites the apostle Paul's words,

> Let every person be subject to the governing authorities. For there is no authority except from God, and those that exist have been instituted by God . . . for he is God's servant for your good. But if you do wrong, be afraid, for he does not bear the sword in vain. For he is the servant of God, an avenger who carries out God's wrath on the wrongdoer.[146]

In light of this, he argues that the church needs to exercise a more prominent role in public and political authority. He laments the political marginalization of the church that has seen Christian public influence diminish with the rise of modernity. Equally troubling for Bell is that the reality that the church has developed a strain of "political laryngitis" stemming from, "modernity's depoliticizing of the church and the cordoning it off safely in a disembodied realm of spirit, where it trades in abstract values and principles" is often celebrated by Christians as a grand achievement rather than regretted as a tragic loss.[147] However, Bell realizes that when he calls for the church to speak up and be heard in the political discourse, the fractured nature of the church makes for a cacophony of opinions rather than a cohesive doctrinal authority. Bell confesses that "historically, to the extent that the just war tradition functioned, it did so, at least in part, because the church was able to speak with a unified voice."[148]

Regrettably, for most Protestant churches at least, such a unified voice does not exist. Even on issues like abortion where normally divergent denominations' views are more or less consistent, the church is pigeonholed into the role of just another special interest lobby and has been severely limited in its ability to affect change in public policy. This problem is exacerbated when the issue is a war where such a unified ecclesial position is highly unlikely. In this instance, those who shape public policy, like many

---

145. Bell, *Just War as Christian Discipleship*, 104.
146. Rom 13:1, 4.
147. Bell, *Just War as Christian Discipleship*, 118.
148. Bell, *Just War as Christian Discipleship*, 118.

parishioners, are free to "shop around" until they find a church whose views coincide with their own and use it to justify their position.

Despite these difficulties, *Just War as Christian Discipleship* takes the criterion of legitimate authority as a challenge to the church to "reclaim its identity as an exemplary form of human community."[149] To revive its political voice, the church must be concerned, first and foremost, with forming the character and consciences of its members but also with "reminding the governing authorities of this world of their responsibility to work for the common good by making concrete judgements about justice and war."[150] For the Christian church to embody what it means to be a just-war people, it must overcome the marginalization it accepted with all too little resistance as part and parcel of the dawn of modernity. Bell writes that if the church wishes to support the state in properly exercising its God-given authority adequately, the church must reassert itself as an independent political entity that, though it would not fight to defend itself, is compelled by the love for both its innocent and enemy neighbors to protect and preserve the common good.[151]

Here Bell exposes one of the limits of placing the just-war tradition exclusively within the ecclesial context. The church will always be dependent on the state in which it exists for the appropriate execution of war. As the church does not have a standing army, it can never be more than what Bell calls "a kind of independent contractor."[152] This critique could be levelled at each criterion, but it is essential to foreground it as a significant obstacle for locating the just-war tradition exclusively within the church.

In his treatment of just cause, Bell challenges the conventional thinking that the most ironclad justification for war is self-defense. When self-defense is the *prima facie* cause for war, the collective conscience is tempted to become ingrown, prioritizing *our* rights over *the* right. "Justice for all" becomes an ideal that is too costly to attain, so the nation is content to settle for "justice for us." The understanding of just cause has deteriorated in this manner because national sovereignty and territorial integrity have become sacrosanct. For this reason, it is far easier to legitimate an act of war in one's interest rather than interceding on behalf of others by breaching another nation's sovereignty and territory.

However, self-defense is not an entirely unambiguous term. This is particularly true when the notion of sovereignty is inflated and made synonymous

---

149. Bell, *Just War as Christian Discipleship*, 124.
150. Bell, *Just War as Christian Discipleship*, 124.
151. Bell, *Just War as Christian Discipleship*, 125.
152. Bell, *Just War as Christian Discipleship*, 125.

with the perpetuation and protection of national values and interests on a global scale.[153] One can easily see how self-defense became the preeminent cause of armed conflict when a nation feels that its best interests are also advantageous to all other nations.[154] This has not always been the case.

According to Bell, "justice prior to the advent of modernity was understood as a virtue concerned with ordering the life of all in accord with a common good."[155] The order in which one seeks justice is important. Instead of saying, "what's best for me is best for everyone," Bell argues it is more appropriate to say, "what is best for everyone (the common good) is best for me." This is directly opposed to the principle of non-intervention, which under the guise of justice can result in malicious neglect of the neighbor and flagrant injustice.

The UN has taken steps to prevent another Rwanda or Bosnia by writing rules, in response to 2001's "Responsibility to Protect" sub-committee report, into 2005's World Summit Outcome Document. In paragraphs 138 and 139 the General Assembly affirmed their responsibility to protect their own populations from genocide, war crimes, ethnic cleansing and crimes against humanity and accepted a collective responsibility to encourage and help each other uphold this commitment. In addition to this the heads of states also declared their readiness to intervene in states when national authorities clearly fail to protect their citizens.[156]

Just War as Christian Discipleship sees intercession on behalf of the innocent, weaker neighbor as the most justifiable cause for war and renders self-defense anathema. Bell reminds his readers that the church has "consistently qualified the legitimacy of self-defense."[157] In an argument that could easily be mistaken for a pacifist's, he opposes self-defense because "Christians follow one who accepted the cross instead of simply slaying sinners, one who told his disciples to turn the other cheek and take up the cross. Thus, as Augustine said, we would rather be killed than kill an enemy-neighbor . . .

---

153. Bell, *Just War as Christian Discipleship*, 130.

154. This line of reasoning is featured prominently in Elshtain's work as we have outlined above as well as in Walzer, *Arguing About War*, 40–43.

155. Bell, *Just War as Christian Discipleship*, 133.

156. UN General Assembly, "Genocide Prevention and the Responsibility to Protect." No interventions have been undertaken under this resolution. The case of Syria may demonstrate why. Bashar al-Assad has used chemical weapons on his own citizens but has framed the war as a terrorist insurection. This fact, coupled with Assad's staunch ally Russia's veto power, insures intervention will be slight if it happens at all.

157. Bell, *Just War as Christian Discipleship*, 134.

[while] Aquinas asserted [that] Christians could defend themselves so long as they did so without the intention of killing their assailant."[158]

Like all elements of just war, the habit of seeking justice for others over and above one's self will not suddenly prevail over humans' naturally selfish bent if it is not practiced by the church in times of peace. Bell admonishes Christians:

> [I]f we are not a people who desire justice for the neighbors who are unemployed, uninsured, homeless, battered, the victims of crime and the perpetrators of crime, and so on; if we are not in the habit of giving our lives to and for others; then it should come as no surprise when the plight of Croatians, Sudanese, Haitians, or Timorese fails to move us. It should come as no surprise that we are not able to recognize or act on just cause.[159]

This virtue is far more easily cultivated within the church than it is in the state. For the latter, survival is a priority. Therefore, it will always privilege its well-being over others. Christians are free to live magnanimously in service of others since they understand that "there are worse things than dying and more important things than living."[160]

Right intent is perhaps the most easily equivocated of the *jus ad bellum* criteria. As it is traditionally understood as an instrument of secular statecraft, it is satisfied as long as the aggressor nation's stated objective is peace, and it has forsworn vengeance. However, the difficulty of surveying the gulf that exists between what one intends to do and what one does becomes incalculably more difficult to assess when the acting party is a state.

As noted earlier, invariably the church and state mean entirely different things when each uses the word peace to describe its goal. The state means that conditions are stable enough for each citizen to pursue his or her private good provided that their pursuits neither impair nor impinge on other individuals' pursuits of their self-interests. The same narrowly focused self-interest is the priority of nations as well, and Bell maintains that this cannot yield authentic peace, merely truces among competing interests.[161] Genuine peace is the outgrowth of people lovingly seeking

---

158. Bell, *Just War as Christian Discipleship*, 134. See also Aquinas, *Summa Theologica*, II/II 64.7. Here in Aquinas, we find the origin of the principle of "double effect," the notion that an action can have both intended and unintended consequences. This principle has figured prominently in moral philosophy's participation in the just-war discussion ever since.

159. Bell, *Just War as Christian Discipleship*, 149.

160. Bell, *Just War as Christian Discipleship*, 150.

161. Bell, *Just War as Christian Discipleship*, 132.

the collective good. However, even the notion of the common good can be manipulated to be expedient in serving the interests of the state. Bell describes this in the following manner:

> Throughout history, great empires have claimed for themselves with some regularity a kind of exceptionalism that prompts them to declare that what is good for them is good for the world, by which they mean that they are the privileged carriers of a universal interest that subsumes and supersedes the interests of all others ... [some] have suggested that the United States, as an indispensable nation whose political power ought to be extended in a kind of benevolent empire, embodies a universal interest. In each case, the peace that is the object of right intent becomes synonymous with the advancement of a particular nation or people's interest, which is now declared to be universal.[162]

Although Bell does not mention Elshtain by name, this is a succinct synopsis of her argument in *Just War Against Terror*. After reading her book, it is clear that the reports of the death of American exceptionalism are greatly exaggerated. There are many glaring difficulties when any nation declares its interests to be internationally normative for the common good. The two most obvious are that other nations may vehemently disagree with a foreign power's vision for imposing good upon them, and self-deception on the part of the munificent power can quickly cloud its ability to sympathize with perspectives that are not its own.

However, love as the right intention is not without its difficulties as well. Undeniably, Jesus's call to love one's neighbor includes one's enemy neighbors also.[163] The difficulty is reconciling love with killing the enemy neighbor that, though not its aim, is inevitable in war. At first glance, it seems that this requires a hierarchy or preferential ordering of love that privileges the innocent over the guilty. This understanding that "we love the innocent more than the guilty, and therefore we will take up arms to defend the innocent and kill the guilty,"[164] is the conventional reconciliation of this seeming paradox. Bell thinks that a more nuanced explanation is needed to demonstrate how love for the enemy is not an inferior kind of love. He builds upon Paul Ramsey's line of reasoning that just war is an "alien act

---

162. Bell, *Just War as Christian Discipleship*, 157.

163. "But I say to you, Love your enemies and pray for those who persecute you ... For if you love those who love you, what reward do you have? Do not even the tax collectors do the same?" Matt 5:44, 46.

164. Bell, *Just War as Christian Discipleship*, 159.

of love."[165] This is true because love restrains the types of and duration of violence one is willing to employ and holds the restoration rather than the destruction of the enemy as its objective.[166]

What is distinctive about just war as Christian discipleship's understanding of last resort is the depth of the commitment required of its adherents to devote time, energy, creativity, and resources to developing unconventional means of addressing injustices.[167] The idea of "just peacemaking" did not originate in Bell's work[168] but it is consistent with his premise that just war is not an activity exclusive to wartime. If Christians are not devoted to such practices when there is peace, then war will not be the last measure attempted after many other options have been exhausted. War is essentially the only option for states with few and fallow alternatives like diplomacy and sanctions to armed conflict at its disposal that more often than not herald an impending war rather than avoid it.

For Bell, the distinguishing mark of a reasonable chance of success is that it is considered not only before the commencement of the war but also on a regular basis throughout the war. He also uses "reasonable chance of success" as opposed to the more traditional "probability of success" to underscore the fact that the concept is more convoluted than a simple cost versus benefit analysis that gives a precise answer to whether or not war is winnable.[169] Instead, it takes wisdom and judgement to discern if the expressed purpose of the war articulated by the just cause criterion is attainable and this question is one that must be continually revisited throughout a war.

The criterion of discrimination is essentially the deciphering of who and what constitute legitimate military targets. It is the differentiation of barracks from hospitals and soldiers from school children. Unfortunately, the dichotomy is not always as easily discerned as these obvious examples would indicate. Many parts of a nation's infrastructure serve both civilian and military purposes. The same electrical plant that allows the hospital to run respirators may also power the computers that control weapons installations. In guerrilla, insurgent, and terrorist warfare, combatants can also purposefully take advantage of the ambiguity between civilians and military hiding behind a human shield of noncombatants. Classically what has demarcated

---

165. Bell, *Just War as Christian Discipleship*, 162. For Ramsey's original argument see Ramsey, *Speak Up for Just War or Pacifism*, 73, 83, 129.

166. Bell, *Just War as Christian Discipleship*, 163.

167. Stanley Hauerwas takes up a similar argument concerning the necessity of creativity devoted to peace although the virtue (patience) and the means (pacifism) are different than those espoused by Bell. See above, "Taking Time for Peace."

168. For the origins of the concept, see Stassen, *Just Peacemaking*.

169. Bell, *Just War as Christian Discipleship*, 202.

the lawful destruction of any of these targets (infrastructure or human) from the illegal and immoral destruction of them has been the intent of the attacker. The intentional decimation of civilians or facilities that primarily serve them has always been considered beyond the pale in the tradition. However, the unintentional destruction of both is permissible.

This concession, known as "double effect" has its origin in the work of Thomas Aquinas. In Bell's assessment, the quandary presented by double effect in international law is the result of "holding on to the basic idea while jettisoning the moral vision in which it was nestled."[170] Bell asserts that the concept of double effect has become too permissive. Rather than prioritizing the protection of noncombatants, states have used the doctrine to excuse their failure to safeguard the innocent. Bell charges, "it is not about embodying a responsibility to protect non-combatants from harm; rather, it is about the permissibility of harming non-combatants so long as such harm can be construed as collateral damage unfortunately incurred in the pursuit of a greater good."[171]

For a fuller theological understanding of double effect, Bell delves into Aquinas's exegesis of the parable of the wheat and the tares found in Matthew 13:24–40, about which Aquinas writes, "our Lord teaches that we should rather allow the wicked to live, and that vengeance is to be delayed until the last judgement, rather than the good be put to death with the wicked."[172] The emphasis is that right authority will demonstrate its power in executing the iniquitous neighbor only when it can do so without endangering the innocent neighbor.[173]

Even when one has rightfully discriminated the enemy from the innocent, the just response must be carried out with proportionate force. These two criteria are often considered together, but the purpose of each is distinct. Bell reminds his readers that proportion, as opposed to discrimination, is a measure of means rather than ends. It is not a quantification of anticipated good outcomes versus negative ones; instead it is the assessment of the *minimum* amount of force necessary to accomplish the goal of restoration of the common good. Seen in this light, a rightly intended act is still immoral if it is carried out with disproportionate force. Bell uses swatting a fly from a friend's forehead with a sledgehammer as an example of an act

---

170. Bell, *Just War as Christian Discipleship*, 216.

171. Bell, *Just War as Christian Discipleship*, 214.

172. Aquinas, *Summa Theologica*, II/II 64.2. The parable of the wheat and tares seems much more fitting as a theological basis for pacifism than for just war since the judgment is reserved for the end time and the perpetrators of wrong are allowed to remain or even thrive until then.

173. Bell, *Just War as Christian Discipleship*, 217.

that, though discriminate, violates the principle of proportion in a such a manner that it would be best not to commit the act and allow the fly to live to be swatted on another day.[174]

At the core of Bell's argument is the truth that belief in God makes a tangible difference in how one wages war. The secular version of the just-war tradition has thoroughly scrubbed away any such theological presuppositions so that the resulting international law would apply to all. It is precisely for this reason that war is viewed as a lesser evil, since "it is thought that God is *not present* now, making us capable of the good."[175] Such a tradition can only serve people and policies that neither "know the power of God or the gift of the resurrection, faith, and hope."[176] Even the most thorough laws are reactionary at best. Military technology evolves faster than international law, which inevitably means the rules for engagement are always at least one war behind.

For Bell, to ask what it means for America to wage a just "war on terror" is to begin in the wrong place. He would modify the question slightly, yet pointedly, to ask what it means for *Christians* to wage such a war. As an American Christian, I applaud his attempt to extensively recalibrate the tradition according to its Christian heritage. The church can ill afford to be a silent partner in America's pursuit of justice. At every turn, the church must petition its rulers, reminding them that the love of its neighbors is the only acceptable *end* and *means* for waging war. Also, we cannot hide the fact that this love will, at times, requires us to cede our "legal right" to reparation for the sake of the common good.

If Bell's account of just war needs thickening, it is precisely in the area of how the church is to overcome its modern marginalization that he describes so well. The Protestant diaspora leaves the church too hoarse to speak loudly enough to be earnestly taken into account by government leaders. Bell has yet to wrestle with the Constantinian problem that his predecessors have articulated clearly.[177] If the church can be no more than

---

174. Bell, *Just War as Christian Discipleship*, 218.

175. Bell, *Just War as Christian Discipleship*, 242. Emphasis in the original.

176. Bell, *Just War as Christian Discipleship*, 242.

177. Hauerwas summarizes Yoder's "Constantinian problem" that the church became invisible under Constantine. He writes, "Prior to Constantine it took exceptional conviction to be a Christian. After Constantine, it takes exceptional courage not to be a Christian . . . Before Constantine, one knew as a fact of everyday experience that there was a church, but one had to have faith that God was governing history. After Constantine, people assumed as a fact that God was governing history through the emperor, but one had to take it on faith that within the nominally Christian mass there was a community of believers. No longer could being a Christian be identified with church membership since many 'Christians' in the church clearly had not chosen to follow Christ." Hauerwas, *Performing the Faith*, 43. See also Yoder, *The Priestly Kingdom*, 135–49.

a "kind of private contractor" to the state as it wages a "war on terror," it seems that the church would become powerless to affect policy yet culpable for its outcome. As noted earlier, one of the largest difficulties with situating the just-war tradition exclusively within the church is that the church does not wage war. So in this sense it will always be dependent on the state within which it resides to provide this police function on its behalf. Perhaps the church should assume the posture of clergy towards the emperor that Augustine describes as "fighting invisible enemies on your behalf by praying, while you struggle against visible barbarians on their behalf by fighting."[178] At best, the church can hope to be a moral compass to stir up the political conscience in society. Even to this end, the church's effectiveness will be limited to its ability to speak the truth in unison.

Lisa Sowle Cahill—"If You Want Peace, Work for Justice."[179]

In her book *Love Your Enemies: Discipleship, Pacifism, and Just War Theory*, Lisa Sowle Cahill raises many of the same questions at the core of this book—chiefly, "What does it mean *today* to live as a follower of Jesus?"[180] Cahill rightly identifies that one of the fundamental dilemmas of the Christian life is how to simultaneously embrace the gospel while embedded in a world seemingly inimical to it.[181] Both projects are particularly concerned by this "enmity with the world" as it is exposed by the juxtaposition of Christian discipleship and violence.

Unlike most of my other interlocutors, Cahill seems to share my reticence for unequivocally embracing Augustine's premise that love can innervate violence, killing, and war. This is the seemingly unavoidable contradiction when drawing upon Augustine's just war: his social ethics are centered around properly ordered goods and loves, and, when the two openly conflict as in war, Augustine calls upon love to restore the ordered social accord.[182]

Cahill underscores that Augustine did not think it theologically inconsistent to consider earthly peace to be a corollary of love and, in turn, for social order (a genus of provisional peace) to also be a form of love.[183]

---

178. Augustine, *Letters*, 189/5.
179. Pope Paul VI, "Celebration of the Day of Peace."
180. Cahill, *Love Your Enemies*, ix. Emphasis mine.
181. Cahill, "Just War and the Gospel," 1.
182. Cahill, *Love Your Enemies*, 57–8.
183. Cahill, *Love Your Enemies*, 62.

Although she concedes that for Augustine *caritas*[184] more often chastised the deepest values of secular politics than it endorsed them, Cahill writes that Augustinians must reconcile Augustine's "willingness to allow considerable leeway in history for Christian compromise with secular and civic values and 'necessities,'[185] deferring eschatological transformation of major dimensions of Christian practice from history to heaven."[186] The most conspicuous theological move that Augustine makes corroborating Cahill's premise is the cordoning off of Jesus's teachings against violence and resisting evil to the "inward disposition of the heart" rather than existential praxis. There is no margin for justified Christian violence unless the kingdom of God is forced to recede from history to become a vague ideal that can only be realized eschatologically. Cahill writes that the heavenly kingdom was most eschatologically detached from history when Augustine advocated for the use of political and physical coercion against the Donatists in order to preserve the unity of the church.[187]

This is one of the few instances in which my analysis of Augustine diverges significantly from Cahill's. My (perhaps too charitable) reading of the conflict is that Augustine was simply calling on the state to perform its essential police function by protecting the Catholic Church from Donatist assaults after Augustine's appeals to theological diplomacy were turned back.[188] Cahill's (perhaps too cynical) interpretation of the same histori-

184. Augustine concisely explains how he is framing *caritas* and its foil *cupidas* in his *Teaching Christianity*: "What I mean by charity or love is any urge of the spirit to find joy in God for his own sake, and in oneself and one's neighbor for God's sake; by cupidity or greed any impulse of the spirit to find joy in oneself and one's neighbor, and in any kind of bodily thing at all, not for God's sake." Augustine, *Teaching Christianity*, III/16.

185. The "necessities" referenced here are those from which Augustine's "wise judge" prays that God will deliver him—i.e., torturing the innocent in *City of God* XIX/6. The judge's dilemma is frequently viewed as a metaphor for Christian political engagement.

186. Cahill, *Love Your Enemies*, 66. In footnote 50, Cahill contrasts Augustine's view of lying with his position on killing. While Augustine maintained that killing was permissible if it occurred under the proper authority, for the sake of others, and was not fueled by hatred, he made no such caveats for even the shadow of a lie. Neither purity of heart nor the protection of the innocent from unjust harm pardoned mendacity.

187. Cahill, *Love Your Enemies*, 79.

188. Even Augustine's biographer Peter Brown, who is *more* critical of Augustine's coercive concession than is Cahill, admits that "The army was the only effective police-force; it was indispensable to [Augustine] in applying the policy of suppression against the Donatists." Brown, *Augustine*, 425. Furthermore, he confesses that "The policy of coercion did not in itself require a great show of force; but force was necessary to hold in check the disturbances that might follow in its wake. In Africa, the police were conspicuous by their absence." Brown, "Religious Coercion in the Later Roman Empire," 283–305.

cal events is that Augustine was importing civil society's instruments for establishing order into his religious community. She concludes that in Augustine's "ambition for the success and defensibility of Christianity, he loosens his grip on those qualities that distinguish the life of the disciple from that of other citizens."[189]

Cahill's critique is seemingly more apropos for Augustine's concession to Christian participation in violence of *any* kind than it is for entreating the earthly city to exercise its most fundamental *raison d'être* by protecting its citizens from one another. In tracing the former argument, Cahill eruditely uncovers the crux of the dilemma that violence and specifically war created for Augustine's epistemology. He struggled to hold two seemingly incongruent beliefs, one political and the other theological, in tension with each other without acknowledging the conspicuous contradiction between them. On one hand, he maintained that humans are inherently social beings and that order is a necessary prerequisite for the social life that should be preserved—by force when necessary. Yet on the other hand, he held the conviction that love is the mechanism that innervates all moral life. Ardently adhering to both beliefs painted Augustine into a rhetorical corner from whence he would claim that love not only motivates but morally obliges violent coercion when it is defending one's neighbor, disciplining an evil person, and protecting the common good. Cahill puts her finger on the "paradoxical norm" in Augustine's just-war theory—that coercively ordered love can be the essence of peace.[190] Despite Cahill's pointed criticism of Augustine, she ultimately gives him the benefit of the doubt by acknowledging that his point of departure is that war and violence *are* dubious in the light of Jesus's teaching[191] and she ultimately concludes that "The core of Augustine's approach to violence is not found in any of the excusing rationales he gives for it, precisely because he *does* realize that it is an activity to be excused in relation to the evangelical requirement of love."[192]

---

189. Cahill, *Love Your Enemies*, 76.
190. Cahill, *Love Your Enemies*, 74–75.
191. Cahill, *Love Your Enemies*, 79.
192. Cahill, *Love Your Enemies*, 80. Emphasis mine. I recognize Cahill's struggle with Augustine because it is mine as well. His writings are predominantly pastoral and, as such, he encouraged everyone he could to actively constrain violence and extend mercy with love in its stead. The unanticipated and unfortunate side effect of Augustine's genuinely compelling petitions is that many have emphasized Augustine's modicum of tolerance for violence and prioritized *that* over and against its necessary precursor, love. The small opening through which Augustine allowed exceptional circumstances of justified violence to pass through has been torn asunder and used to justify all manner of malevolence including many forms of violence that Augustine would have likely found abhorrent. Augustine was no warmonger. In his defense, I would reaffirm John

Regardless of how compelling one finds Augustine's conclusions, at a minimum he provided inimitably fruitful points of departure from which to advance a Christian social ethics discourse as old as the church itself surrounding the restraint of violence. Cahill traces, somewhat remorsefully, the Christian epistemic devolution from Jesus's nonviolent example in the gospels and the early church's admonishment against killing and military service to Augustine's fourth century defenses of Christian participation in government, the military, war, and killing as necessary to punish evil, preserve the social order, achieve temporal peace, and express love of neighbor. Cahill resolves that "There is surely something paradoxical if not self-contradictory about Christians, starting with Augustine (and his teacher Ambrose), who justify killing in the name of love and the Gospel."[193] In her view, this paradox is likely intentional, salutary, and permanent. While Christians believe that Jesus's ministry supernaturally augmented the human capacity for justice and reconciliation by inaugurating the immanent kingdom of God's love and peace, we simultaneously confess that these capacities are somewhat impeded by what Cahill describes as a deep and existential "Augustinian undertow" in a world still marred by sin and evil.[194]

Cahill seeks to resist the Augustinian undertow by calling on the church to prioritize a doctrine of "just peace" over "just war." She articulates just peace as, "conflict-transforming practices such as direct nonviolent action, diplomatic initiatives, interreligious political organization in civil society, unarmed civilian peacekeeping, public rituals of repentance, and initiatives of reconciliation."[195] Her account of "just peace" cannot be casually dismissed by those, who like Nigel Biggar above, consider nonviolent political mobilization and resistance to be utopian, naïve, and marginal at best. Far from inaction, Cahill describes peacebuilding as the leaven that the

---

Milbank's thoughts above that it is the ontological priority of peace that undergirds the whole of Augustinian thought. This priority of peace was not merely an inward disposition of the heart but outwardly manifested in Augustine's opposition to the death penalty and torture, his use of church funds to buy back those who were kidnapped and sold into slavery, and his opening up the church as a sanctuary for people threatened with torture or imprisonment over failure to pay burdensome taxes.

193. Cahill, "A Church for Peace?" Cahill also uniquely highlights Ambrose's influence on Augustine's view of justice. Within her quotation of Ambrose, one can see the foreshadows of Augustinian positions on justice and order. "The splendor of justice is great. Justice exists for the good of all and helps to create unity and society among us . . . Those who love justice must first direct it to God; second, to their country; third, to their parents; and last, to all people. This is the way in which nature reflects it . . . Courage reflects justice when it protects one's country in time of war or defends the weak and oppressed." Ambrose, "Duties of the Clergy," 1/27-28, 59.

194. Cahill, "A Church for Peace?"

195. Cahill, "A Church for Peace?"

church must work throughout societies—both those dreadfully tormented by violence suffered as well as those with violent histories of international misdeeds undertaken. She thickens her call to action by adding that,

> Gospel peacemaking is an integral dimension of discipleship and a powerful form of real-world politics, to which the global Catholic Church is not yet as committed as it should and could be. Catholics who are not directly touched by violence too rarely appreciate not only the devastating effects it has on other people's lives and societies, but also their own complicity in that devastation and their own power to bring change.[196]

Here again I find my project overlapping with Cahill's. Initially, it is the confession of complicity with violence and the subsequent call to repentance that resonates deeply with the American experience as I have outlined it in the introduction and chapter 1. It is also the recognition of the clarion call that the most constructive heavy lifting that remains to be done in this field of theological ethics is to make the promotion and deployment of "just peacebuilding" more powerfully determinative than "just war–making."[197] My contribution to this discussion will follow in chapter 4.

R. A. Markus—Just War in the Saeculum

Markus began his paper "Saint Augustine's Views on the 'Just War'" with a backhanded compliment of sorts: "A long and very respectable tradition of thinking about the morality of warfare has accustomed us to looking at Augustine's views on the 'just war' through the wrong end of the telescope."[198] With this analogy, he wryly and succinctly highlights the error common to many of my interlocutors in this chapter—that is, they have imbibed a tradition that has conditioned them to let their present obscure Augustine instead of allowing Augustine to clarify their present. This is the admonishment that has guided the methodology of this work since I am acutely aware that we are born on the wrong side of the telescope.[199]

Any heuristic that does not attempt to re-orientate itself right way around with Augustine leaves a very pliable and flimsy hermeneutic,

---

196. Cahill, "A Church for Peace?"
197. Cahill, "Just War and the Gospel," 13.
198. Markus, "Saint Augustine's Views on the 'Just War,'" 1.

199. Perhaps more appropriately stated, we are stuck in the "middle" of the telescope in the Bonhoefferian sense with knowledge of neither the beginning nor the ends of our history. Bonhoeffer, *Creation and Fall*, 28–32.

particularly when it comes to war. Such malleability leads to divergent readings of the same passages. Markus explains:

> The assertion that under certain specifiable circumstances killing in war may be morally justifiable looks like a simple, unambiguous statement. It could, however, serve quite opposed ends: either to raise or to lower the barriers against violence in a society. But it will encourage one set of attitudes in a society in which war is unthinkable as a human activity and quite different attitudes where it is readily accepted as normal and sanctioned by the current norms of conduct. In the one case, the assertion would tend to reconcile men to the possibility of envisaging warfare as occasionally justifiable in some specified circumstances: *to make the unthinkable thinkable*. In the other it would act as a restraining force: it would engender the reflection that what is accepted as allowable or virtuous is so only under special conditions which are spelt out: *it makes the unquestioned questionable*. The force of the notion of the just war is determined by the antecedent assumptions current in the society.[200]

It is not difficult to determine on which side of the spectrum the US falls. Chapter 1 demonstrated that America's "antecedent assumptions" are bellicose and have been since the nation's inception. Concerning the "war on terror," it is fair to ask has Augustine been used to justify the merely unquestioned or the unthinkable?

After tracing the chronology of Augustine's contemplations on war, Markus found it most surprising that "the core of his view was and remained that warfare, and especially killing in war, must be subject to the generally valid norms set for human conduct."[201] This consistency of thought is precisely why subsequent generations have been able to excise a "theory of just war" in isolation from the complexity and nuances of the mind in which its origins were embedded. He concludes that, "Augustine's thought on the 'just war' has suffered more perhaps than any other idea from the uprooting to which it has been subjected by medieval lawyers and theologians in search of *authorities* and by modern historians in search of a homogenous doctrinal tradition."[202]

Though his message remained more or less consistent, Augustine did mature into a reluctant realist rather than an overly zealous one. Markus summarizes the evolution of Augustine's disposition by surmising that,

---

200. Markus, "Saint Augustine's Views on the 'Just War,'" 2. Emphases are mine.
201. Markus, "Saint Augustine's Views on the 'Just War,'" 11.
202. Markus, "Saint Augustine's Views on the 'Just War,'" 11.

He did not repudiate the possibility, even the necessity, of fighting a "just war"; what he came to repudiate was a whole set of attitudes towards it induced by the euphoria which encouraged Christians to invest wars such as Theodosius's with a religious significance. He did not need to check his contemporaries' "pacifist inclinations"—few of them can have had any. What he challenged was a more fundamental mood of Christian self-identification with a whole social structure, a system of institutions and functions, including that of war.[203]

Augustine would find much to challenge in a country where both war and Christianity are deemed normative and the two coalesce far too readily. How then can Christians engage American structures and institutions without syncretizing the predominant cultural values with those of the gospel? Chapter 4 is my attempt at parsing this problem.

---

203. Markus, "Saint Augustine's Views on the 'Just War,'" 12.

IV

Imperial Pilgrims

> The difference between a witness to government that is explicit, and one that we give in spite of ourselves by our silence, is not a difference between being involved in politics and not being involved; it is a matter of whether we are conscious, and responsibly careful, about what we say.[1]
>
> —John Howard Yoder

To help Christians be "conscious and responsibly careful about what we say" is the most economical synopsis of my motive in writing this book. As inherently communal creatures, the question is not whether we participate in or withdraw from the body politic but that we do either in a conscientious and purposeful manner. The primary aim of this chapter is to consider peculiarly Christian ways of inhabiting the American context given that the claims of the previous chapters are true.

These claims include that, despite its popular self-understanding, the United States of America has had imperial pretensions since its inception. In light of this, Augustine is a constructive guide for contemporary American Christians, given his rich theological contemplation of empire and his pastoral counsel to its citizens. To so read him offers a unique deployment of Augustine, whose voice has more often been used to accommodate the American imperial project and "war on terror" rather than interrogate them. No less than Augustine, American Christians are imperial pilgrims—citizens of the city of God negotiating their way through

1. Yoder, "Things That Are Caesar's, Part I," 4–5, 34.

the city of man. The ethical question is how we sojourners should conduct ourselves within such an unconsciously imperial context.

This chapter begins by offering up repentance as the primary act of Christian political participation. This very act can be disarming to those who are used to Christians speaking in "prophetic" judgement rather than with the humility of one being judged. Micah 6:8 offers a simple yet profound refrain for Christian engagement in the *polis*: "He has told you, O man, what is good; and what does the Lord require of you but to do justice, and to love kindness, and to walk humbly with your God?" Each requirement represents an unpretentious request, yet each is derailed by the impediment of our inherently ingrown spirit. It is more natural for us to demand justice when we feel aggrieved than to do so for others. The kindness we love is that which we receive, harder still is to love giving it away. Lastly, to the extent that we can adhere to either of the first two commands, pride percolates from our hearts more readily than humility. This is why repentance—orthopraxy preceding orthodoxy—is the entrance for Christians into the political arena, particularly when it is filled with those who though they do not know God can admire and respect justice, kindness, and humility.

In developing repentance further, this chapter turns to the unique ways citizenship in a democracy inculpates Christians. The choice is not between abstention or participation in national sins committed on one's behalf—it is between varying degrees of complicity or resistance. As voters (or non-voters), taxpayers, and potentially elected officials American Christians participate in a political microcosm as co-sovereigns in a manner that was unfathomable among early Christians. In light of this, political participation is incumbent upon Christians whether there is a natural predilection to do so or not.

Beyond repentance, Christians are called to not merely *do* justice but to *be* justice, particularly for their poor and disenfranchised neighbors who historically have had few advocates. In this way we pursue *caritas* for those society has deemed the "least of these," for as Augustine reminds us justice without *caritas* is not justice at all.

The culmination of this humble repentance that *is* justice and loves kindness is a radically different kind of patriotism. Not the flag waving, slogan chanting, mouth foaming that so easily devolves into nationalism at international sporting events, but a thicker, richer patriotism that can simultaneously say "I love my country, but when it does wrong it needs to change." I can think of no other loves in my life—my wife, children, or even myself—that go unreproved, yet for most that's what patriotism is—"My country, right or wrong." Instead, following Augustine as a political iconoclast, Christians should be able to put forward uncomfortable questions to their government about the actions undertaken in their names without being accused of subversion.

One example that is combustible political fodder is being holistically pro-life. The evangelical right has whittled down the phrase to refer to the rights of fetuses. The conversations often turn uncomfortable when one wants to expand pro-life to health care, education, and other social services for the fetuses once they are born. It gets more uncomfortable still if you intend to suggest that pro-life also means that you would raise these babies to reject violence and the kill-or-be-killed binary.

The Humility of Political Repentance

Micah 6:8 offers an unpretentious, yet profound point of departure for Christian political participation,

> He has told you, O man, what is good;
> And what does the Lord *require of you*
> But to do justice, and to love kindness,
> And to walk humbly with your God?

These three requirements provide a type of supernatural scaffolding from which Christian disciples can discover eternal inroads among the temporal paths of the earthly city. In doing so, the Christian citizen also cultivates a fuller understanding of the heart of the God who exists eternally in perfect relationship in the Trinity wanting for nothing yet continuing to pursue the restoration of communion with his image-bearing creatures amidst their well-documented propensity for infidelity.

"Do justice . . . love kindness . . . walk humbly with your God"—certainly not the most arduous tasks the Lord has asked of his children. However, what is simple on the lips of God is easily confounded by the prideful hearts and selfish appetites of his people. To do justice requires an extraordinary fortitude not normally associated with humility and loving kindness. However, to do justice without being mindful of kindness and humility is also to succumb to the temptation of the prodigal son's older brother who possessed a much thicker sense of justice than of kindness. Likewise, loving kindness and walking humbly are excellent ways to live, but if they are the fruit of a life that is also oblivious to injustice, the whole of their character is tainted by their disregard for their neighbors and the second greatest commandment, for they "have neglected the weightier matters of the law: justice and mercy and faithfulness. [It is these they] ought to have done without neglecting the others."[2] There are two Christian practices that, when combined, hold all three elements—doing justice, loving kindness, and walking humbly—in proper equilibrium.

The first practice that calibrates the Christian in her right place before God and in the *polis* is repentance. Repentance is rarely advanced as a political act, but it is a chiefly diplomatic virtue in which the believer professes that she enters the discourse concurrently burdened by her own iniquities and complicit in the sins of her nation.[3] When faced with the presence of God filling the temple Isaiah bellowed, "Woe is me! For I am lost; for I am a man of unclean lips, and I dwell in the midst of a people of unclean lips."[4] Proximity to the divine has a way of laying bare our anthropologies, both of ourselves and our people. This is the nature of the repentance for which I am advocating. The confessor is not an apolitical prophet or counter-culture warrior enthusiastically picking out the specks in her government's eye. She is more contrite than prophetic, more akin to a chastened co-conspirator than a sanctimonious adjudicator of history. Repentance keeps the Christian citizen humble as it reminds her of the Augustinian assertion that even on her most impeccable day of discernment she still must arbitrate prudently as one simultaneously under judgment.

Repentance is the indispensable opening move of Christian civic participation. Conscientious participation in this arena, like many others, is frequently arrested by our being born malformed by our selfish natures. Repentance is not merely the opening prelude to more meaningful civic engagement later, but the dynamic chorus that is echoed with such frequency that our neighbors and children ask us what they mean. The allusion to the *shema* in Deuteronomy 6 is purposeful here. "You shall teach them diligently to your children, and shall talk of them when you sit in your house, and when you walk by the way, and when you lie down, and when you rise."[5] Repentance is a distinctive kind of listening and remembering—more than being delivered from our enemies and receiving a promised parcel of land, repentance rejoices in the second Passover that brings new life, an inheritance for those covered in paschal blood that

---

2. Matt 23:23b.

3. Although forgiveness is the cornerstone of the gospel, forgiveness is a mostly forgotten relic in political affairs. Hannah Arendt called forgiveness Jesus's most radical and important teaching because it was "the exact opposite of vengeance," which set in motion chain reactions. Jesus's message taught "freedom from vengeance, which encloses both doer and sufferer in the relentless automatism of the action process." Arendt, *The Human Condition*, 238–42.

4. Isa 6:5.

5. Deut 6:7.

cannot be forfeited. For this reason, the Christian pilgrim cleaves to her God with all her heart, soul, and mind and teaches her children to do the same lest they forget all that he has done and grow so comfortable in a foreign land they are seduced by false gods.

The consistent public confession of both personal and national sin is a peculiarly Christian political habit. It is a declaration of meekness that's existence is unsettlingly out of place in a paradigm fashioned from one power struggle after another. The prayer, "Forgive us our sins as we forgive those who sin against us"[6] is the penitential plumb line against which the sojourner can measure his endeavor to participate in the public square without, "think[ing] of himself more highly than he ought to think," but instead "considers himself with sober judgement."[7]

Chapter 1 of this book is rife with examples that should give American Christians fertile grounds for sober reflection about the US pursuit of economic self-interest writ large as foreign policy.[8] In repenting of national sin and how the church has been complicit with and benefited from unjust machinations of power, the Christian citizen can express solidarity with her fellow citizens while concurrently confessing that there needs to be more staunch resistance to such practices. Humility, not jingoism, is the natural derivative of repentance. Like repentance, humility is an atypically civic virtue largely estranged from the political sphere due to its perception as a feeble instrument rather than a powerful tool.[9]

Repentance and humility may seem like too lofty a calling for nation states that intrinsically prioritize the perpetuation of their self-interested subsistence over and against that of other nations. However, governments

---

6. Matt 6:12.

7. Rom 12:3.

8. There are also issues that I did not explore that would cause a similar sobering of American self-perception. The exploitation of America's indigenous people, slavery, lynching, and Jim Crow laws that were supported by many professing Christians immediately come to mind. In fact, the history of African Americans in the US has led James Cone to ask, "How could any theologian explain the meaning of Christian identity in America and fail to engage white supremacy, its primary negation?" Cone, *The Cross and the Lynching Tree*, xvii. While I have not dealt with white supremacy, I have addressed "American Supremacy."

9. Immigration is but one example of a heated political polemic that is at least partially defanged by practicing repentance and its related by-product humility. If American Christians repented of the nefarious ways in which most of the continental US was secured for white Europeans, they would also be hard pressed not to temper the boldness with which they appeal to their inalienable rights as citizens that inherently castigates the foreign outsiders' lives as "other" or "ungrievable." The appropriate next move would be to "do justice" on behalf of the families that are separated at the border and the men and women who are applying for asylum.

are not ordained to be ingrown, survivalist think-tanks obsessed primarily with their self-preservation. John Howard Yoder expresses that,

> The denunciation of national selfishness is part of the Christian testimony to the state as it is, in favor of the state as it should be. When we challenge national selfishness, we are not challenging the state—we are calling the local state to be what the state should be in principle, an organ not of selfishness, but of justice and equality.[10]

What distinguishes genuine repentance from the subversive denigration of the state is the humble confession of complicity with national sin. In this respect, contrition, an uncharacteristic act of the state, is patriotic because it challenges the state to pursue its professed ideals rather than merely its interests.

Such a penitential posture is counterintuitive in a political landscape that rues admission of culpability, much less atonement for it. This is why few, regardless of their moral convictions, will bear such an arduous yoke in front of their colleagues. However, doing so is not counterproductive. Given the paucity of genuine humility within the political discourse, it is concurrently disruptive and disarming when encountered. It draws people in precisely because it is the diametric opposite of hypocritically feigned moral superiority only capable of underscoring the deficiencies of one's adversaries but impotent to help anyone overcome them.[11] Being honest about one's own collusion with the formidable status quo is the precursor to speaking truth to power. It is the epitome of removing the log from our eye so we can see more clearly to cleanse the speck from our brother's eye. Repentance is not an ephemeral accessory the Christian citizen may flippantly adorn herself with or discard in the global public square. The current polarized American political climate does not afford the imperial pilgrim such latitude. Instead, repentance has grown in stature from an encouraged best practice of the pious to a requisite spiritual discipline for

---

10. Yoder, "Things That Are Caesar's, Part II," 16–17.

11. Unfortunately, much of what is called Christian engagement in the political has assumed this righteous, prophetic posture that uses the Christ of scripture to denigrate current state practices but stops well short of attempting to transform and redeem them. These are Christians who would engage their culture's maladies by lobbing diagnoses at it from a safe distance without ever getting close enough to effectively treat the roots of its infirmities or getting infected by them. This is reminiscent of the apostle Paul's treatment of the law and sin in Romans 7. The law is presented as a diagnostic tool that makes the heretofore undetected cancer of Paul's sin abundantly evident to him. However, Paul quickly recognizes that the law that so precisely uncovered his malady is a rather ineffectual remedy for the disease it has exposed. Paul recognized that the "rescue from this body of death" must come externally from Jesus, the great physician.

all Christians who desire to meaningfully influence the *saeculum* with the gospel. The dramatic paradigm shift is attributable to the pride of place given to democracy in the US context.

The Citizen as Fully Vested Shareholder

Despite its admirable qualities, democracy inevitably obfuscates aspects of the Christian's pilgrimage through the earthly city. This is true because there is a real sense in which each democratic citizen is also a partial co-sovereign—an actual steward, however arguably slight, of the formation and maintenance of the same authority that will rule over her. Ostensibly, when the United States wins or loses domestically and overseas, so too do her citizens. At least this is the fundamental idea behind the false bill of goods sold as "trickle-down economics" that was popularized by the Reagan administration in the 1980s and peddled by conservatives ever since.

Therein lies the rub for the American Christian citizen. Since the US is a democracy, its citizens are characterized by outsiders, whether fairly or not, as legitimizing and sanctioning their government's policies. This is the principal reason the claim that repentance is the foremost political act is emphasized so heavily. Though the Christian US citizen may be viewed by other nations as indissolubly complicit with the misconduct of her government, the persistent practice of repentance would enable her to highlight a small, but vocal counter-narrative that proclaims that things must not remain how they are because there are alternatives to the bellicose injustices perpetrated in the name of their "national security."[12] In light of this, the gravitas of the political onus borne by rulers *should* also weigh upon the consciences of Christian voters just as profoundly as it does upon those of their governing ministers.

---

12. Obviously, the numbers behind the repentance as civil disobedience movement mustn't always remain small. Consider the copious amount of pressure put on the Johnson and Nixon Administrations by protestors calling for the end the Vietnam war. It is worth noting that these protests gathered substantially greater leverage once the Pentagon Papers were smuggled out by Daniel Ellsberg and the public learned the truth that the actual US progress in Vietnam was greatly exaggerated. See Ellsberg, *Secrets*. I will concede that this was a secular, not religious, movement, but there is no reason to believe that US churches in their great numbers, even as fractured as they are from one another, are not more than capable of using their considerable size and purchase to tip the scales of public sentiment towards justice, if they were absolutely convicted to speak the truth, repudiate injustice, and repent of their complicity with the immoral actions of their government.

Rowan Williams describes the unique burden that arises from Christian participation in governance by noting that the Christian ruler[13] is hampered by an "insoluble dilemma" that his secular counterparts are under no compulsion to consider.[14] The enigma is that the Christian is not free to deify the state's continued temporal survival to the preeminent place it occupies among so many other peoples because in doing so he would subjugate and betray others worldly goods like justice, true peace and love.

The Christian ruler who relinquishes the exploitation of unjust weapons and maneuvers at his disposal must develop a manifestly superior agency for innovative diplomacy. The Christian will engage in the political realm differently than her secular humanist counterpart simply by the terms in which they understand what politics is *for*. For example, disciples of Jesus will forswear "holy wars" and false "clash of civilizations" dichotomies and refuse that a victory secured despite its moral expenditures is still an authentic triumph. Williams elucidates the disposition of a Christian ruler who willfully submits to such encumbrances while they are readily abjured by his peers: "he has the alarming task of discerning the point at which what he is defending has *ceased to be defensible* because the means of defense beyond this point undermine the real justice in the state by implicitly treating it as an absolute, to be preserved at all costs."[15] If the ruler forfeits the utilization of all unjust means of defense, he in effect retains only one, particularly unpalatable, alternative—to resign his *civitas* to defeat.[16] However, even the most incomparably meticulous reader of history would be hard pressed to produce even one occurrence outside of Jesus's crucifixion in which a Christian sovereign resigned his society to defeat rather than exhaust every option at his disposal regardless of how unjustly exorbitant.[17] This is far less likely attributable to the inadequacy

---

13. Given our recent discussion, I would include every Christian citizen here, particularly those who are eligible to vote.

14. Williams, *On Augustine*, 122.

15. Williams, *On Augustine*, 122. Emphasis mine.

16. Williams, *On Augustine*, 122.

17. However, two American Presidents come to mind, but for less than exceptional reasons. First is Harry S. Truman, a professed Baptist, who authorized the only use of nuclear weapons in a war killing nearly 200,000 Japanese citizens, 95 percent of whom were noncombatants. Many deaths were mercifully instantaneous. Many had much longer battles against radiation induced cancers. Truman's choices were not of the same kind as Williams's "insoluble dilemma." Truman was not forced to choose between injustice and defeat of his nation but rather between expediency and justice. Avalon Project, *Atomic Bombings of Hiroshima and Nagasaki*. The other President is George W. Bush who is by all accounts an earnest evangelical Methodist. In his autobiography, Bush called Jesus the "author of a divine plan that supersedes all human plans." Bush, *A*

of their faith than it is to their inordinate desire to rule, particularly when exacerbated by their self-preservation instinct.

If contemplated earnestly by Christian democratic citizens, this quandary provokes a great deal of moral, cognitive, and emotive dissonance because we share the burden of discerning when our defense has traversed the borderline into the inexcusable. Williams's depiction of this muddled dilemma as intrinsic to Christian embodiments of democracy is one of the most concise yet thick synopses of political-theological ethics that could be written. Yet, this is precisely the moral imagining that increasingly few Christians are equipped to undertake, largely because they have conflated the survival of their temporary earthly city with that of the pilgrims en route to their heavenly home.[18]

The truth that competing allegiances often hinder faithful obedience gives rise to my suggestion that many American Christians may have incrementally and imperceptibly allowed their worship of the Holy Trinity to be diluted by their deification of the polity. If the state is given such a prominent place in the Christian's heart, the citizen will more readily

---

Charge to Keep, 6. In light of this statement, it seems difficult to square the continuous "war on terror," torture, and assassinations by remotely controlled drones with a "divine plan." They much more resemble retribution, an instrument more familiar in the hand Machiavelli's *Prince* than the Prince of Peace.

18. The confounding of one's place within an oppressive empire is reminiscent of Malcolm X's parable of the house negro. The house negro was always close to his master. He usually lived in the master's house—most likely in the attic or the basement—but still inside the house. The house negro ate the food scraps left on the master's table. He even looked like his master because he would wear his secondhand clothing. In the mind of the house negro, he and his master were so close that whenever the house negro identified himself, he always identified himself in the same sense that his master did. When his master said, "We have good food," the house negro would say, "Yes, we have plenty of good food." When the master said that, "We have a fine home here," the house Negro said, "Yes, we have a fine home here." When the master would be sick, the house negro identified himself so much with his master he'd say, "What's the matter boss, we sick?" His master's pain was his pain. And it hurt him more for his master to be sick than for him to be sick himself. When the house started burning down, that type of negro would fight harder to put the master's house fire out than the master himself would. Fast forward to the twentieth century and Malcolm X said the mentality had not changed much at all. "And when you [a field negro] say, 'your army,' he says, 'our army.' He hasn't got anybody to defend him, but anytime you say 'we' he says 'we.' 'Our president,' 'our government,' 'our Senate,' 'our congressmen,' 'our this and our that.' And he hasn't even got a seat in that 'our'—[not] even at the end of the line." Both the contemporary house Negro and his older equivalent knew that his privileged status depended on preserving the status quo. Accordingly, he would betray his fellow slaves to stay in his master's good graces. Malcolm X, *The Race Problem*. Christians cannot likewise become so enamored with the empire's distinct version of peace and our comfortable place within the empire that we enthusiastically finance and fight for it even if by doing so we betray our fellow pilgrims around the globe.

defend their *civitas* by any means available rather than see it suffer defeat. Parsing the morality of what qualifies as "necessary means of survival" is a superfluous and onerous chore for those who have syncretized the destinies of the cities of God and man. After all, people staunchly convinced that they are ensconced in God's will because they are fighting on "God's side" for the expansion of the eternal city rarely hesitate to baptize all expedient means they find necessary.[19]

John Howard Yoder illuminates how the relatively recent phenomena of sharing the locus of power in a democracy has momentous repercussions for political theology: "The claim is not simply made that the people benefit from being ruled but that they help to rule themselves and that the actions of government are taken on their behalf and in an indirect but real sense at their behest."[20] This consideration opens up a fresh and fertile space for ethical reflection about complicity with and accountability for governmental improprieties with which many previous generations of Christians including Augustine's have not had to contend.

"National sin" is not a new idea as it is found throughout the Old Testament. The development introduced by democracy is not national sin but the citizens's proximity to it. The notion of governmental authority is no longer embodied by a Caesar so far removed from those over whom he reigns that he is largely disinterested in their very existence (save perhaps for their ability to pay taxes or serve in the army) much less their opinions. Caesar had no pretensions of ruling over the Jews either at their behest or for their benefit. Regardless of the deity he may have claimed had ordained him to be emperor, it was not the Hebrew God. Consequently, Yoder writes that "it would never have occurred to anyone to hold Palestinian Jews responsible for the atrocities or even the routine injustices committed in the name of Caesar by his armies and administrators."[21]

The tectonic shift that has separated contemporary American politics from those of first century Palestine is that the modern bureaucrat, every individual from the city councilman of the nation's smallest municipality to the president of the country, requires citizens's votes to triumph in an election in a well-defined locale. Whether or not today's politician genuinely values the sentiments of her constituency or will govern with their welfare in mind, she

---

19. For example, Sarah Palin, former governor of Alaska and continuing conservative evangelical and political activist, has said that "Waterboarding is how we baptize terrorists." Blake, *Palin*. What I am sure was meant as a punchline for the amusement of her political base is a sad amalgamation of a gospel sacrament with a dehumanizing defense of nationalism.

20. Yoder, "Limits of Obedience to Caesar," 6.

21. Yoder, "Limits of Obedience to Caesar," 6.

is unlikely to be elected if she does not at least feign the empathy to do so for her electorate. In this respect, each citizen is responsible for the very same government that is reciprocally responsible to her. Among democracies it is true that "Every nation has the government it deserves."[22]

The assumption of the United States is that, as a nation that democratically elects its government, it deserves an administration that ostensibly acts on behalf of its citizens. Thus, the novel crucible that democracy poses to Christian Americans is that "Any American citizen who does not wish to be counted co-responsible for the action taken in his name must therefore disavow it in a way that would not have been conceivable and of course not necessary in the time of Jesus."[23]

Such is the liability of Christian citizens within an imperial democracy: we cannot easily absolve ourselves from the injustices committed by the state in our name. I have advocated for public and tireless repentance from American Christians because complicity with national sin cannot be hastily alleviated by private penance. The world is as familiar with US power—economic, political, and military—as it is with the US evangelical self-perception.[24] These realities cannot be flippantly dismissed as there is no shortage of voices calling US citizens to account for the actions of their government. Furthermore, there are smaller, more sinister factions eager to see US citizens atone for their government's policies by suffering violence similar to that which the US has trafficked in other nations.

In his November 2002 *fatwa*,[25] a "Letter to the American People,"[26] Osama bin Laden argued for precisely this kind of individual moral accounting. Bin Laden's letter is a reckless misappropriation of *Sharia* just-war theory.[27] However, the portion of his lurid diatribe most germane to this

---

22. Though French moralist Joseph de Maistre most likely meant the quote sardonically, it is certainly true of democracies. Maistre, *Lettres et Opuscules*, 76.

23. Yoder, "Limits of Obedience to Caesar," 6.

24. Here, I am using evangelical in the religious sense as well as highlighting the American propensity to enthusiastically attempt to baptize the world in its brands of economic and political freedom.

25. A *fatwa* is a non-binding Islamic legal decree, disseminated by an authority in religious law known as a *mufti* and is intended to resolve a matter in which Islamic law is unclear. The qualifications to be a *mufti* are quite rigorous. A *mufti* must know both the *Quran* and *Hadith* (sayings attributed to Muhammad) in their entirety and with such specificity to identify whether a chapter was revealed in Mecca or Medina. Kabbani, *What is Fatwa?*

26. Bin Laden, "Letter to the American People."

27. Not the least of which is the fact that Islam expressly forbids anyone who is not a *mufti* from issuing a *fatwa*. Muhammad went so far as to say, "Whoever gives fatwa without knowledge, the angels of the heavens and the earth curse him." Bin Laden's

discussion is his argument for stripping American civilians of non-combatant immunity—the most fundamental of human rights guaranteed by international law and both the Christian and Islamic just war traditions—on the grounds that as citizens of a democracy Americans share the responsibility for the fruit of their government's decisions.

Bin Laden attempts to rationalize the inexcusable murder of non-combatants by casting aside the anticipated argument that American civilians are being punished for crimes they did not commit. He says that the very nature of the claim contradicts the American refrain that it "is the land of freedom, and its leaders in the world."[28] He continues that Americans exercise their free will in choosing their government and in doing so tacitly approve of their policies—the most insidious of which, in his opinion, is the American support for Israeli oppression of Palestinians by the occupation of their homeland. Since American citizens have the power to change the government and its policies but choose not to, argues bin Laden, they are as culpable for the suffering of the Palestinians as they would be if they committed the atrocities with their own hands.

Not only do Americans show their approval for the crimes committed against the Palestinians by their votes, but they are also guilty of paying the taxes that fill American and Israeli war chests. He concludes the diatribe by invoking the right of self-defense. *Al Qaeda*, he argues, is only attacking those who first attacked them. It seeks to destroy the homes and wealth of those who first perpetrated the same crimes in Muslim lands. Likewise, *al Qaeda* refuses to treat non-combatants as inviolable when they are citizens of the very nations that have haphazardly butchered Muslim civilians.[29]

Regardless of one's opinion of the Israeli occupation of Palestinian territory, bin Laden's critique of voting and paying taxes as two principal practices that solicit civilian participation in the American project was piercingly accurate. These kinds of political participation, whether done out of obligation or self-interest or avoided out of apathy or greed, are inherently ethical endeavors and engender a measure of complicity with the ultimate ends they serve. However, the argument he constructs from these two premises does not follow. It is impossible to fashion any substantive culpability from the negligible amounts of capital and political purchase wielded by the overwhelming majority of citizens. Neither did the planes

---

overreach transgressed *Shariah* law a second time by declaring *jihad*, an authority that the *Quran* says belongs exclusively to an *Imam*.

28. Bin Laden, "Letter to the American People."
29. Bin Laden, "Letter to the American People."

on 9/11 discriminate between victims who supported nefarious US practices and those who did not.

Though pardoned from ultimate accountability for its national transgressions, the Christian conscience should be no less profoundly pricked by its complicity with injustice meted out under the guise of national interest. The best cure for a conscience so wounded is repentance and humility, and the realization that both are formative practices for those wish to remain politically engaged.

Repentance is a yoke that Christians are uniquely fit to bear, even in public. This is so because repentance and its by product humility are load-bearing practices of Christian discipleship. The only thing that makes these 2,000-year-old spiritual disciplines radically political in contemporary American society is the short walk outside of the sanctuary of the church or the privacy of one's home required to make the habits public.

For some, this claim may be scuttled straightaway by Jesus's admonition in the Sermon on the Mount against public displays of self-aggrandizing religious practice: "Beware of practicing your righteousness before other people in order to be seen by them, for then you will have no reward from your Father who is in heaven."[30] He continues by specifically underscoring benevolence to the poor, prayer, and fasting as Christian practices that should only be exercised covertly for the sole audience of the heavenly father where it is safely hidden from unfettered public gaze and the temptation that frequently accompanies it: circuitously courting human praise, of which hypocrites are fond.

However, when Jesus teaches about forgiveness in Matthew 6:14-15, there is no mention of a similar public/private dichotomy. The emphases here are the communal and reciprocal natures of the practice—forgive others their trespasses and your heavenly father will also forgive you yours; but be mindful that the contrapositive is equally true. What is recurrent public repentance if not an open invitation to engage in mutual forgiveness initiated by humbly confessing one's own offences? That this reconciliation is of great consequence to Jesus is shown earlier in the Sermon on the Mount where he instructs his disciples and the crowds that had gathered that, "if you are offering your gift at the altar and there remember that your brother has something against you, leave your gift there before the altar and go. First be reconciled to your brother, and then come and offer your gift."[31] Those who can endure such a public embarrassment for reconciliation's sake are well on their way to comprehending what Jesus

---

30. Matt 6:1.
31. Matt 5:23-24.

meant when he chastised the Pharisees to "Go and learn what this means: 'I desire mercy, and not sacrifice.'"[32]

To the non-believer, repentance is a peculiar practice that disrupts and disorients political discourse as it is classically understood. It does so because it enters the conversation not with the expected lust to dominate but much more tenderly begins by saying "forgive me" and "forgive us." This is disarming to non-Christians who expect Christians politicians to be enthusiastic participants in the same manipulatively coercive power struggles as their secular counterparts, merely to achieve different ends. If public repentance is the initial politically Christian act, it is closely followed by the embodiment of Christian civic witness. Witness of this sort is how Christians respond to their newly rediscovered civic responsibility. It is witness in the fullest sense of the word martyr. Witness is the logical first fruit of disciples pruned by repentance and steeped in humility.

Witnessing Justice

When Jesus is interrogated by Pilate in John 18, Jesus testifies to the fundamental role witness played in his life's mission, "For this purpose I was born and for this purpose I have come into the world—to bear witness to the truth."[33] Christians should take their cue from their crucified Lord and emphasize bearing witness to gospel truth while on their pilgrimage in this world. However, it is altogether possible that Christians will find common ground by extolling the necessity for and virtues of Christian witness in the public sphere while ascribing different meanings to the word. Like much of the language found in the New Testament, the Greek word rendered "witness" in English carries multiple layers of meaning: "one who testifies in a legal matter, witness; one who witnesses at the cost of life, martyr."[34]

As depicted in the gospels, witness contains deeper nuance than many contemporary Christians realize. Jesus drew Jewish ire for healing a crippled man on the Sabbath near the pool of Bethesda. When confronted by the Jews over the healing, Jesus only exacerbates their rage by declaring, "My Father is working until now, and I am working."[35] While the modern reader will likely find this statement to be obscure and innocuous, to the ears of devout first-century Jews it was an unambiguous and patent provocation. John tells us that, "This was why the Jews were seeking all the more to kill

32. Matt 9:13a.
33. John 18:37.
34. Bauer, *Greek-English Lexicon*, 619.
35. John 5:17b.

him, because not only was he breaking the Sabbath, but he was even calling God his own Father, making himself equal with God."[36]

Never one to shy away from a teachable moment, despite his audience's hostility, Jesus elaborates:

> Truly, truly, I say to you, the Son can do nothing of his own accord, but only what he sees the Father doing. For whatever the Father does, that the Son does likewise ... If I alone bear witness about myself, my testimony is not true ... For the works that the Father has given me to accomplish, the very works that I am doing, bear witness about me that the Father has sent me. You search the Scriptures because you think that in them you have eternal life; and it is they that bear witness about me, yet you refuse to come to me that you may have life.[37]

The scriptures are Jesus's witnesses, but many of the seemingly pious could not recognize the very messiah of whom the scriptures testified. Instead, many who considered themselves spiritual had erroneously sought salvation in the same scrolls of the witness rather than in the one of whom they attested.

The chapter also says that Moses, John the Baptist, and God the Father were witnesses who corroborated the truth of Jesus's claims about himself, but their testimonies fell on deaf ears and hardened hearts. Frustrated by the crowd's incredulity, Jesus rhetorically wondered aloud "how will you believe my words?"[38] in light of their refusal to believe those who had testified about him. It is a good question asked at the most appropriate moment, particularly for American Christians who aspire to be contemporary witnesses of Jesus but who also cannot be faulted for finding John 5 more than a little disconcerting. What do today's disciples of Jesus offer as testimony that has not already been entered into evidence or in what manner is their witness more compelling than the collective testimonies of scripture, the saints, and the incarnate word? The witness can be comforted knowing that we are only responsible for the truthfulness of our testimony and not for its efficacy to change hearts and minds.

John 5 reveals more than just the frustration of gospel witness. Upon a closer reading of the chapter, Jesus through his polemic with the Jews is describing a more robust notion of witness that goes deeper than a verbal reiteration of the gospel. As we discovered above, Jesus laments that his own testimony is likely to be as ineffectual as the testimonies that have preceded

36. John 5:18b.
37. John 5:19, 31, 36, 39–40.
38. John 5:47.

him. However, the crucial distinction here is that Jesus does not hamstring witness altogether by limiting it to rhetorical acumen. Jesus calls the work he *does* in imitation of his Father his witness. The work of Jesus ordained by his father for him to fulfil shaped a more compelling, comprehensive, and enduring narrative—in a fashion that no verbal or written testimony could emulate—of Jesus's origin, mission, and purpose.

Equipped with this understanding of witness, Christian disciples testify about their experience with Jesus through imitating him as he imitated his Father. While it is difficult to distill the whole of Jesus's life and ministry into a pithy slogan, our earlier point of departure, Micah 6:8, is a remarkably concise encapsulation of Jesus's life: "do justice . . . love kindness . . . walk humbly with your God." We have covered how public repentance is an act of loving kindness whose fruit is humility. Now we will turn to doing justice as the quintessential act of Christian witness.

Christian citizens, rather than lobbying for a strictly self-centered agenda, are well equipped to doggedly pursue equitable care (*caritas*) for their most vulnerable neighbors who have neither the clout nor the means to repay their sole advocates.[39] This would be the rarest breed of genuine political activism and consistent with the work of Jesus in the gospels. Political participation of this nature is the embodiment of the Augustinian assertion that justice without love is no justice at all.

For Augustine, justice was a profoundly dense construct. Robert Dodaro describes how Augustine fused together layers of meaning beginning with Greco-Roman philosophy's description of justice as "the habit of the soul or the virtue whereby one gives to each individual his due."[40] This layer of understanding was augmented by the scriptural clarification that love is the nature of the debt owed to both God and neighbor.[41] Augustine further nuances justice with the Pauline notion of righteousness (*dikaiosune*), a descriptor of how the soul stands before God its creator in a "right" (because it is properly ordered) relationship. This appropriately positioned relationship is declared righteous.[42]

---

39. Recalling that Elshtain is an excellent reader of Augustine, she frames the discussion this way: "Authentic compassion (*com*, together; *pati*, to suffer) eradicates contempt and distance. The Christian is not afraid that he or she will lose something by offering him or herself. That is what the ethic of *caritas* is all about—not moralistic self-abnegation but an abundant overflowing of the fullness of life." Elshtain, *Augustine and the Limits of Politics*, 36.

40. Dodaro, *Christ and the Just Society*, 4.

41. Dodaro, *Christ and the Just Society*, 4.

42. Dodaro, *Christ and the Just Society*, 4.

In *The Trinity* VIII/4, Augustine fleshes out how love exercises justice by drawing upon Paul's admonition in Romans 13:8 to "Owe no one anything, except to love each other, for the one who loves another has fulfilled the law." Justice is giving everyone the love they are due because they are already in right relationship with God *or* so that they might become so. Augustine adds that it is precisely this understanding of justice that enables the Christian disciple to "love his neighbor as himself" without the danger of self-indulgence.

That Augustine turns to Romans 13 to discuss justice will surprise few American Christians, as it often quoted by the religious political conservatives as the basis for government and much criminal (including capital) punishment.[43] Read apart from Romans 12 however, it is easy to miss what Augustine understood: that love is the crux of justice.

We cannot meaningfully interpret Paul's account of justice in chapter 13 but through the magnifying lens of chapter 12:

> Bless those who persecute you; bless and do not curse them. Repay no one evil for evil but give thought to do what is honorable in the sight of all. If possible, so far as it depends on you, live peaceably with all. Beloved, never avenge yourselves, but leave it to the wrath of God, for it is written, "Vengeance is mine, I will repay," says the Lord. Do not be overcome by evil but overcome evil with good.[44]

Romans 12 is how the city of God must dwell within the city of man that requires as it does the governing authorities in Romans 13. However, chapter 13 does not underwrite all manner of governance. Rather it exposes the provisional legitimacy of human authority. Wielding the sword purposefully is not synonymous with wielding it justly. Pilate wielded the sword purposefully but not justly. Furthermore, Jesus's trial and crucifixion undermine any idealistic hope in human law because they expose "*par excellence* that both religious and imperial law may produce injustice rather than justice . . . Jesus was condemned by religious law (the laws of Moses) and state law (the laws of the Roman empire). Neither could affect justice, and Jesus was executed

---

43. Former US Attorney General Jeff Sessions cited the chapter of Romans in order to justify the separation of immigrant children from their parents at the border saying, "Concerns raised by our church friends about separating families are not fair or logical. I would cite you to the Apostle Paul and his clear and wise command in Romans 13 to obey the laws of the government because God has ordained them for the purpose of order." BBC, *US Child Migrants*. In response, I would remind Mr. Sessions that "Jesus said, 'Let the little children come to me and do not hinder them, for to such belongs the kingdom of heaven.'" Matt 19:14.

44. Rom 12:14, 17–19, 21.

as a threat to law and order."⁴⁵ In the cross, we see firsthand how the living sacrifice of Jesus could not be conformed to human conceptions of justice. For on it, the one who owed no one anything suffered unduly to become the love that gives each one everything that they are not due. The city of man wields the sword because it knows of no other way to bring about justice, but in the city of God justice innervated by love is manifested by bearing the cross instead of wielding a sword.

Augustine's multifaceted construal of justice invariably complicates the Lord's admonition to do justice in Micah 6:8. One cannot merely "do justice" in an Augustinian sense because it is not a chore that can ever be accomplished and marked off a list. Instead, it is a practice to be continuously inhabited. Perhaps it is more instructive to consider justice as a virtue we *are* rather than one we *do*. It is appropriate to call one another to *be* justice unto one another because it influences every relationship we have with our neighbors and calibrates our lives with the heart of our Lord.

The indelible earmark of faithful Christian political practice is that it inhabits justice in a way that has been unmistakably transformed by love. In light of this, Christian civic engagement ought to cultivate rather than excoriate the fruit of the Spirit, against which "there is no law." This enables those who do justice, love kindness, and walk humbly with the Lord to maneuver through contentiously fraught political landscapes in a peculiarly peaceful manner while simultaneously disarming and convicting others at the table. If Paul can write without contradiction that Christians should "Pay to all what is owed them: taxes to whom taxes are owed, revenue to whom revenue is owed, respect to whom respect is owed, honor to whom honor is owed," and at the same time to "Owe no one anything, except to love each other," it is reasonable to consider what is properly due one's country.

To this point I expect the suggestions offered for Christian political participation have been fairly mild and uncontroversial. Repentance, humility, kindness, witness, and justice are unlikely to be provocative either among Christians or their non-believing counterparts. This was purposeful as there are many who believe faith already overly determines Christian political agendas to the point where evangelicals are spoken of as another extreme political lobby to whom politicians must pander. The practices advanced were purposely chosen because they follow scriptural claims upon disciples and at the same moment, they can disarm critics of faith-based political engagement by rejecting the politics of manipulation and domination pervasive at every level of government. To be clear, I am not advocating for flaccid accommodation to the status quo. The politician

45. Reed, *Theology for International Law*, 47, 52.

of faith will undoubtedly upset the proverbial applecart by approaching governing from a pilgrim's perspective. The sheep would do well to head Jesus's advice that when they are among wolves they should "be wise as serpents and innocent as doves."[46] The political virtues discussed so far have purposely fallen into the "dove" category to earn a seat at the table and right to be heard. Once granted them, what can the Christian statesman wisely say from the platform she has been given?

A thicker understanding of how the pilgrim makes use of earthly polity must include the obligation to name the practices of that earthly city antithetical to even the most anemic understanding of peace as the absence of war. As a people bound by more than blood, soil, or common interest, the church can uniquely equip women and men able to challenge dubious civil practices and affect ostensibly impossible changes through persistent and patient obedience to God's Holy Spirit. This claim is qualified by Paul's admonition in Romans 12 against being conformed to the world since the fruit of national and religious syncretism is more often complacency or complicity rather than countercultural dissent.

It is crucial to demonstrate that even dissent grows out of a place of repentance. Repentance that does not call for a change in practice is merely a vacuous religious platitude. Robert Dodaro writes that contrition is not inimical to political involvement but rather that it fleshes out a morally fuller understanding of patriotism.[47] On Dodaro's reading, Augustine finds that genuine love for one's homeland lies in a "shared understanding of the nature of reconciliation."[48] Moreover, the essence of civic virtue and thus patriotism is the practices of penitence—"self-examination, confession, prayer for pardon, and forgiveness of others," especially of the enemy other.[49] However, Dodaro notes that to be efficacious to govern the wider *civitas* the citizens must exercise their penitential habits by repudiating moral perfectionism and spiritual autonomy[50] and embracing, "the freedom to live interiorly as citizens in God's 'city.'"[51]

Repentance is rarely lauded as a patriotic endeavor. However, when guarded from becoming idolatrous, repentance *can* be patriotic and serve as a check against more pugnacious patriotisms' devolution into bellicose

---

46. Matt 10:16.

47. Dodaro, *Christ and the Just Society*, 218.

48. Dodaro, *Christ and the Just Society*, 218. This sounds like a framework for understanding repentance.

49. Dodaro, *Christ and the Just Society*, 218.

50. The two vanities that, over time, come to tempt even the most contrite confessors.

51. Dodaro, *Christ and the Just Society*, 218.

nationalisms[52] of the "my country, right or wrong" sort.[53] Repentance safeguards against such tyranny by questioning a nation's more charitable glosses on its polarizing policies at home and abroad. In doing so, it also presses to the foreground penetrating questions like what kind of ethics are required or expunged, whether implicitly or explicitly, from the faithful citizen of this state.

Here Augustine proves a trustworthy example of Christian witness. Although criticized by some for being too accommodating to power, he was more political iconoclast than apologist. The occasions and audiences varied widely, but the content and posture of his political writings unswervingly revealed the gospel as both impetus and paradigm for consequential political involvement. His gift lay in his ability to seamlessly employ the familiar rhetoric of Roman philosophers and historians to challenge the incongruences inherent within the empire's predominant moral myths. On the same page, Augustine could rhetorically expose the deficiency of Roman virtue and offer the gospel as a more cogent and comprehensive counternarrative and praxis.

52. There is a compelling case to be made that religiously zealous nationalism killed Jesus. After Jesus raised Lazarus, John gives us insights into the unexpected and politically charged conversation among the chief priests and the Pharisees. What kept the religiously powerful awake at night was the notion that Jesus might develop a large enough following to be considered a political rival to Rome. This would invite the empire's wrath, stripping the privileged Jews of their "place and nation." They reasoned, "If we let him go on like this, everyone will believe in him, and the Romans will come and take away both our place and our nation" (John 11:48). Caiaphas, the high priest, had an answer: "it is better for you that one man should die for the people, not that the whole nation should perish" (John 11:50). Caiaphas was inadvertently prophetic in ways the council could not have possibly understood. Jesus would die for the people but not just for their people or to preserve their nation. Hebrew nationalism not only indicted Jesus but it also returned his conviction and sentence. When Pilate sought to release Jesus, the crowd accused them both of political misconduct. They censured Pilate reprimanding him, "If you release this man, you are not Caesar's friend. Everyone who makes himself a king opposes Caesar" (John 19:12). Thus Pilate was thrust into an administrative catch-22: be indicted as Caesar's opponent or continue to prosecute a man in whom he could find no fault. "Shall I crucify your king?" he asked. The chief priests provided yet another politically charged response: "We have no king but Caesar." In this declaration, the crowd reversed Jesus's response to the Pharisees and Herodians concerning the lawfulness of paying taxes to Caesar—for they were eager to render unto Caesar what rightly belonged only to God, his only begotten Son.

53. Stephen Decatur, nineteenth-century US Naval Officer, has been (in)famously quoted as toasting the US by saying, "Our Country! In her intercourse with foreign nations, may she always be in the right; but our country, right or wrong." Mackenzie, *Life of Stephen Decatur*, 295. His toast has been both supported and disparaged numerous times but none better than when G. K. Chesteron wrote, "'My country, right or wrong,' is a thing that no patriot would think of saying. It is like saying, 'My mother, drunk or sober.'" Chesterton, "A Defense of Patriotism," 166.

To be authentically Augustinian in the political sense is to steadfastly interrogate how governing authorities delineate and administer morally pregnant practices like justice and the common good. In *Saeculum*, Robert Markus compellingly contends that one of Augustine's most crucial rhetorical moves was to desacralize human history.[54] One seemingly counterintuitive corollary to Augustine's secularization of human history is that it compels Christians to more vigorously inhabit the political realm rather than cede the task to nonbelievers.

Markus develops this idea further, explaining that Augustinianism is, by its very nature, politically radical. It is radical because it is unremittingly critical of its inherited social order, regardless of the type, since the prevailing social order is inevitably deficient when measured against the eschatological kingdom that is "the fully human community of love promised by God, [that] discloses injustice and inhumanity in the best of social structures."[55]

This is not criticism for criticism's sake but an appraisal of the status quo that is instigated by Christian hope that things need not remain as they are. This variety of hope is not an inert longing for things to be made as they will be in the eschaton. Instead, it is an unsettling spotlight that, when turned on its social milieu, creates an indispensable and enduring tension with the world. Markus reminds us that, "this tension should be a fruitful one, from which awkward questions are continually being put to the world."[56]

Christian political theology that is not somewhat critically inquisitive is likely too comfortable with and compromised by the established system. Augustinianism's "awkward questions" are a rebuke to those who are comforted by complicity with morally bankrupt practices of power as well as those who abdicate all manner of political responsibility. The lamentable irony is that both positions are merely sinister forms of the same complicity that enables systemic injustice. The politically radical Augustinianism that Markus describes has been largely abandoned in American political theology in favor of more comfortably accommodationist tendencies.

---

54. Augustine's attack on the "sacral" conception of the empire liberated the Roman state, and by implication, all politics, from the direct hegemony of the sacred. Society became intrinsically "secular" in the sense that it is not as such committed to any particular ultimate loyalty. It is the sphere in which different individuals with different beliefs and loyalties pursue their common objectives in so far as they coincide. His "secularization" of the realm of politics implies a pluralistic, religiously neutral civil community. Markus, *Saeculum*, 173.

55. Markus, *Saeculum*, 168.

56. Markus, *Saeculum*, 169.

Patriotism is often too narrowly defined as flag-waving apologetics for a baptized nationalism, but there must be room for constructive critique if a nation is to approach its idealized self-perception. Patriotism is complex and includes a natural affinity for and honest appraisal of one's country. As a Vietnam protestor turned Vietnam veteran turned protestor again, former Secretary of State John Kerry reminds us that patriotism is more nuanced than simply toeing the party line: "I saw courage both in the Vietnam War and in the struggle to stop it. I learned that patriotism includes protest, not just military service. But you don't have to go halfway around the world or march on Washington to learn about bravery or love of country."[57] The lines that follow examine a few areas in the American political context where coherent, consistent, and critical Christian reflection promises to prove fruitful.

Holistically Pro-Life

The most distinctive witness available in the contemporary American context is to be pro-life. Yet this term encompasses much more than the abortion debates to which it has been traditionally confined. While this is undoubtedly included, there is much more to life than being born. A consistently pro-life witness will exercise nonviolent *caritas* for her neighbors long after they are born. She is an advocate not only for the unborn but also those born disadvantaged by poverty, disease, and/or location. She believes that justice does not culminate in preemptive and retributive killing and that black lives matter *because* all lives matter and historically that "all" has not included the minority other.[58]

Nearly four out of five of American conservatives identify as Christians.[59] Conservatives overwhelmingly identify as ardently pro-life, pro-war, pro-gun, and pro–capital punishment.[60] Yet they seek to limit immigration and social welfare benefits for the poor. Although these issues are normally addressed in isolation from one another, they are each a consequential nuance of what it means to be holistically pro-life. It is hypocritical to defend

57. Shapiro, "Hype and Glory."

58. Consider that in the US, slaves were designated as three-fifths of a person in the nation's constitution, a status that would not change until the addition of the thirteenth amendment seventy-eight years later.

59. Nearly 80 percent of the Republican Party identify as Christians, while white Christians constitute 73 percent of the party. See Lipka, "U.S. Religious Groups and Their Political Leanings," and Singer, "White Christians Decline in U.S., but Still Dominate Republican Party."

60. One of the pro's seems glaringly out of place with the others.

fetuses while simultaneously advocating to defund food, health, education, and housing assistance programs that many of those children will need as they grow.

Despite immense wealth in the US, poverty is a significant problem. According to a 2018 UN report by the human rights council, approximately forty million Americans live in poverty, eighteen and a half million live in "extreme poverty," while over five million live in "third world conditions of absolute poverty."[61] Furthermore, 13.3 million children, nearly 1 in 5, live in poverty while US government spending on children is near the bottom for developed countries. These statistics would be even more dire if the nation's safety net programs are cut further. To be consistently pro-life means protecting the unborn as well as those born underprivileged.

Another hurdle to a pro-life witness is warfare. By the end of the twentieth century, over 75 percent of those killed in war were civilians.[62] This is difficult to square with the just-war tradition. So too are the opaque practices of torture and drone strikes to preemptively execute those who are on US kill lists.

Conservatives are also notoriously against taxes because they feel that bloated government agencies misappropriate their resources. If Christians begrudge the government their tax dollars over sub-standard stewardship, perhaps they should cut defence spending which is usually a non-starter for conservatives.[63] The US senate approved $716 billion defense budget for 2019, which represents 17 percent of America's $4 trillion budget.[64] To put this into perspective, twenty-four cents of every dollar paid in taxes goes to fund the US defense budget.[65] Unless you are a member of Congress, you will not have much say on how your federal tax dollars are spent. In light of this, what form might a pro-life witness take?

John Howard Yoder, a Mennonite and vociferous advocate for non-violence intentionally withheld the percentage of his taxes he knew would be directed toward non-peaceful purposes. In lieu of paying in those funds, he donated to the Mennonite Central Committee for overseas war sufferers' relief. He also included a letter to the Internal Revenue Service (IRS) explaining why he had sent less than he owed: "I could not take the moral responsibility of forwarding to [the] government funds which I

61. Stein, "U.N. Report Shows America's Safety Net was Failing."

62. BBC, *In an Ethical War, Whom can you Fight?*

63. Although they have looked the other way while President Trump has reallocated $18.5 billion from the defense budget to build a border wall. Miroff, *Trump Planning to Divert Additional $7.2 Billion in Pentagon Funds for Border Wall*.

64. Stein, "U.S. Military Budget Inches Closer to $1 Trillion Mark."

65. National Priorities Project, *2017 Tax Receipt*.

knew would be used for a purpose contrary to that which government is supposed to be serving."[66]

As a second mile gesture, Yoder including his banking information so the IRS could easily find and seize the amount he had not paid conventionally. Yoder clarifies that the point of the exercise is not to keep the money from the government, evade taxes, or maintain "moral purity" but rather to "give a testimony to government concerning its own obligation before God."[67]

The enthusiasm with which Christians participate in and support wars of all kinds is also an obstacle to a pro-life witness. American Christian complicity with state violence is the byproduct of generations of deficient moral imagining. It is difficult to envisage peace when raised in a country that has never known a time without war. It is incumbent upon those of us who baulk at the legitimization of much violence as a moral imperative to advocate and employ more robust and creative alternative praxes.

Few Americans contemplate the possibility of inhabiting a republic where perpetual war is not the unchallenged norm. It is doubtful that many could do so if directly charged with the task. More doubtful still is whether anyone would be troubled by their inability to conceive of such a country or wonder what type of trauma had created such a conspicuous blind spot in their perception. The moral training necessary to form and inhabit a polity that does not privilege violence over peace is inconceivable to most. However, these facts do not make the priority of peace any less feasible. Consider that for the majority of history the right to own another person as property was an unquestioned assumption of many societies. Yet it took a relatively few short generations to shift the prevailing moral consensus on slavery, an institution as old as civilization itself, from commonly justified practice to a morally repugnant deed.

Another such American practice contrary to life that history will likely look back upon with disdain is its liberal use of drones as instruments of targeted killing. The ability to kill with impunity makes drones intrinsically unjust weapons. Any child who plays video games, to which drone operation is often compared as it utilizes a joystick and screen, knows that the ability to kill while being unassailable in the same way is cheating. Former airman Michael Haas, who amassed over 5,000 hours operating Predator and Reaper drone missions over Afghanistan and other conflict zones 8,000 miles away in the safety of Creech Air Force base outside Las Vegas, described the experience in the following manner:

66. Yoder, "Why I Don't Pay All of My Income Tax," 81, 92.
67. Yoder, "Why I Don't Pay All of My Income Tax," 81, 92.

Ever step on ants and never give it another thought? That's what you are made to think of the targets—as just black blobs on a screen. You start to do these psychological gymnastics to make it easier to do what you have to do—they deserved it, they chose their side. You had to kill part of your conscience to keep doing your job every day—and ignore those voices telling you this wasn't right.[68]

Try as they might, Haas and other drone operators have difficulty circumventing the gravity of their duties as evidenced by the similar proportions of depression and post-traumatic stress disorder (PTSD) among drone operators and soldiers deployed in the battlefield.[69]

While US administrations will say that their drone policies have reduced the likelihood of terrorism in the US, it has magnified terror many times over in the countries where they are used. The kill lists are created and carried out surreptitiously. Even innocent civilians in countries like Yemen and Pakistan have learned to fear blue skies lest they become inadvertent collateral damage. The Bureau of Investigative Journalism estimates that since 2004 there were at least 6,176 confirmed strikes killing between 8,459 and 12,105 people, of whom between 769 and 1,725 were estimated to be civilians and between 253 and 397 were children.[70] The US use of drones for targeted killing has increased precipitously with each new US administration—tenfold from the George W. Bush to Obama presidencies.[71] According to the BBC, Trump has followed suit having ordered more strikes in his first two years in office than Obama did in his entire presidency.[72] In this way, the drone policy foments rather than deters the galvanization of terrorist organizations. In his 2013 testimony before the US Senate subcommittee on the Constitution, Civil Rights and Human Rights Yemeni journalist Farea al-Muslimi describes the result of drone strike in his village, "What radicals had previously failed to achieve

---

68. Pilkington, *Life as a Drone Operator*.

69. Dao, *Drone Pilots*. For a fascinating article describing the moral injuries that drone operators often suffer, see Press, *Wounds of the Drone Warrior*.

70. Bureau of Investigative Journalism, *Drone Warfare*. Drone data is notoriously difficult to pinpoint precisely and varies from source to source. Though the Obama administration released annual reports on the strikes and civilian casualties, the data was misleadingly lower than independent reports because they counted every male of military age as a combatant. The Trump administration has done away with the report in its entirety and along with it any attempt to feign transparency or accountability.

71. Bureau of Investigative Journalism, *Obama's Covert Drone Wars*.

72. BBC, *Trump Revokes Obama Rule on Reporting Drone Strike Deaths*.

in my village, one drone strike accomplished in an instant: there is now an intense anger and growing hatred of America."[73]

It is difficult to find fault with al-Muslimi or his neighbors for harboring such sentiments. Imagine the US response if the situation was reversed. What if every sunny sky brought with it the potential for you to suffer your own personal 9/11 whether or not you are an actual enemy of the foreign power that is clandestinely killing your neighbors? It is difficult to fathom the would-be depths of US incredulity if even one foreign drone was captured over American soil. The nation would become more apoplectic still if foreign drones killed US citizens in their homes without charge, trial, or any hint of due process. We would have little difficulty properly naming the fear under which we lived as "terror" and its agents "terrorists." Yet, the hypocrisy of the US government, whose drone policy and practice is *de facto* terrorism committed under the pretense of making its citizens safer, barely registers with most American consciences.

How should American Christians respond when their government acts unjustly under the guise of their defense? Above I have supported the cultivation of Christian witnesses, formed by repentance and humility, that seek to *be* justice for their neighbors—even their distant neighbors, as far removed as the Samaritan was from the Hebrew traveler. The following is a list of specific iterations this might take when applied to the US drone policy.[74]

- Release the results of all government investigations promptly about specific strikes, subject to redactions only where families of those killed or injured have requested privacy or to ensure their physical safety, or only as strictly necessary for legitimate national security reasons.
- Explain all past and future cases in which there are credible allegations of unlawful killings or civilian harm.
- Record, acknowledge, and explain to families and the public every civilian death or injury.
- Compensate the families of innocent civilians killed or injured by strikes conducted or authorized by the United States.
- Publish the kill lists so innocent civilians can keep themselves out of harm's way.[75] Include the legal basis for individual strikes with the

---

73. Al-Muslimi, *Drone Wars*.

74. This bulleted list is an amalgamation of my thoughts, al-Muslimi's testimony above, and the report from Columbia Law School Human Rights Clinic and Sana'a Center for Strategic Studies, *Out of the Shadows*.

75. I can hear the retort that publishing the list will only push the targets deeper into hiding. However, generous bounties and self-preservation are just as likely to cause the communities in which these men attempt to hide to ostracize them and turn them in.

names of the targeted, including all Office of Legal Counsel and other agency legal memoranda that set forth the basis for force against all persons targeted, whether US citizen or non-citizen.

There is no assurance that violence in any of its forms (abortion, poverty, capital punishment, or war) will decrease if censured by American Christians becoming holistically pro-life. However, our ethics, no more than our witness, are not determined by their expediency or effectiveness. They are formed instead by our understanding of faithful discipleship as illumined by the Holy Spirit and scripture.[76] The manner in which Christians convey our ethics in a world with malleable and porous principles can be a clarion invitation to enter the kingdom of heaven or a stumbling block to the tone deaf that impedes their passage. Stanley Hauerwas reminds us that capitulation to such violence may guarantee our survival, but it is not capable of ensuring our lives.[77] The powers that claim to "give us the security to be at peace, in fact are not capable of such security. Instead, we believe that God has done all that is necessary to give us time to learn to be at peace in a world at war."[78]

A crucial component of a witness with the fortitude to speak this way to power is to be confident that one's testimony is true. Politically, this is increasingly difficult because journalism has become sensationally commodified to sell ads to keep some of its dying mediums on life support. The news is as problematic as it is stylized and crafted for a narrow target audience. Conservatives and liberals alike have their preferred echo chambers where their biases are confirmed yet never challenged. Anything that contests our prefabricated worldviews is dismissed as "fake news," and compromise is an illusory goal when everyone begins with his or her own alternative facts.

For Christians, the truth is not an arbitrarily flexible idea that can be expediently manipulated to suit our purposes. Instead, truth is a person, a way, and a life that sets us free by conforming us to itself. Speaking truth to power is speaking the gospel of Jesus to power. This is sorely needed even

---

76. Following Dietrich Bonhoeffer and Karl Barth, I believe that any notion of ethics that considers itself thoroughly theological must be pliable and obedient to the command of God.

77. Hauerwas, "Taking Time for Peace," 99.

78. Hauerwas, "Taking Time for Peace," 99.

in a country in which the President,[79] Vice President, and 91 percent of Congress confess to be Christians.[80]

Martyn Percy explains that the American project was uniquely suited to cause such moral relativism concerning the truth.[81] Percy notes that the American churchgoer long ago embraced the ecclesial free market, which has led to competition for members between individual churches and an organizational and theological diversity that differentiates the US from other Christian societies. The unintended consequence of the commodification of worship was doctrinal incoherence. If everyone is entitled to a personally tailored religious experience, Percy writes, "then faith will mean almost anything—and therefore almost nothing."[82] This devolution has affected life outside the church, since a market-driven approach to religion has yielded a malleable conception of truth. Percy goes on to claim that America's implicit religion, "In God we trust," is appropriately written on every dollar bill since "Godly providence and worldly prosperity are spiritual and material realities for Americans, and politics and pragmatism their agents. Trump is merely the natural progeny of a nation where the intercourse of God and mammon is seldom questioned."[83]

The US policy of plausible deniability stands in direct opposition to responsible truth-telling. Speaking the truth is more challenging yet necessary in an age of blatant disinformation. While governments cannot always operate with full transparency, they must govern in a manner that allows for multiple layers of oversight and accountability because the most insidious acts in our history were committed when the right hand was haplessly oblivious to what the left hand was doing.

John Quincy Adams was prescient when he proclaimed the US is better served when it "goes not abroad in search of monsters to destroy." However, when the US travels the globe furtively assassinating people on its classified kill list, it acts imperially. Under President Trump, "America first" has become de facto domestic and foreign policy, but this should be

---

79. Trump's religious convictions are difficult to pin down. He is a baptized Presbyterian but rarely discusses his faith publicly. Martyn Percy has written that "Trump's interior religious landscape is a kind of politico-spiritual Ponzi scheme [of] opportunism, pragmatism and positivism." Percy, "To Know Donald Trump's Faith Is to Understand His Politics."

80. This number includes 99 percent of Republicans and 80 percent of Democrats. Sandstrom, *Faith on the Hill.*

81. Percy, "To Know Donald Trump's Faith Is to Understand His Politics."

82. Percy, "To Know Donald Trump's Faith Is to Understand His Politics."

83. Percy, "To Know Donald Trump's Faith Is to Understand His Politics."

unsettling for a group of people taught to believe that the "last will be first and the first last."[84]

For Augustine, empire was ultimately a theologically neutral concept.[85] In light of this, it is important to take up Peter Leithart's question as to what kind of empire the United States has become. Americanism is the worship of a profiteering empire. In retrospect, American intervention in world affairs has been one blatantly, commercially driven and militarily supported venture after another. Remember that Leithart differentiated between better or worse empires based on how they treated the people of God. It is difficult to pin down precisely how the United States fares in this respect, as its treatment of Christians by the government, which considers itself predominantly Christian, undulates between marginalizing apathy and ebullient pandering depending on which point in the election cycle the question is asked. An united church that is holistically pro-life would be much more difficult to either marginalize or pander to as it would call for radical consistency throughout government domestic and foreign policy that seeks to do justice by giving each her due.

Conclusion

The United States has by no means cornered the market on national exceptionalism or revisionist history, but the nature of American cultural, economic, political, and military dominance since World War II have led some to christen this period the "American Century." Like Augustine before me, I have tried honestly to recollect my homeland's history rather than merely recite its popular mythos.

The American Christian shares Augustine's lot because we are all imperial pilgrims. The former's situation is further complicated by the element of national complicity that democracy introduces. However, this newfound civic responsibility also creates a substantial basis from which to conscientiously challenge the government one has helped to create.

---

84. Matt 20:16.

85. This is a recurring in theme Markus's *Saeculum* and *Christianity and the Secular*. His thoughts regarding Roman exceptionalism are just as applicable to the contemporary American context, "The bond that linked the Roman Empire and Christianity was now a contingent historical fact, which might at any future time be dissolved, even reversed. The Empire had no specially privileged place in God's providence either as an instrument of or an obstacle to the achievement of his purposes. There was nothing intrinsically sacred about it; it was a *res publica* among others." Markus, *Christianity and the Secular*, 37.

Speaking truth to power must always begin with humbling repentance instead of arrogant triumphalism thinly veiled as prophetic judgement. Rather than surrender to the obsessive-compulsive desire to keep our hands "clean from sin," it is the confession that we were also born with "dirty hands" that humanizes us. To such a common humanity we appeal with unpretentious gospel witness—the most poignant aspect of which is to pursue justice with the experience of the peace that surpasses all understanding. In a nation where war is normative, this genuine peace underwritten by *caritas* is the most uniquely Christian political act of a people conformed to Jesus's death on the cross—the ultimate act of nonviolent resistance and the only authentic example of truly redemptive violence in history. Rather than fight, the kingdom resists evil by bearing witness to the truth that imitates the work of God the Father by caring for its neighbor from the womb to the grave.

Conclusion—Who Would Jesus Drone?

> Victory in Iraq was declared a week before Palm Sunday in 2003 as American Abram tanks rolled into the central square of Baghdad. Christ chose a donkey and not a chariot to mark his entry into Jerusalem for his own final confrontation with the forces of evil. Pilgrims from Judea marked his path not with swords but palm branches as he rode towards the temple. At his trial and in his preparedness to go the way of the cross, Christ called the bluff of the reigning powers, not appeasing but resisting their claims to dominion through the ultimate weapon of the weak, his preparedness "to lay down his life for his friends" (John 15:13).[1]
>
> —Michael Northcott

The reason I continue to find Michael Northcott's words so poignant is that they resonate deeply with both what I read in the gospels and my experience of the political realities of growing up as an American. The apostle Paul wrote to the church in Corinth that the mere mention of the "cross,"

> is folly to those who are perishing, but to us who are being saved it is the power of God . . . But God chose what is foolish in the world to shame the wise; God chose what is weak in the world to shame the strong; God chose what is low and despised in the

---

1. Northcott, "The Weakness of Power and the Power of Weakness," 88–101.

world, even things that are not, to bring to nothing things that are, so that no human being might boast in the presence of God.²

Although he spoke with authority concerning God's kingdom, Christ refused to engage in the political power struggles of his day and instead usurped the power that governors and the Sanhedrin had claimed for themselves over life and death by laying down his own life on a tree.³ Refusing to violently defend one's self against violence is regarded as unqualified foolishness by the world's standards, yet enduring violence without returning it in kind shames the world's blunt and vulgar use of its meager power to defend everything from their ephemeral possessions to their fleeting lives. I have read enough scripture to understand that when *Yahweh* tangibly acts within history, he does so in such a way that those who witness it know that it is unmistakably him who has intervened in such a way so peculiar to himself that no other person could reasonably boast and mitigate God's glory. These paradoxes or dichotomies—perishing and power, foolishness and wisdom, weakness and strength—they are the Father's *modus operandi* so that no disciple can brag as if we had anything good at all that had not been given to us.⁴

Empire

Chapter 1's historical reading established the backdrop for the American Christian's struggle to reconcile her identities. Every chapter is built upon one or more of these contradictions. The introduction drew out some of the violent parallels between my contemporary American context and the Roman empire of Augustine's time. To call into question the American republic's self-perception as a "city on a hill" that the world should long desire to emulate and that the US is obligated to spread to the corners of the earth is viewed as foolish and seditious, particularly in the deep south of the country where I was raised and still reside. The usual response is to be suspicious of anyone who questions the coercive means through which

---

2. 1 Cor 1:18, 27–29.

3. Talal Asad has called the crucifixion "the most famous suicide in history, whose horror is transmuted into the project of redeeming universal humanity—again, through a combination of cruelty and compassion." Asad, *On Suicide Bombing*, 3. While the reader may initially find the suggestion that crucifixion of Christ was a suicide, it does resonate with Jesus's parable of the Good Shepherd: "For this reason the Father loves me, because I lay down my life that I may take it up again. No one takes it from me, but I lay it down on my accord. I have the authority to lay it down, and I have the authority to take it up again. This charge I have received from my Father" (John 10:17–18).

4. 1 Cor 4:7.

American brands of freedom, liberty, and economic policies have been advanced with evangelistic zeal—first throughout the continental US, then the Western hemisphere, and ultimately the globe.

When the US has acted in this manner, it is what I have labelled "classically imperial." These overt means of direct manipulation of foreign proxies for another nation's self-interested purposes fell out of favor after World War II. The death of colonialism forced the United States to find more creative ways to conceal its thumb on the scales of international commerce and justice to ensure that they stayed forever tilted in the United States' favor. The aspects of US policy that have been deployed and persist after the second World War to maintain America's hegemony—like the ubiquitous network of military bases, interference in foreign democracies, and drone assassinations—are the reasons I have labelled the US an "unconventional empire."

Unlike classical empires, the US does not need to simultaneously occupy much of the world's land mass and control the seas to manage and influence what happens there. The US has replaced the colony with the military base—over 700 military hubs dispersed around the planet ready to serve as points of departure from which it can mobilize full-scale war anywhere in the world in a matter of days. When coupled with the advancement of instant surveillance and communication technologies like satellites and the internet, the borders of an empire are pulled ever closer to the metropole of power. Unmanned aircraft that can simultaneously relay real-time reconnaissance and surreptitiously assassinate enemies is another unconventional form of imperial policing that does not require the physical boots on the ground of antiquity's empires. When taken together, the military base and technology greatly mitigate the imminent threat of imperial overstretch, which was previously the leading cause of imperial failure in classical empires because empires have the habit of growing too large and unwieldy to efficiently manage themselves before they succumb to and suffocate under the burden of their own girth.

Beyond its military reach, there is also the pervasive use of the US dollar as the world's global reserve currency. This fact endows the US with outsized influence in global markets, particularly in petrochemical trading that must be denominated in US dollars thanks to the many magnanimous arms deals between Saudi Arabia and the US. This adds teeth to economic sanctions against its enemies like Iran, which cannot sell its primary natural resource because potential trading partners fear incurring the wrath of the US. Chapter 1 is rife with other examples of the confounding of American economic and military doctrine until the two are often indistinguishable.

The US also once wielded liberal amounts of what Joseph Nye called "soft power," which can best be described as an enticing cultural magnetism that others nations wanted to emulate.[5] Since September 11, 2001, the US has lost much of this soft power as details emerged about its many morally deficient practices such as extraordinary rendition, suspension of the habeas corpus rights of detainees, advanced interrogation techniques, targeted killings, and the physical and sexual abuse that came to light at *Abu Ghraib* military prison. These realities should give American Christians sufficient grounds to question whether the "war on terror" is indeed a just war as the Christian discourse has historically understood it.

Just War

What is truly at stake in the US imperial question? Many will deem the US incapable of exercising imperial practices given its republican origins and its historically professed aversion to the task. Others are comfortable with the United States as a modern empire, hegemon, or sole remaining superpower. Those in this camp argue that the absence of a stabilizing US presence on the global stage will merely create a power vacuum that may well be filled by a less scrupulous and more sinister faction or conglomeration thereof.

It is difficult to parse the just-war tradition apart from the imperial context in which it was conceived. Though it has undergone innumerable revisions since its inception, just war—whether in its theological, legal, philosophical, or political incarnations—has always been the prerogative of the most powerful political entities. The poor, weak, or decimated are never privileged with determining what qualifies as justified violence. Rarely has just war been used as Augustine intended, to constrain and even prevent violence. Augustine intended to excise or at least confine the cancer of violence before it rapidly metastasized into the lust to dominate and consumed its host along with his neighbors. In this book, the crux of both the imperial and just-war dilemmas hinge on one critical question: "Can the unconventionally imperial United States wage a 'just war on terror?'" Answering this question required a thicker account of both empire and just war so the research naturally led to an examination of the concepts through Augustine's meticulously theological lens.

Augustine

War assumes as many qualifiers as there are ways for men to impose their will upon one another. It accepts the adjectives defensive, holy, guerilla,

---

5. See Nye, *Soft Power*.

just, nuclear, cyber, but they are all wars nonetheless. Each evolution of war seems to send a new generation of theologians flocking to recalibrate Augustine's contemplations on just war to the newest manifestation of combat. This book is seemingly unique because it has attempted to gather examples from its own political landscape and latest machinations of warfare—this one being "against terror"—that resonate with Augustine's own pastoral voice. From my perspective, to speak of Augustine's pastoral voice is redundant, but necessarily so. It is redundant in the sense that the *only* voice of Augustine that has survived is that of a wise shepherd nurturing his sheep. It is *necessarily* repetitive because the temptation for Augustinian scholars has been to form some systematic homogeny from such a variegated author. This pastoral emphasis is the most unifying element of Augustine's corpus. This is not to say that more ambitious projects such as understanding what "political Augustinianism" might entail is fruitless labor, but it risks becoming so if it is not secured on all sides by the scaffolding that is Augustine's ministerial guidance.

Rather than make Augustine over in the guise of a liberal democrat as some of my contemporaries have done in search of support for their projects, this book acknowledges that Augustine was an acutely self-aware imperial citizen whose fourth-century Roman framework is not entirely different from the American milieu. Augustine was leery of imperial overstretch, preferring smaller governing entities to bloated empires. Perhaps this was because he ministered within an immense landscape surrounded by boundaries in constant flux due to the internal and external pressures of violence. Augustine's flock was under threat from all sides—the barbarian invaders of Rome, the Roman pagans who faulted the Christians for the empire's atrophy, and the Donatist Christians who violently resisted integration into the Catholic Church.

In light of this, there is little wonder he advocated for the defensive protection of one's neighbors even if it escalated to physical coercion motivated by love. Given the scope of his letters to Roman officials arguing against the death penalty and pleading for leniency even for violent criminals, I concur with John Milbank who emphasized the "ontological priority of peace" in Augustine's work. This is why I characterized Augustine as a reluctant realist rather than as an excessive realist (as Reinhold Niebuhr's characterized him) or an overly enthusiastic realist (my characterization of Nigel Biggar's interpretation). Even as a reluctant realist, as long as he allowed even the thinnest of margins where justified violence could foment there were those who were happy to cart their instruments of war and torture into the camp and baptize their practices as Augustinian. Sadly, the repurposing of Augustine's pastoral theology is common, but more often than not it yields a horribly disfigured replica of his idyllic intentions that is unrecognizable as anything remotely resembling Augustine's original thought.

Repurposing Augustine

Chapter 3 represent my engagement with the contemporary landscape of Augustinian scholarship focusing primarily on the post–September 11 context. My most extensive interaction is with Jean Bethke Elshtain. In 1995, Elshtain contributed to Augustinian scholarship when she wrote *Augustine and the Limits of Politics*. It was a tightly argued, thick, and faithful interpretation of Augustine's political writings. That was before four airplanes were weaponized against American civilians on US soil. Afterwards, the emphases within her exegesis shifted dramatically. She was consistently found working the George W. Bush apologia circuit defending the administration's response to the terrorist attacks.

A short time later she published another book, more loosely Augustinian, *A Just War Against Terror*, which defended the invasions of Afghanistan and Iraq, not as acts of self-defense, which are beyond the pale for Augustine, but rather on humanitarian grounds. It is a substantial footnote that she failed to mention these same conditions existed in 1995 when her previous work was published. The title to her book preemptively declares the Bush administration's "war on terror" to be a just one, and the subtitle belies a justification for the neoconservative agenda of war in perpetuity: "The Burden of American Power in a Violent World." Affirming my prior assertion that empire and just war are merely two hands crafted to sustain each other, Elshtain argues for a new American imperialism that polices the global community protecting it from failed states.

Given the perspicacity of her earlier Augustine scholarship, one could easily construe Elshtain's arguments in *Just War Against Terror* as simply a distraught and disproportionate response to the collective violence and trauma suffered on September 11. With that hypothesis in mind, I searched Elshtain's later lectures, interviews, and journal articles—she unfortunately passed away before completing her next project with the working title *Torture and Terror in a Time of Troubles*—to see if the subsequent revelations regarding US improprieties and circumvention of international laws during its prosecution of the "war on terror" had deterred any of her enthusiasm for her conviction that the "war on terror" was in fact a just war in the Augustinian sense.

Though she would learn of the US use of torture, suspension of habeas corpus, and targeted killing before she died in 2013, she never wavered in

CONCLUSION—WHO WOULD JESUS DRONE?

her certitude that the US was fighting a just war. Instead of walking back her earlier claims, she doubled down on them. She turned to moral casuistry to justify the "limited but necessary" use of torture and developed *jus post bellum* criteria to rationalize the indefinite occupation of war torn countries like Afghanistan and Iraq.[6] Augustine put a premium on civil order and peace, but he did not do so by underwriting asymmetrical warfare and occupation in perpetuity. My apprehension is that if prodigious fear could turn such a meticulous reader of Augustine as Elshtain into an ardent jingoist who advocated torture and American garrisoning of the globe,[7] the typical Christian layperson may be far more easily provoked to such bellicose positions unless her church is intentional about instructing their members in persistent peace building. Lisa Sowle Cahill encourages precisely this kind of discipleship, but before we turn our focus to Cahill's elucidation of Augustine it is worth considering the input of Elshtain's British counterpart Nigel Biggar. He effectively composed a theological work shielding former UK prime minister Tony Blair much as Elshtain had for Bush.

Biggar's case, as detailed in his book *In Defence of War*, is more appropriately understood as an offensive against pacifism rather than a defense of just war. He is more critical of the pacifists's sins of omission rather than the just warriors's sins of commission. He points to Rwanda and Bosnia as genocides the blood from which stains the very hands of the pacifists whom he calls parasitic because they enjoy the peace that war provides without lifting a finger to participate in the cause for fear of getting their hands dirty.

He then moves from this harsh appraisal of pacifists, some of whom are his Christian sisters and brothers, to redeploy Augustine's maxim that only love should induce violence. This includes love for the recipients of one's violence, even when the violence will foreseeably lead to their death. This seems to be a hyper extension of the Augustine metaphor of how a loving father disciplines his disobedient son. Although the father would prefer the son respond to a reasoned verbal command, the father would rather physically discipline the child than see his son ruined. However, discipline that results in the death of the recipient has ceased to be discipline regardless of the original intention. I am also skeptical of Biggar's assertion that love is powerful enough to motivate a Christian to slay a would-be attacker yet somehow too impotent to enable her to restrain or subdue the same aggressor until he could be turned over to the proper policing authority.

---

6. This latter move is reminiscent of "classical imperialism" as she holds up the continued American presence in Europe, Japan, and South Korea for several decades after fighting has ceased in those places as successful models.

7. Augustine was decidedly not a nationalist, argued against the use and effectiveness of torture, and advocated garrisoning for peaceful rather than belligerent purposes.

The two most compelling readings of Augustine in chapter 3 belong to Daniel Bell and Lisa Sowle Cahill. Though they utilize different language, their arguments are similar enough to each other to be treated together. Both Bell and Cahill interpret Augustine to advocate for meaningful praxes rooted within the church—an argument difficult to disregard on Augustinian terms. Bell calls his praxis "just war as Christian discipleship" while Cahill's is aptly named "just peace-making." Both practices are contingent upon becoming part and parcel of the regular work of the church, not merely a peculiar set of habits or strange dispositions that are dusted off and awkwardly applied in times of war. Both Bell and Cahill would agree that the church and her just-war discourse have been largely ineffective at impeding wars abroad because the church is sorely out of practice at propagating peace at home. The church, by and large, has lost the collective muscle memory needed to regularly practice the kingdom's work. Worse yet, it may be more accurate to say there are many parts of Christ's body where the muscles required to do the heavy lifting of justice and *caritas* have atrophied altogether. A church that does not equip its disciples routinely to advocate for justice and rehearse peace in the smaller conflicts of the Christian life in times of relative peace will have little of substance to say and even less to contribute during times of war.

Imperial Pilgrims

The veracity of the ultimate chapter and the cogency of the ethical implications that logically progress from its premises will primarily be based upon how convincing the reader has found the arguments in the previous chapters. In order to develop a compellingly prescriptive course of action, it must first be preceded by an accurate and thorough appraisal of the context of the problem.

Inherent in each of the three preceding chapters is a central premise. Each premise has meaningful ramifications that help to unearth an intelligible answer to this book's central research question—"how Christian Americans are to reconcile the competing claims of their faith and citizenship."

Chapter 1's primary supposition is that the United States of America has had imperial pretensions since its inception. Replacing America's historically republican narrative with an imperial one casts aspersions on the United States's many military engagements, the public justifications given for them, and Christian participation in them. In light of these new questions, chapter 2 sought the council of Augustine as a useful guide for contemporary Christian Americans as he was well versed in imperial citizenship, justifying coercive force, and reconciling Christian involvement in both respects.

The third chapter explored contemporary Augustinian studies primarily since September 11, 2001, and found that a great deal of theological work since that day has used Augustine to accommodate American imperialism and underwrite moral justifications for its "war on terror." As far as I can discern, I am alone among Christian ethicists in my use of a pastoral reading of Augustine to criticize rather than champion American imperialism and its "war on terror."

Chapter 4 borrows its title from Augustine's metaphor for Christians while we inhabit the earthly city. We are pilgrims, sojourners, travelers, little more than tourists who have overstayed our visas on Earth. Nonetheless, Augustine encouraged pilgrims to make use (*uti*) of and actively seek the peace of our hosts within the city of man. He also wrote that those so gifted should participate in more executive capacities. The chapter is my conception of what practices might comprise such participation.

Micah 6:8 offers a modest yet substantial commission for Christian involvement in politics: "He has told you, O man, what is good; and what does the Lord require of you but to do justice, and to love kindness, and to walk humbly with your God?" When phrased in this manner, it does not seem like a casual addendum to God's covenant that Christians may opt in or out of at their discretion. These three things *Yahweh* requires: do justice, love kindness, and walk humbly with him. These behaviors are not easily cultivated or maintained because they are antithetical to our natural proclivities for selfishness, pride, and the lust to dominate.

The initial and quintessentially Christian act of political engagement is repentance. It is unmistakably political because it is public testimony amongst our peers, yet it is also irrevocably Christian because it is simultaneously the confession we have fallen well short of our call to do justice, love kindness, and walk humbly. It can also be highly disorientating for the casually or non-religious who are more accustomed to religious faith used as a partisan tool to either rally the base or bludgeon the opposition.

Few would object if American Christians' repentance ended there. However, as citizens of a liberal democracy we are also stakeholders, however slight, in the policies, purse strings, and power of the republic. As patriotic patrons, we are also complicit when our nation miscarries justice, repudiates kindness, and harms our neighbors. We must also repent of our collusion with national sin. To be clear, this repentance is not the guilty, heavy-hearted, and ham-handed apologies of a people powerless to do anything other than sin.

In the spirit of genuine repentance, the American Christian turns away from the objects of her contempt and towards the praxes that are the negation of that contempt—justice, kindness, and humility. She inhabits justice by giving each—especially those the world has relegated as the least of these—their due, which is the *caritas* that we learn by walking humbly with Christ. This is a politically radical amendment that would transfigure patriotism from ordinary love of country to an extraordinary love of countrymen.

The palpable fruit of such a political revolution would be the thickening of previously partisan issues. For example, since 1973 the term pro-life has been narrowly pigeon-holed to mean the right for an unborn fetus to be carried to full term. It is no exaggeration to claim that in the United States there is not a more polarizing political issue. Many cast their ballots on this issue alone—which has traditionally been a boon for the conservative party. However, to do justice, love kindness, and walk humbly on this issue requires more intricately nuanced thinking than it is usually afforded. I have argued for a more extensive policy I have called being holistically pro-life. Those who argue most vigorously to protect the lives of fetuses are also, more often than not, likely to argue just as vociferously against increased funding for the social-safety-net programs that help feed, educate, and provide medical care needed for many of those children born into poverty. The aim of being holistically pro-life is to raise thriving adults, not merely give birth to babies.[8]

In the United States, the political left urges people to *do* good while the right urges people to *be* good. However, the gospel reminds us that God alone *is* good. The rest of us are born with a congenitally selfish bent that must be continually straightened by God's Holy Spirit, his word, and his people. In a world where cities of men and God coalesce and conflict, the most unambiguous witness is the capacity to tell the truth responsibly. To that end, my hope is that this book has been a witness to its readers.

---

8. There are other issues on which conservatives are decidedly *against* the thriving of life. Their positions on gun ownership rights, capital punishment, the privatization of mass incarceration and liberal use of the death penalty that disproportionately targets minorities, climate change denial, military spending, and winnowing pensioners's social security immediately come to mind.

Bibliography

Adams, John Quincy. "She Goes Not Abroad in Search of Monsters to Destroy." *The American Conservative*. July 4, 1821. http://www.theamericanconservative.com/repository/she-goes-not-abroad-in-search-of-monsters-to-destroy/ (accessed February 15, 2016).

Agamben, Giorgio. *Home Sacer: Sovereign Power and Bare Life*. Translated by Daniel Heller-Roazen. Stanford: Stanford University Press, 1998.

———. *State of Exception*. Translated by Kevin Attell. London: The University of Chicago Press, 2005.

Allande, Salvador. "Last Words of Salvador Allande." *MR Zine*. November 11, 2006. http://mrzine.monthlyreview.org/2006/allende110906.html.

Al-Muslimi, Farea. *Drone Wars: The Constituional and Counterterrorism Implications of Targeted Killing*. April 23, 2013. http://www.judiciary.senate.gov/pdf/04-23-13Al-MuslimiTestimony.pdf.

Ambrose, "The Duties of the Clergy." in *Morality and Ethics in Early Christianity*. Edited and translated by Jan L. Womer. Philadelphia: Fortress, 1987.

American Civil Liberties Union. *Guantanamo by the Numbers*. May 2018. https://www.aclu.org/issues/national-security/detention/guantanamo-numbers.

Aquinas, Thomas. *Summa Theologica*. trans. Fathers of the English Dominican Province, five vols. Westminster, MD: Christian Classics, 1981.

Arendt, Hannah. *The Human Condition*. London: University of Chicago Press, 1998.

Aristides, *Orations*. 26/22. Cambridge: Harvard University Press, 1973.

Asad, Talal. *On Suicide Bombing*. New York: Columbia University Press, 2007.

Augustine. *Answer to Faustus, a Manichean*. Edited by Boniface Ramsey. Translated by S.J. Roland Tesk. Vol. I/20. 49 vols. Hyde Park, NY: New City, 2007.

———. *The City of God (1-10)*. Edited by Boniface Ramsey. Translated by William Babcock. Vol. I/6. 49 vols. Hyde Park, NY: New City, 2012.

———. *The City of God (11-22)*. Edited by Boniface Ramsey. Translated by William Babcock. Vol. I/7. 49 vols. Hyde Park, NY: New City, 2013.

———. *The Confessions*. Edited by O.S.A. John E. Rotelle. Translated by Maria Boulding, O.S.B. Vol. I/1. 49 vols. Hyde Park, NY: New City, 1997.

———. *Expositions of the Psalms (51-72)*. Vol. III/17. 49 vols. Hyde Park, NY: New City, 2016.

———. *Letters 100-155*. Edited by Bonifce Ramsey. Translated by S.J. Roland Teske. Vol. II/2. Hyde Park, NY: New City, 2003.

———. *Letters 156-210*. Edited by Boniface Ramsey. Translated by S.J. Roland Teske. Vol. II/3. Hyde Park, NY: New City, 2004.

———. *Letters 1-99*. Edited by O.S.A. John E. Rotelle. Translated by S.J. Roland Teske. Vol. II/1. 49 vols. Hyde Park, NY: New City, 2001.

———. *Political Writings*. Edited by E. M. Atkins, & R. J. Dodaro. Cambridge: Cambridge University Press, 2007.

———. *Revisions*. Edited by Teske, S.J. Roland. Translated by Boniface Ramsey. Vol. I/2. 49 vols. Hyde Park, NY: New City, 2010.

———. *Sermons (341-400)*. Edited by O.S.A. John E. Rotelle. Translated by O.P. Edmund Hill. Vol. III/10. 49 vols. Hyde Park, NY: New City, 1992.

———. *Teaching Christianity (De Doctrina Christiana)*. Edited by O.S.A. John E. Rotelle. Translated by O.P. Edmund Hill. Vol. I/11. Hyde Park, NY: New City, 2013.

———. *Teaching Christianity*. Edited by O.S.A. John E. Rotelle. Translated by O.P. Edmund Hill. Vol. I/11. 49 vols. Hyde Park, NY: New City, 2013.

———. *The Trinity*. Edited by O.S.A. John E. Rotelle. Vol. I/5. 49 vols. Hyde Park, NY: New City, 2012.

Avalon Project: Documents in Law, History and Diplomacy. *The Atomic Bombings of Hiroshima and Nagasaki: Chapter 10–Total Casualties*. 2008. https://avalon.law.yale.edu/20th_century/mp10.asp.

Barth, Karl. *Epistle to The Romans*. Translated by Edwyn C. Hoskyns. Oxford: Oxford University Press, 1968.

———. *Pride and Fall of Man*. Vols. IV,1, in *The Church Dogmatics*, by Karl Barth, edited by Geoffrey William & Torrance, Thomas Forsyth Bromiley, translated by Geoffrey William Bromiley, 358–513. Edinburgh: T&T Clark, 1956.

Bauer, Walter. *A Greek–English Lexicon of the New Testament and other Early Christian Literature, 3rd Edition*. Edited by Frederick William Danker. London: The University of Chicago Press, 2000.

BBC. *In an ethical war, whom can you fight?* 2014. http://www.bbc.co.uk/ethics/war/just/whom_1.shtml.

———. "Trump Revokes Obama Rule on Reporting Drone Strike Deaths." March 7, 2019. https://www.bbc.com/news/world-us-canada-47480207.

———. *US child migrants: 2,000 separated from families in six weeks*. June 15, 2018. https://www.bbc.com/news/world-us-canada-44503318.

Bell, Daniel M. Jr. *Just War as Christian Discipleship: Recentering the Tradition in the Church rather than the State*. Grand Rapids, MI: Brazos, 2009.

Bernstein, Jared. "After All These Years, 'Welfare Reform' is the Same Racist Dog Whistle it Always Was." January 8, 2018. https://www.washingtonpost.com/news/posteverything/wp/2018/01/08/after-all-these-years-welfare-reform-is-the-same-racist-dog-whistle-it-always-was/?noredirect=on&utm_term=.9b22b31651ad.

Biggar, Nigel. *In Defence of War*. Oxford: Oxford University Press, 2013.

Bin Laden, Osama. "Letter to the American People." *The Guardian*. November 24, 2002. https://www.theguardian.com/world/2002/nov/24/theobserver.

Blake, Aaron. "Palin: 'Waterboarding is how we Baptize Terrorists.'" April 28, 2014. https://www.washingtonpost.com/news/post-politics/wp/2014/04/28/palin-waterboarding-is-how-we-baptize-terrorists/?utm_term=.b35bbebe2a9c.

Bobbitt, Philip. *The Shield of Achilles: War, Peace and the Course of History*. London: Penguin, 2002.

———. *Terror and Consent: The Wars for the Twenty-First Century*. London: Penguin, 2008.

Bonhoeffer, Dietrich. *Creation and Fall: A Theological Exposition of Genesis 1-3*. Edited by John W. de Gruchy. Translated by Douglas Stephen Bax. Minneapolis: Fortress, 1997.

Bowden, Mark. "The Dark Art of Interrogation." October 2003. https://www.theatlantic.com/magazine/archive/2003/10/the-dark-art-of-interrogation/302791/.

Brown, Peter. *Augustine of Hippo: A Biography*. London: University of California Press, 2000.

———. "Religious Coercion in the Later Roman Empire: The Case of North Africa." *History*, vol. 48, no. 164 (1963): 283–305. JSTOR, www.jstor.org/stable/24405550.

Bruno, Michael J.S. *Political Augustinianism: Modern Interpretations of Augustine's Political Thought*. Minneapolis: Fortress, 2014.

Bureau of Investigative Journalism, "Drone Warfare." n.d., https://www.thebureauinvestigates.com/projects/drone-war, (accessed 23 June 2019).

Burton, Paul. "Pax Romana/Pax Americana: Perceptions of Rome in American Political Culture, 2000–2010." *International Journal of the Classical Tradition* (March 2011): 66–104.

Bush, George W. "Bullhorn Address to Ground Zero Rescue Workers." September 11, 2017. https://americanrhetoric.com/speeches/gwbush911groundzerobullhorn.htm.

———. *A Charge to Keep: My Journey to the White House*. New York: Perennial, 2001.

———. *A Distinctly American Internationalism*. November 19, 1999. https://www.mtholyoke.edu/acad/intrel/bush/wspeech.htm.

———. "President Bush Outlines Iraqi Threat." *Whitehouse.gov*. October, 2002. https://georgewbush-whitehouse.archives.gov/news/releases/2002/10/20021007-8.html.

———. *President Bush's Acceptance Speech to the Republican National Convention*. September 2, 2004. http://www.washingtonpost.com/wp-dyn/articles/A57466-2004Sep2.html.

Butler, Judith. *Frames of War: When is Life Grieveable?* London: Versi, 2010.

Cahill, Lisa Sowle. "A Church for Peace? Why Just War Theory Isn't Enough." *CommonWealMagazine.com*. July 11, 2016. https://www.commonwealmagazine.org/issues/2016-09-09.

———. *Love Your Enemies: Discipleship, Pacifism, and Just War Theory*. Minneapolis: Fortress, 1994.

———. "Just War and the Gospel." in *Can War be Just in the 21st Century? Ethicists Engage the Tradition*. eds. Tobias Winright and Laurie Johnston. 1–13. Maryknoll, NY: Orbis, 2015.

Campolo, Tony. "Undoing the Mess that America Made." October 9, 2013. https://www.redletterchristians.org/undoing-mess-america-made/.

Carpenter, F.B. *Six Months at the White House with Abraham Lincoln*. New York: Hurd and Houghton, 1866.

Cavanaugh, William T. "Terrorist Enemies and Just War." *Christian Reflections* (Center for Christian Studies at Baylor University), 2004: 27–35.

———. *Torture and Eucharist: Theology, Politics, and the Body of Christ*. Oxford: Blackwell, 2011.

Central Intelligence Agency. "CIA Activiites in Chile." September 18, 2000. https://www.cia.gov/library/reports/general-reports-1/chile/#17.

———. "CIA and Assassinations: The Guatemala 1954 Documents." *The National Security Archive at George Washington University*. Edited by Kate Doyle, & Peter Kornbluh. Undated. http://nsarchive.gwu.edu/NSAEBB/NSAEBB4/.

———. *The CIA and the House of NGO: Covert Action in South Vietnam, 1954–63*. Washington: Center for the Study of Intelligence, 2009.

———. *National Security Archive at George Washington University*. Undated. http://nsarchive.gwu.edu/NSAEBB/NSAEBB435/docs/Doc%202%20-%201954-00-00%20Summary%20of%20Wilber%20history.pdf.

———. *The World Factbook–Country Comparison: Military Expenditure*. 2016. https://www.cia.gov/library/publications/the-world-factbook/rankorder/2034rank.html.

Chadwick, Henry. *Augustine of Hippo: A Life*. Oxford: Oxford University Press, 2010.

Chapin, Harry. "Cat's in the Cradel." *Verities and Balderdash*. Comp. Harry Chapin. 1974.

Chesterton, G.K. "A Defense of Patriotism." in *The Defendant*. Freeport, NY: Books for Libraries, 1972.

Cicero. *On the Commonwealth and On the Laws*. Edited by James E. G. Zetzel. Cambridge: Cambridge University Press, 1999.

Clausewitz, Carl von. *On War*. Edited by Beatrice Heuser. Translated by Peter Paret Michael Howard. Oxford: Oxford University Press, 2007.

Coll, Steve. *Directorate S: The C.I.A. and America's Secret Wars in Afghanistan and Pakistan*. New York: Penguin, 2018.

———. *Ghost Wars: The Secret History of the CIA, Afghanistan, and Bin Laden, From the Soviet Invasion to September 10, 2001*. London: Penguin, 2005.

Columbia Law School Human Rights Clinic Sana'a Center for Strategic Studies. *Out of the Shadows: Recommendations to Advance Transparency in the Use of Lethal Force*. New York: Columbia University Press, June 2017.

Colvin, Jill. *Trump Signs Executive Order Pushing Work for Welfare*. April 11, 2018. https://www.apnews.com/6e1cc4a1ebf14cd0bba369254670c8eb/Trump-signs-executive-order-pushing-work-for-welfare.

Comittee on Oversight and Government Reform. "House Hearing, 110th Congress - Blackwater USA." *www.govinfo.gov*. October 2, 2007. https://www.govinfo.gov/content/pkg/CHRG-110hhrg45219/html/CHRG-110hhrg45219.htm.

Cone, James H. *The Cross and the Lynching Tree*. Maryknoll, NY: Orbis, 2011.

Congressional Budget Office. *The Federal Budget in 2017: An Infographic*. March 5, 2018. https://www.cbo.gov/publication/53624.

Copp, Tara. "Immigrant Soldiers Now Denied US Citizenship at Higher Rate than Civilians." May 15, 2019. https://www.mcclatchydc.com/latest-news/article230269884.html.

Coughlan, Sean. "2018 'Worst Year for US School Shootings.'" December 12, 2018. https://www.bbc.com/news/business-46507514.

Cullather, Nicholas. "Operation PBSUCESS: The United States and Guatemala 1952–1954." *National Security Archive at George Washington University*. 1994. http://nsarchive.gwu.edu/NSAEBB/NSAEBB4/docs/doc05.pdf.

Dao, James. "Drone Pilots Are Found to Get Stress Disorders Much as Those in Combat Do." February 22, 2013. https://www.nytimes.com/2013/02/23/us/drone-pilots-found-to-get-stress-disordersmuch-as-those-in-combat-do.html?_r=0.

Delaney, Arthur, and Ariel Edwards-Levy. *Americans Are Mistaken About Who Gets Welfare*. 5 February, 2018. https://www.huffingtonpost.com/entry/americans-welfare

-perceptions-survey_us_5a7880cde4b0d3df1d13f60b?ojs (accessed June 16, 2018).
De Las Cases Emmanuel–August-Dieudonné. "Mémorial de Sainte Hélène." *Journal of the Private Life and Conversations of the Emperor Napoleon at Saint Helena* 4.7 (1823) 250–52.
De Lubac, Henri. *Theological Fragments*. Translated by Rebecca Howell Balinski. San Francisco: Ignatius, 1989.
De Maistre, Joseph. *Lettres et Opuscules*. Sydney: Wentworth, 2018.
Department of Defense Joint Advertising, Market Research and Studies. "Reports: Youth Poll 20." *JAMRS.Defense.Gov*. September 2011. http://jamrs.defense.gov/Market-Research-Studies/Reports/.
Director of National Intelligence. "Summary of Information Regarding U.S. Counterterrorism Strikes Outside Areas of Active Hostilities." *DNI.gov*. n.d. https://www.dni.gov/files/documents/Newsroom/Press%20Releases/DNI+Release+on+CT+Strikes+Outside+Areas+of+Active+Hostilities.PDF.
Dodaro, Robert. *Christ and the Just Society in the Thought of Augustine*. Cambridge: Cambridge University Press, 2004.
Douglas, James W. *JFK and the Unspeakable: Why he Died and Why it Matters*. Maryknoll, NY: Orbis, 2009.
Dulles, John Foster. "Radio and Television Address on Communism in Guatemala." *Milestone Documents*. June 30, 1954. https://www.milestonedocuments.com/documents/view/john-foster-dulles-radio-and-television-address-on-communism-in-guatemala/text.
Dwyer, Colin. *U.S. Announces Its Withdrawal From U.N. Human Rights Council*. June 19, 2018. https://www.npr.org/2018/06/19/621435225/u-s-announces-its-withdrawal-from-u-n-s-human-rights-council.
Eckstein, Arthur. *Mediterranean Anarchy, Interstate War, and the Rise of Rome*. Los Angeles: University of California Press, 2006.
Ellsberg, Daniel. *Secrets: A Memoir of Vietnam and the Pentagon Papers*. London: Penguin, 2003.
Elshtain, Jean Bethke. *Augustine and the Limits of Politics*. Notre Dame, IN: University of Notre Dame Press, 2018.
———. "The Ethics of Fleeing: What America Still Owes Iraq." *World Affairs* 170.4 (Spring 2008): 91–98.
———. "Foreword." In *The Impact of 9/11 on Religion and Philosophy: The Day That Changed Everything?*, by editor Matthew J. Morgan, xi–xv. Hamshire, England: Palgrave Macmillan, 2009.
———. *Just War Against Terror: The Burden of American Power*. New York: Basic, 2003.
———. "Just War and an Ethics of Responsibility." In *Ethics: Beyond War's End*, edited by Eric Patterson. Washington, DC: Georgetown University Press, 2012.
———. "Reflection on the Problem of 'Dirty Hands'" in *Torture: A Collection*, edited by Sanford Levinson, 77–89. Oxford: Oxford University Press, 2004.
———. "A Response." *International Relations* 21.4 (2007): 502–9.
———. *Women and War*. London: University of Chicago Press, 1995.
Ferguson, Niall. *Colossus: The Rise and Fall of the American Empire*. London: Penguin, 2004.
Gay, Doug. *Honey from the Lion: Christianity and the Ethics of Nationalism*. London: SCM, 2013.

Gentry, Caron E. *Offering Hospitality: Questioning Christian Approaches to War.* Notre Dame, IN: University of Notre Dame Press, 2013.

Goff, Stan. *Borderline: Reflections on War, Sex, and Church.* Eugene, OR: Cascade, 2015.

Gregory, Eric. *Politics & the Order of Love: An Augustinian Ethic of Democratic Citizenship.* Chicago: University of Chicago Press, 2008.

Grose, Peter. *Gentleman Spy: The Life of Allen Dulles.* New York: Houghton Mifflin, 1994.

Grossman, Lt. Col. Dave. *On Killing: The Psychological Cost of Learning to Kill in War and Society.* London: Back Bay, 1996.

Grotius, Hugo. *The Rights of War and Peace.* Edited by Richard Tuck. Indianapolis: The Liberty Fund, 2005.

Gwynn, David M. *The Roman Republic: A Very Short Introduction.* Oxford: Oxford University Press, 2012.

Haines, Geral K. "CIA and Guatemala Assassination Proposals 1952–1954." *The National Security Archive at George Washington University.* June 1995. http://nsarchive.gwu.edu/NSAEBB/NSAEBB4/.

Hardt, Michael, and Antonio Negri. *Empire.* London: Harvard University Press, 2000.

———. *Multitude: War and Democracy in the Age of Empire.* New York: Penguin, 2004.

Harris, Shane, and Matthew Aid. "Exclusive: CIA Files Prove America Helped Saddam as He Gassed Iran." August 26, 2013. http://foreignpolicy.com/2013/08/26/exclusive-cia-files-prove-america-helped-saddam-as-he-gassed-iran/.

Hauerwas, Stanley. *After Christendom? How the Church Is to Behave If Freedom, Justice, and a Christian Nation Are Bad Ideas.* Nashville: Abingdon, 1991.

———. "How Real Is America's Faith?" October 16, 2010. http://www.theguardian.com/commentisfree/belief/2010/oct/16/faith-america-secular-britain.

———. *Performing the Faith: Bonhoeffer and the Practice of Nonviolence.* London: Society for Promoting Christian Knowledge, 2004.

———. "September 11, 2001: A Pacifist's Response." *The South Atlantic Quarterly* 101.2 (Spring 2002): 425–33.

———. "Taking Time for Peace: The Ethical Significance of the Trivial." In *Christian Existence Today: Essays on Church, World, and Living in Between.* Durham, NC: Labyrinth, 1988.

———. *War and the American Difference: Theological Reflections on Violence and National Identity.* Grand Rapids: Baker Academic, 2011.

Hauerwas, Stanley, Paul Griffiths, and Jean Bethke Elshtain. "War, Peace & Jean Bethke Elshtain." *First Things.* October 2003.

Hearn, J. *Rethinking Nationalism: A Critical Introduction.* Basingstoke: Palgrave Macmillan, 2006.

Hersh, Seymour M. *The Killing of Osama bin Laden.* London: Verso, 2016.

Howard, Micheal. "Smoke on the Horizon." *Financial Times*, September 7–8, 202:1.

Howe, Julia Ward. *Civil War Music: The Battle Hymn of the Republic.* n.d. http://www.civilwar.org/education/history/on-the-homefront/culture/music/the-battle-hymn-of-the-republic/the-battle-hymn-of-the.html?referrer=https://www.google.com/.

Howe, Stephen. *Empire: A Very Short Introduction.* Oxford: Oxford University Press, 2002.

Human Rights Watch. *Guantanomo: Facts and Figures.* March 30, 2017. https://www.hrw.org/video-photos/interactive/2017/03/30/guantanamo-facts-and-figures.

Ignatieff, Michael. *The Lesser Evil: Political Ethics in an Age of Terror*. Edinburgh: Edinburgh University Press, 2005.

Immerman, Richard H. *Empire for Liberty: A History of American Imperialism from Benjamin Frankilin to Paul Wolfowitz*. Oxford: Princeton University Press, 2010.

Immerwahr, Daniel. *How to Hide an Empire: A History of the Greater United States*. New York: Farrar, Straus, and Giroux, 2019.

James, Harold. *The Roman Predicament: How the Rules of International Order Create the Politics of Empire*. Woodstock, Oxfordshire: Princeton University Press, 2006.

Jerome. *Letter 127: To Principia*. In *Nicene and Post-Nicene Fathers*, edited by Kevin Knight, translated by G. Lewis and W. G. Martley W. H. Fremantle, vol. 6. Buffalo: Christian Literature, 1893.

Johnson, Chalmers. "On Garrisoning the Planet." January 15, 2004. http://www.tomdispatch.com/post/1181/chalmers_johnson_on_garrisoning_the_planet.

Kabbani, Shayk Muhammad Hisham. *What is Fatwa?* n.d. http://www.islamicsupremecouncil.org/understanding-islam/legal-rulings/44-what-is-a-fatwa.html.

Kataluyi. *The Arthashastra*. Translated by L. N. Rangarajan. London: Penguin, 2010.

Kay, David. "No Evidence Iraq Stockpiled WMDs Former Chief U.S. Inspector Faults Intelligence Agencies." January 24, 2004. http://edition.cnn.com/2004/WORLD/meast/01/25/sprj.nirq.kay/.

———. "Text of David Kay's Unclassified Statement." October 3, 2003. http://edition.cnn.com/2003/ALLPOLITICS/10/02/kay.report/.

———. "Transcript: David Kay at Senate Hearing." January 29, 2004. http://edition.cnn.com/2004/US/01/28/kay.transcript/.

Kerry, John. "Announcement Speech." p2004.org. September 2, 2003. http://p2004.org/kerry/kerr090203sp.html.

Kinzer, Stephen. *All the Shah's Men: An American Coup and the Roots of Middle East Terror*. Hoboken: John Wiley & Sons, 2008.

———. *The Brothers: John Foster Dulles, Allen Dulles, and their Secret World War*. New York: Times Books; Henry Holt, 2013.

———. *Overthrow: America's Century of Regime Change from Hawaii to Iraq*. New York: Times, 2006.

———. *The True Flag: Theodore Roosevelt, Mark Twain, and the Birth of American Empire*. New York: Henry Holt, 2017.

Kornbluh, Peter. *The Pinochet File: A Declassified Dossier on Atrocity and Accountability*. London: The New, 2003.

Layne, Christopher. "The End of Pax Americana: How Western Decline Became Inevitable." *The Atlantic*, April 26, 2012.

LeFebre, Walter, ed. *John Quincy Adams and American Continental Empire: Letters, Papers, and Speeches*. Chicago: Quadrangle, 1965.

Leithart, Peter J. *Between Babel and Beast: America and Empires in Biblical Perspective*. Eugene: Cascade, 2012.

———. *Defending Constantine: The Twilight of an Empire and the Dawn of Christendom*. Downers Grove: InterVarsity, 2010.

Lewis, C.S. *Surprised By Joy: The Shape of My Early Life*. New York: Harcourt, Brace and World, 1955.

Lipka, Michael. "U.S. Religious Groups and their Political Leanings." February 23, 2016. http://www.pewresearch.org/fact-tank/2016/02/23/u-s-religious-groups-and-their-political-leanings/.

Livy. *The History of Rome: Book 1-5*. Translated by Valerie M. Warrior. Cambridge: Hackett, 2006.

MacGregor, Sarah, and Katherine Greifeld. *China Holdings of U.S. Debt Rose in 2017 by Most in Seven Years*. February 15, 2018. https://www.bloomberg.com/news/articles/2018-02-15/china-2017-holdings-of-u-s-treasuries-rise-most-in-seven-years.

Mackenzie, Alexander Slidell. *Life of Stephen Decatur, a Commodore in the Navy of the United States*. Boston: Little and Brown, 1846.

Makamson, Collin. "Praise The Lord and Pass The Ammunition!" October 12, 2012. http://www.nww2m.com/2012/10/praise-the-lord-and-pass-the-ammunition/.

Markus, R.A. *Christianity and the Secular*. Notre Dame: University of Notre Dame Press, 2006.

———. *Saeculum: History and Society in the Theology of St. Augustine*. Cambridge: Cambridge University Press, 2007.

———. "Saint Augustine's Views on the 'Just War.'" In *The Church and War: Papers Read at the 21st Summer Meeting and the 22nd Winter Meeting of the Ecclesiastical History Society*, edited by W. J. Shiels, 1–13. Oxford: Blackwell, 1983.

Maslow, Abraham. *Toward a Psychology of Being*. NY: John Wiley and Sons, 1999.

Mathewes, Charles. *The Republic of Grace: Augustinian Thoughts for Dark Times*. Cambridge: William B. Eerdmans, 2010.

———. *A Theology of Public Life*. Cambridge: Cambridge University Press, 2008.

Mattox, John Mark. *Saint Augustine and the Theory of Just War*. London: Continuum, 2008.

Mayer, Jane. *The Dark Side: The Inside Story of How the War on Terror Turned into a War on American Ideals*. London: Doubleday, 2008.

McCarthy, Niall. "The Top 15 Countries For Military Expenditure In 2016." April 24, 2017. https://www.forbes.com/sites/niallmccarthy/2017/04/24/the-top-15-countries-for-military-expenditure-in-2016-infographic/#780273f843f3.

McGlinchey, Stephen. "Richard Nixon's Road to Tehran: The Making of the U.S.–Iran Arms Agreement of May 1972." *OxfordJournals.org*. April 12, 2013. http://dh.oxfordjournals.org/content/37/4/841.

McGregor, Sarah, and Katherine Greifeld. "China Holdings of U.S. Debt Rose in 2017 by Most in Seven Years." February 15, 2018. https://www.bloomberg.com/news/articles/2018-02-15/china-2017-holdings-of-u-s-treasuries-rise-most-in-seven-years.

Milbank, John. *Theology & Social Theory: Beyond Secular Theory*. Oxford: Blackwell, 2006.

Miroff, Nick. "Trump planning to divert additional $7.2 billion in Pentagon funds for border wall." January 13, 2020. https://www.washingtonpost.com/immigration/trump-planning-to-divert-additional-72-billion-in-pentagon-funds-for-borderwall/2020/01/13/59080a3a-363d-11ea-bb7b-265f4554af6d_story.html.

———. *Why the U.S. Base at Cuba's Guantanamo Bay is Probably Doomed*. May 15, 2015. https://www.washingtonpost.com/news/worldviews/wp/2015/05/15/why-the-u-s-base-at-cubas-guantanamo-bay-is-probably-doomed/.

Moaveni, Azadeh. *Roxana Saberi and How Journalism Works in Iran*. June 1, 2009. http://content.time.com/time/world/article/0,8599,1902080,00.html.

Multatuli. *Max Havelaar Or the Coffee Auctions of the Dutch Trading Company*. Edited by Roy Edwards. Translated by Roy Edwards. London: Penguin, 1995.

Murphy, Cullen. *Are We Rome? The Fall of an Empire and the Fate of America*. New York: Mariner, 2007.

National Commission on Terrorist Attacks Upon the United States. "The 9-11 Commission Report." August 12, 2004. http://govinfo.library.unt.edu/911/report/911Report.pdf.

National Priorities Project. *2017 Tax Receipt*. n.d. https://www.nationalpriorities.org/interactive-data/taxday/2017/taxespaid/1/.

Neuman, Scott. *Trump Signs Order To Keep Prison At Guantanamo Bay Open*. January 31, 2018. https://www.npr.org/sections/thetwo-way/2018/01/31/582033937/trump-signs-order-to-keep-prison-at-guantanamo-bay-open.

Niebuhr, Reinhold. *The Essential Reinhold Niebuhr: Selected Essays and Addresses*. Edited by Robert McAfee Brown. London: Yale University Press, 1986.

Northcott, Michael. *An Angel Directs the Storm: Apocalyptic Religion and American Empire*. London: I. B. Taurus, 2004.

———. "The Weakness of Power and the Power of Weakness: The Ethics of War in a Time of Terror." *Studies in Christian Ethics* 20.1 (2007): 88–101.

Nye, Joseph S. Jr. *Soft Power: The Means to Success in World Politics*. New York: Public Affairs, 2004.

Obama, Barack. "Nobel Lecture: A Just and Lasting Peace." *NobelPrize.org*. December 10, 2009. https://www.nobelprize.org/nobel_prizes/peace/laureates/2009/obama-lecture_en.html.

O'Daly, Gerard. *Augustine's City of God: A Reader's Guide*. Oxford: Oxford University Press, 2009.

O'Donovan, Oliver. *Common Objects of Love: Moral Relfection and the Shaping of Community*. Cambridge: Eerdmans, 2002.

———. *The Desire of the Nations: Rediscovering the Roots of Political Theology*. Cambridge: Cambridge University Press, 2003.

———. *The Just War Revisited*. Cambridge: Cambridge University Press, 2003.

———. *The Ways of Judgement: The Bampton Lectures, 2003*. Cambridge: Eerdmans, 2005.

O'Donovan, Oliver, and Joan Lockwood O'Donovan. *From Irenaeus to Grotius: A Sourcebook in Christian Political Thought*. Cambridge: Eerdmans, 1999.

Office of Management and Budget. "Budget of the United States Government, Fiscal Year 2019." *Whithouse.gov*. February, 2018. https://www.whitehouse.gov/wp-content/uploads/2018/02/budget-fy2019.pdf.

Orwell, George. "Notes on Nationalism." *England Your England and Other Essays*. Edited by T. R. Fyvel. London: Secker & Warburg, 1953.

Orwell, George. Review of *The Men I Killed by Brigadier-General F.P. Crozier*. Vol. 1, in *George Orwell: An Age Like This 1920–1940*. Edited by Ian Angus Sonia Orwell, 282–283. Boston: Nonpareil, 2000.

Percy, Martyn. "To Know Donald Trump's Faith is to Understand his Politics." February 6, 2018. https://www.theguardian.com/commentisfree/2018/feb/06/donald-trump-faith-politics-religious-presidency.

Peyrefitte, Alain. *C'était de Gaulle*. Paris: Gallimard, 2002.

Pilkington, Ed. "Life as a Drone Operator: 'Ever Step on Ants and Never Give it Another Thought?'" November 19, 2015. https://www.theguardian.com/world/2015/nov/18/life-as-a-drone-pilot-creech-air-force-base-nevada.

Platt, Orville. "Milestones:1899-1913. The United States, Cuba, and the Platt Amendment, 1901." *U.S. Department of the State*. March 2, 1901. https://history.state.gov/milestones/1899-1913/platt.

Plutarch. *The Lives of the Noble Grecians and Romans*. Edited by Arthur Hugh Clough. Translated by John Dryden. London: John Lane the Bodley Head, 1974.

Possidius, *Life of Saint Augustine*. Translated by Herbert T. Weiskotten. Merchantville, NJ: 2008.

Press, Eyal. "The Wounds of the Drone Warrior." June 13, 2018. https://www.nytimes.com/2018/06/13/magazine/veterans-ptsd-drone-warrior-wounds.html.

Raheb, Mitri. *Faith in the Face of Empire: The Bible Through Palestinian Eyes*. Maryknoll, NY: Orbis, 2014.

Ramsey, Paul. "How Shall the Counter-Insurgency War Be Conducted Justly?" in *The Just War: Force and Political Responsibility*, 427–64. Oxford: Rowman and Littlefield, 1983.

———. "The Just War According to St. Augustine." In *Just War Theory*, edited by Jean Bethke Elshtain. London: New York University Press, 1992.

———. *Speak Up for Just War or Pacifism: A Critique of the United Methodist Bishops' Pastoral Letter "In Defense of Creation."* London: Pennsylvania State University Press, 1988.

Reed, Esther D. *Theology for International Law*. London: Bloomsbury, 2013.

Reuters. "China Raises 2018 Military Budget by 8.1 Percent." March 4, 2018. https://www.cnbc.com/2018/03/04/china-raises-2018-military-budget-by-8-point-1-percent.html.

Roosevelt, Theodore. "Trasncript to Theodore Roosevelt's Corollary to the Monroe Doctrine." *ourdocuments.gov*. December 6, 1904. http://www.ourdocuments.gov/doc.php?flash=true&doc=56&page=transcript.

Rude, Emelyn. "The Very Short History of Food Stamp Fraud in America." March 30, 2017. http://time.com/4711668/history-food-stamp-fraud/.

Sandstrom, Aleksandra. *Faith on the Hill: The Religious Romposition of the 115th Congress*. January 3, 2017. http://www.pewforum.org/2017/01/03/faith-on-the-hill-115/.

Savage, Charlie. *U.S. Transfers First Guantánamo Detainee Under Trump, Who Vowed to Fill It*. May 2, 2018. https://www.nytimes.com/2018/05/02/us/politics/guantanamo-detainee-transferred-trump-al-darbi.html.

Scahill, Jeremy. *Blackwater: The Rise of the World's Most Powerful Mercenary Army*. London: Serpent's Tail, 2008.

Schaeffer, Carol. *US Citizens Own 40% of All Guns in World–More Than Next 25 Top-Ranked Countries Combined, Study Suggests*. June 19, 2018. https://www.independent.co.uk/news/world/americas/gun-ownership-country-us-legal-firearm-citizens-statistics-a8406941.html.

Senate Select Comittee on Intelligence. "Committee Study of the Central Intelligence Agency's Detention and Interrogation Program." *Senate Torture Report- FOIA*. April 24, 2017. https://www.aclu.org/cases/senate-torture-report-foia.

Shapiro, Isaac, Danilo Trisi, and Raheem Chaudhry. "Poverty Reduction Programs Help Adults Lacking College Degrees the Most." February 16, 2017. https://www.cbpp.org/research/poverty-and-inequality/poverty-reduction-programs-help-adults-lacking-college-degrees-the.

Shapiro, Walter. "Hype and Glory." September 18, 2003. https://usatoday30.usatoday.com/news/opinion/columnist/shapiro/2003-09-18-hype_x.htm.
Sherman, Nancy. *Stoic Warriors: The Ancient Philosophy Behind the Military Mind*. Oxford: Oxford University Press, 2005.
Siems, Larry. *The Torture Report: What the Documents Say About America's Post 9/11 Torture Program*. Kindle edition. London: OR, 2011.
Singer, Paul. "White Christians Decline in U.S., but still Dominate Republican Party." September 6, 2017. https://www.usatoday.com/story/news/politics/2017/09/06/white-christians-decline-but-still-dominate-republican-party/634536001/.
Slahi, Mohamedou Ould. *Guantanamo Diary*. Edited by Larry Siems. London: Back Bay, 2015.
Smith, J. Warren. "Augustine and the Limits of Preemptive and Preventitive War." *Journal of Religious Ethics* (2007): 141–62.
Smith, John Stafford (composer), and Francis Scott (lyricist) Key. "The Star Spangled Banner. Notated Music." *The Library of Congress*. Oliver Ditson. 1918. https://www.loc.gov/item/ihas.100010134/.
Stassen, Glen. ed. *Just Peacemaking: The New Paradigm for the Ethics of Peace and War*. Cleveland: Pilgrim, 2008.
State of Florida Legislature. *The 2016 Florida Statutes, 776.012*. January 1, 2005. http://www.leg.state.fl.us/statutes/index.cfm?App_mode=Display_Statute&URL=0700-0799/0776/0776.html.
Stein, Jeff. "U.S. Military Budget Inches Closer to $1 Trillion Mark, as Concerns over Federal Deficit Grow." June 19, 2018. https://www.washingtonpost.com/news/wonk/wp/2018/06/19/u-s-military-budget-inches-closer-to-1-trillion-mark-as-concerns-over-federal-deficit-grow/?utm_term=.1867a93ee440.
———. "An Explosive U.N. Report Shows America's Safety Net was Failing Before Trump's Election." June 6, 2018. https://www.washingtonpost.com/news/wonk/wp/2018/06/06/an-explosive-un-report-shows-americas-safety-net-was-failing-before-trumps-election/?utm_term=.2bd4425520e0.
Stirk, Peter M. R. *Carl Schmitt, Crown Jurist of the Third Reich: On Preemptive War, Military Occupation, and World Empire*. Lewiston, NY: Edwin Mellen, 2005.
Stockholm International Peace Research Institute. *Military Expenditure*. May 2, 2018. https://www.sipri.org/research/armament-and-disarmament/arms-transfers-and-military-spending/military-expenditure.
Swift, Louis J. *The Early Fathers on War and Military Service*. Wilmington, DE: Michael Glazier, 1983.
Taber, Robert. *War of the Flea: The Classic Study of Guerilla Warfare*. Dulles, VA: Potomac, 2002.
Taguba, Antonio M. MG. "AR 15–6 Investigation of the 800th Military Police Brigade" May 27, 2004. https://www.thetorturedatabase.org/files/foia_subsite/pdfs/DODDOA000248.pdf.
Texas Department of Criminal Justice. *Death Row Information: Gender and Racial Statistics of Death Row Offenders*. April 25, 2019. https://www.tdcj.texas.gov/death_row/dr_gender_racial_stats.html.
Trainer, Ken. "Just War: Divinity School Professor Jean Bethke Elshtain Considers the Moral Necessities of War." June 2010, http://magazine.uchicago.edu/1006/investigations/just-war.shtml.

Tolstoy, Leo. "Christianity and Patriotism." *The Spiritual Works of Leo Tolstoy*. Translated by Constantine Popoff, Louise Maude, Aylmer Maude, V. Tchertkoff, Nathan Haskell Dole Leo Wiener. Kindle Edition. Antwerp: E-Artnow, April 5, 2016.

———. "What I Believe." *The Spiritual Works of Leo Tolstoy*. Translated by Constantine Popoff, Louise Maude, Aylmer Maude, V. Tchertkoff, Nathan Haskell Dole Leo Wiener. Kindle Edition. Antwerp: E-Artnow, April 5, 2016.

Torreon, Barbara Salazar. "Instances of Use of United States Armed Forces Abroad, 1798–2017." *fas.org*. October 12, 2017. https://fas.org/sgp/crs/natsec/R42738.pdf.

Turabian, Kate L. *A Manual for Writers of Research Papers, Theses, and Dissertations: Chicago Style for Students and Researchers*. 8th ed. Edited by Wayne C. Booth, Gregory G. Colomb, Joseph M. Williams, & The University of Chicago Press Editorial Staff. London: University of Chicago Press, 2013.

UN. "Charter of the United Nations, Chapter VII: Article 51." June 26, 1945. http://www.un.org/en/sections/un-charter/chapter-vii/.

UN General Assembly. "Genocide Prevention and the Responsibility to Protext." *UN.org*. September 16, 2005. https://documents-dds-ny.un.org/doc/UNDOC/GEN/N05/487/60/pdf/N0548760.pdf?OpenElement.

US Census Bureau. *Pop Culture: 1850*. May 30, 2019. https://www.census.gov/history/www/through_the_decades/fast_facts/1850_fast_facts.html.

———. *Quick Facts: Montana*. July 1, 2017. https://www.census.gov/quickfacts/fact/table/mt/PST045217.

US Congressional Committee on Oversight and Government Reform. "House Hearing, 110th Congress–Blackwater USA." www.govinfo.gov October 2, 2007. https://www.govinfo.gov/content/pkg/CHRG-110hhrg45219/html/CHRG-110hhrg45219.htm.

US Department of Defense. "Unified Combatant Commands." *U.S. Department of Defense*. April 06, 2011. http://www.defense.gov/Sites/Unified-Combatant-Commands.

US Department of State. "Foreign Relation of the United States, 1945–1950 Retrospective Volume, Emergence of the Intelligence Establishment, Document 292." *U.S. Department of the State*. June 18, 1948. https://history.state.gov/historicaldocuments/frus1945-50Intel/d292.

———. "SECRET/NODIS, 'Secretary's Staff Meeting, October 1, 1973.'" *The National Security Archive at George Washington University*. October 4, 1973. http://nsarchive.gwu.edu/NSAEBB/NSAEBB110/chile03.pdf.

———. *The Phillipine-American War, 1899-1902*. Undated. https://history.state.gov/milestones/1899-1913/war.

US Marines. *Principles & Values*. 2016. https://www.marines.com/history-heritage/principles-values.

UN Security Council. *Israel's Settlements Have No Legal Validity, Constitute Flagrant Violation of International Law, Security Council Reaffirms*. December 23, 2016. https://www.un.org/press/en/2016/sc12657.doc.htm.

VI, Pope Paul. "Message of his Holiness Pope Paul VI for the Celebration of the Day of Peace." *The Holy See-Vaticano*. January 1, 1972. http://w2.vatican.va/content/paul-vi/en/messages/peace/documents/hf_p-vi_mes_19711208_v-world-day-for-peace.html.

Vine, David. *Base Nation: How U.S. Military Bases Abroad Harm America and the World*. New York: Metropolitan, 2015.

———. *Where in the World is the U.S. Military?* 5W Infographics. July/August 2015. http://www.politico.com/magazine/story/2015/06/us-military-bases-around-the-world-119321.

Vogel, Kenneth P., and Mike Allen. "Koch Donors Uncloaked." October 14, 2015. http://www.politico.com/story/2014/10/koch-donors-111846.html.

Walzer, Michael. *Arguing About War*. New Haven, CT: Yale University Press, 2004.

———. *Just and Unjust Wars: A Moral Argument with Historical Illustrations*. New York: Basic, 2006.

———. "The Triumph of Just War Theory (and the Dangers of Success)." *Social Research: International Justice, War Crimes, and the U.S. Record* (Winter 2002): 925–44.

Will, George. "Scalia Missed Point But Made Right Argument on Separation of Religion." *Durham Morning Herald*, April 22, 1990, section f.

Williams, Rowan. *On Augustine*. London: Bloomsbury, 2016.

Winright, Tobias, and Laurie Johnston. *Can War Be Just in the 21st Century? Ethicists Engage the Tradition*. Maryknoll, New York: Orbis, 2015.

Wynn, Phillip. *Augustine on War and Military Service*. Minneapolis: Fortress, 2013.

X, Malcolm. "The Race Problem." Speech to the African Students Association and NAACP Campus Chapter. Michigan State University. East Lansing, MI: January 23, 1963.

X, Malcolm, and Alex Haley. *The Autobiography of Malcolm X as Told to Alex Haley*. New York: Ballantine, 1999.

Yoder, John Howard. "Limits of Obedience to Caesar." In *John Howard Yoder Digital Collection*, 1–15. Goshen: Goshen College, 1978.

———. *The Priestly Kingdom: Social Ethics as Gospel*. Notre Dame, IN: University of Notre Dame Press, 2001.

———. "The Things That Are Caesar's, Part I." *Christian Living* (July 1960): 4–5, 34.

———. "The Things That Are Caesar's, Part II." *Christian Living* (August 1960): 14–17, 39.

———. "Why I Don't Pay All of My Income Tax." *Gospel Herald*, January 22, 1963: 81, 92.

Subject Index

Abel, offering of, 78
Abraham, 78, 101
absolute poverty, living in, 187
Abu Ghraib military prison, 40n48, 131, 134–35, 198
Achilles, 79
actions, having many consequences, 147
acts, of violence as morally upright, 100
"acts of war," 9/11 attacks as, 122
Adam and Eve, desire to be *Sicut Deus* (like God), 143n122
Adams, John Quincy, 19, 192
Adams-Onis Treaty, 21
Addington, David, 39
Afghanistan, 35n35, 123, 125, 127, 201
African Americans, 2n4, 59n109, 132n80, 169n8
Agamben, Giorgio, 42, 43
agape (neighborly love), Augustine on, 116
agrarian reform, of Arbenz, 32
al Qaeda, 9, 35n35, 42n55, 135, 176
Alaska Purchase, 21
al-Assad, Bashar, 152n156
Alexander the Great, 83
allegiances, competing, 173
Allende, Salvador, 36, 37
al-Muslimi, Farea, 189–90
Alypius, 110
Ambrose, 66, 161n193
America, as an unconventional empire, 9–10, 18–64
American, meaning of being, 5

American business, intercession by the US government on behalf of, 32
American caricature, incarnation of, 2
"American Century," since World War II, 193
American Christians
    conditioned by Niebuhrian realist sensibilities, 6
    deification of the polity by, 173
    failing to see the urgency in practicing just war, 149
    orienting within the contemporary American context, 12
    reconciling the competing claims of their faith and citizenship, 8
    sharing Augustine's lot, 193
    turning away from objects of contempt, 204
    understanding their nation's role in world affairs, 15
American context, Christian ways of inhabiting, 165
American dream, of amassing wealth, 8
American empire, perpetual "war on terror," 8
American experience, immersion in violence, 3
American hegemony, 114, 143
American liberators, refused to leave Cuba, 25
American Republic, 58, 59
American Revolution, 45
American Territorial Acquisitions, 1803–1898, 21

Americanism, 50, 193
Americans
  fated to be "free," 54
  fighting and buying across the continent, 19–20
  forty million living in poverty, 187
  guilty of paying taxes filling war chests, 176
  living in a state of perpetual fear and uncertainty, 56
  rest of the world not wanting to be like them, 51
  small handful wielding clout, 59
Anglo-Iranian Oil Company, 30
Answer to Faustus, a Manichean, 91
"antecedent assumptions," America's as bellicose, 163
Apringius (African proconsul), letter to, 74
Aquinas, Thomas, 153, 153n158, 156
Arabs, US arming, 129n64
Araya, Commander, 37
Arbenz, Jacobo, 29n23, 32
"arbitrary power," 120
Arendt, Hannah, 78, 79, 119, 168n3
Aristides, 63
Armas, Carlos Castillo, 33, 34
armed services, anguishing over moral decisions, 15
Asad, Talal, 196n3
assassination, 29, 29n23, 33, 197
assimilation, of Christianity and Rome, 73
atomic bombs, on Japanese cities, 28n21
atrocity, 125n56
Augustine
  accommodating the American imperial project and "war on terror," 165
  advocated coercion against the Donatists, 159
  agreeing that Rome would not fully obey Christ, 7
  avoided sanctification of government, 116
  becoming Bishop of Hippo, 66
  biographies of, 66n5
  born a citizen of Rome, 107–8
  as both faithful disciple of Christ and subject of the Roman Empire, 70
  calling on the state to perform its police function, 159
  commended the use of coercive force, 95
  as a constructive guide for American Christians, 165
  council for contemporary Christian Americans, 202–3
  on the courage to pursue Christ in a foreign land, 127n60
  as a cypher for liberal democratic participation, 70n18
  disturbed by a sacral conception of the Empire, 72n28
  on effects of Constantine's conversion, 72–73
  on empires, 10–11
  encouraged pilgrims to make use (*uti*) of peace, 203
  faulted Donatists, 105–6
  favoring forgiveness over retribution, 112
  having no political preference, 82
  held tribunals, mediating disputes, 73
  as an imperial citizen, 199
  importing civil society's instruments for establishing order, 160
  imprint upon Christian and Western thought, 66
  intended to excise or confine violence, 198
  inviting Donatist leaders to a public debate, 145
  justifying activities foreign to him, 10
  on Lucretia's response, 76
  on the "lust to dominate," 22
  with Marcellinus and Apringius as Christians, 74
  maturing into a reluctant realist, 163
  on the moral fortifications of Rome, 55
  motivations of, 66

SUBJECT INDEX

mourned the dead's lost margin for repentance, 141
not an advocate for unfettered violence, 7n14
not calling for swift and retributive justice, 125
not concerned with who ruled over the people, 145
not wanting to use coercion against Donatists, 105
political and theological reflections of, 65
providing groundwork for Christian participation in violence, 7
on rather be killed than kill, 152–53
refused to baptize the empire as wholly Christian, 71
rejecting a policy of preventive military action, 90
repurposing, 200–202
route to becoming a Christian disciple, 66n8
as a self-consciously imperial subject, 70, 113
on a "shared understanding of the nature of reconciliation," 183
spending the majority of his final years of life in his library, 109–10
on "splendid vices," 51
supporting a merciful sentence against clerics guilty of violent crimes, 74
on the task of the judge who must torture to assess guilt, 11
theological lens of, 198–200
tilting the scales of justice toward mercy, 74
as too skeptical of government for Niebuhr, 115n14
as a trustworthy example of Christian witness, 184
trying to find a thread through the no-man's-land of war and empire, 118
on war as neither the greatest evil nor peace the highest good, 148
as a wise shepherd nurturing his sheep, 199
would not have advocated for war in perpetuity, 127
Augustine and the Limit of Politics (Elshtain), 117, 118, 200
Augustinian just-war tradition, coopting of, 118
"Augustinian undertow," in a world of sin and evil, 161
Augustus Caesar, 57, 58, 97n126
author of life and peace, fearing, 90
authority, 81, 82, 100, 139, 150, 151, 181
author's father, refusing to place his hand over heart, 4
"auxiliaries," foreign fighters known as, 61
"awkward question," Augustinianism's, 185

Babel, emulating, 50
baptism, 6, 15
"barbarian" immigration, making them Roman, 69n11
barbarian invaders, of Rome, 199
"barbarians," US buying off, 47
barriers, 80, 121
Barth, Karl, 1n1, 191n76
Batista, Fulgencio, 24n12
The Battle Hymn of the Republic, 52
Bay of Pigs invasion, of Cuba, 24n12
belief in God, making a difference in waging war, 157
Bell, Daniel, 114, 146–58, 202
Bible, on the political construct of empire, 50
Biggar, Nigel, 14, 114, 137, 141, 161, 201
bin Laden, Osama, 42n55, 145, 175–76
biographies, of Augustine, 66n5
Bishop of Hippo, Augustine becoming, 66
bishops, 73, 74
Black Americans. *See* African Americans
black lives, mattering because all lives matter, 186
"black sites," CIA's use of, 9

Blackwater, billions in federal contracts, 62
Blair, Tony, 137, 201
Bobbitt, Philip, 41, 63
Bonhoeffer, Dietrich, 191n76
Boniface, letter to, 93–94
border wall, building, 187n63
Borderline: Reflections on War, Sex, and Church (Goff), 16
borders, protecting from attack, 89
Bosnia, genocide, 201
Bowden, Mark, 134
bribes, influencing journalists, 31
British colonization, of the Americas, 19
brothers, rarely governing together equitably, 139
Brown, Peter, 55n99, 64, 66n5, 67n8, 70, 71, 108, 159n188
Budapest Memorandums on Security Assurances, promises to Ukraine, 128n62
"The Burden of American Power in a Violent World," 200
Bureau of Investigative Journalism, statistics on drone strikes, 189
"bureaucrats," modern requiring citizens's votes, 174
Burton, Paul, 56, 58, 60, 63
Bush, George H. W., 38
Bush, George W.
　apologia circuit, 200
　authorization of "enhanced interrogation techniques," 11
　called Jesus the "author of a divine plan that supersedes all human plans," 172n17
　continuous "war on terror," torture, and assassinations, 173n17
　invaded Iraq on the word of a single informant, 124n51
　meaning of "compassionate conservative," 136
　on the story of America as expanding liberty, 18
　use of the term crusade describing the US "war on terror," 129

Bush White House
　Elshtain invited to, 118
　on Geneva Conventions, 39

Caecilian, Catholic bishop of Carthage, 104
Caesar, Julius, 57
Cahill, Lisa Sowle, 114, 158–62, 161n193, 201, 202
Caiaphas, the high priest, 184n52
Cain, 3, 78
Cameron, Ronnie, 49n84
Campolo, Tony, 126, 129n66
capital punishment, 2, 204n8
capitalism, pursuit of material comforts, 53
caritas (equitable care), 117, 120, 159, 166, 180, 180n39, 204
Carthage, 61
Castille, Philando, 132n80
Castro, Fidel, 24n12
casuistry, 135
Catholics, sought protection from violence of Donatists, 69n12, 106
Cato the Younger, 76–77
Cavanaugh, Bill, 122
Central Intelligence Agency (CIA). See CIA (Central Intelligence Agency)
Chadwick, Henry, 44, 66, 66n5, 67, 110, 111
chemical weapons, 38
Cheney, Dick, 39, 122n49
Chesterton, G. K., 184n53
child, striking out of love, 102
childhood memories, of the author's father, 4
children of God, living fearlessly, 90
Chile, 36–38
China, 48, 144n128
Christ. See Jesus Christ
Christian citizens, 8, 64, 169, 175
Christian disciples, 79, 180, 181
Christian discipleship, just war as, 148
Christian emperor, 100

SUBJECT INDEX

Christian engagement, in the political, 170n11
Christian participation, in government, 161
"Christian realist," Niebuhr as, 115
Christian ruler, 172
Christianity, 13, 71, 75, 86
Christianity and America, as two competing stories, 8
Christians
    better equipped to recognize between the liberty and freedom, 52
    bound to a community of servants, 54
    called to be holy, 17
    called to be justice, 166
    empowered to inhabit the good, 6
    engaging American structures and institutions, 164
    fighting against invisible enemies, 94
    fit to bear the yoke of repentance, 177
    as free to live in service of others, 153
    having to rule differently, 100, 164
    helping to be careful about what we say, 165
    as imperial pilgrims, 108
    justifying killing, 161
    not called to be powerful or respectable or patriotic or masculine, 17
    obeying laws that do not violate their religion, 99
    participating in and supporting wars, 188
    persecution of by US allies and recipients of foreign aid, 50
    waging a just war on terror, 157
    witnessing to the gospel truth, 12
church
    American declaring that the US was founded upon Christian principles, 3
    becoming invisible under Constantine, 157n177
    challenging dubious civil practices, 183
    complicity with American use of coercive violence, 7–8
    dependent on the state for the execution of war, 151
    forming character and consciences of members, 151
    fractured nature of, 150
    just-war discourse and, 202
    not waging war, 158
    overcoming marginalization, 157
    as a people called to contemplate "other ways," 141
    propagating peace at home, 202
    reasserting as an independent political entity, 151
    role in public and political authority, 150
    as Rome's evangelist or its convert, 72
    speaking to the world truthfully, 5n7
"church as mixture," 73
churches, 171n12, 192
churchgoer, embraced the ecclesial free market, 192
CIA (Central Intelligence Agency)
    acting without oversight, 29n22
    creation of, 27–28
    lists of political adversaries in Guatemala, 33n31
    pre-emptive coup against Allende, 36
    threatened detainees with harm to their families, 40
    torture report of innocent detainees, 131
"CIA and Assassinations," training manual, 29n23
Cicero, 75, 83–84
cities
    of man and God, 77
    never free from risk, 90
citizens
    encouraged to participate by voting, 59
    faith in the substitutionary atonement, 52

citizens *(continued)*
  as fully vested shareholders, 171–78
  obliged to kill in the name of their countries, 53
  proximity to national sin, 174
  repudiating moral perfectionism and spiritual autonomy, 183
citizen's army, becoming a mercenary force, 61
Citizen's United decision, 49
citizenship, 61, 166
city of Christ, never once fought back, 103
city of God, 96n121, 98, 113, 121, 182
The City of God against the Pagans (Augustine), 68
city of man, wielding the sword, 182
"city on a hill," calling into question, 196
civic idol, elevation of mammon to, 53
civic leadership, Christians to participate in, 99–100
civic participation, repentance as the opening move, 168
civic responsibility, 193
civil authorities, proper authority residing in, 101
civil disobedience movement, repentance as, 171n12
civil servants, resorting to illicit behaviors, 29
Civil War, 57, 58–59, 121
civilians
  butchery of after war has ended, 119
  contributing to their nation's war discourse, 14
  death or injury, 190
  intentional decimation of as beyond the pale, 156
  lacking authority on policy recommendations, 15
  participation in the America project, 176
  percent killed in war, 187
civitas, defending by any means available, 174
civitas terrena (earthly city), self-love and, 115
"clash of civilizations," 126, 172

classic imperialism, embodiment of, 24
Classical Empire, British Empire as, 22
classical empires, expansion of, 19
classical imperialism, as anathema to Americans, 18
"classically imperial" actions, of the US, 197
Clausewitz, Carl von, 44n67
climate change denial, 204n8
"Coalition of the Willing," 124n52
coercion, 53, 93, 112, 134, 136, 139, 159n188, 199
coercive force, Christian deployment of, 70
coercive means, questioning of, 196–97
coercive political rule, for the period after the fall, 81n62
Cold War, between the US and the Soviet Union, 22
collective good, lovingly seeking, 153–54
colonialism, death of, 197
colonists, American wanted a representative in parliament, 45
combatants, hiding behind a human shield, 155
commerce, war as the continuation of, 44–49
commercial interests, US intervened in Cuba to safeguard, 25
commercial republic, taming and domesticating religious fervor, 52
commodification, of worship, 192
common good, 6, 151, 152, 154
"common objects," of Roman society, 87
"common objects of love," of Augustine, 87n86
commonwealth, 84n69, 116
"Communist domino effect," fearing, 35
"Communist imperialism," in Guatemala, 34
Communist lust for power, Dulles accused Arbenz of serving, 33–34
compassion, authentic eradicating contempt and distancing, 120
complicity, varying degrees of, 166

SUBJECT INDEX

compromise, 159, 191
compulsion, problematic potential of, 105
concord, with a good neighbor, 85
concubine, Augustine's relationship with, 67n8
Cone, James, 169n8
Confederate Army, enlisting slaves, 62
confession, of being born with "dirty hands," 194
confessions, secured by torture, 102
The Confessions, Augustine's autobiography, 66n5
conflict, absence of, 90
congruencies, between the US and Rome, 57–64
conscience, 177, 189
conscription, US routinely staffing its military rolls, 62
consent of the ruled, empires based on, 63
conservatives, 186, 204n8
Constantine, 47, 71–74, 71n20, 104, 157n177
consumer choice, freedom to worship the god of, 54
contrition, as patriotic, 170
controversies, regularly finding Augustine, 67–68
conversion, of Paul, 106
corn production, gods and goddesses for, 84
Cornelius, 94
corporate money, influx into the electoral process, 60
corporations, as people, 49
country, not loving unconditionally, 14
courage, reflecting justice, 161n193
court ordered warrants, seeking prior to torture, 136
covenantal loves, placing claim on life, 14
covert operations, of the CIA, 28
Creech Air Force base, outside Las Vegas, 188
Crimea, 140n113
Cronkite, Walter, interview with Kennedy, 36

the cross, 54, 81n63, 138
crucifixion, of Christ as a suicide, 196n3
Crusades, Elshtain's defense of, 129n66
Cuba, wresting away from Spanish control, 24–25
Cuban missile crisis, in 1962, 24n12
cultural magnetism, of the US, 197–98
cultural production, attractiveness of, 60
cyber weapons, sending, 48

Count Darius, letter to, 94
David, 94
de Gaulle, Charles, 47
de Lubac, Henri, 70n15
death penalty, 199, 204n8
death sentences, on people of color in Texas, 2n4
death-avoidance practices, of America, 8
Decatur, Stephan, 184n53
December 7, 1942, 16
deeds, 79, 91
DeFazio, Peter, 49n84
Defending Constantine (Leithart), 72
defense, 16, 47, 172
defense budget, 47, 187
defense contractors, 62
defensive protection of one's neighbors, advocated by Augustine, 199
defensive war, 89n96, 96–97
dehumanization, of inmates at *Abu Ghraib*, 135
democracies, 171, 197
democratic republic, complicating repentance, 12
deontology, 134
depression, among drone operators, 189
Dershowitz, Alan, 136
detainees, detention and torture of, 39
detention, of an intellectually challenged man, 40n50
Diem, Ngo Dinh, 35, 36
diplomacy, money spent on compared to defense, 47
disciples of Jesus, 79, 88, 179
discipleship, 148
discipline, 101, 140, 201

disposition, evolution of Augustine's, 163–64
"dispositions of the heart," 93
disputes, as seeds of animosity, 68
dissent, growing out of a place of repentance, 183
diversity, US, 192
"divine disturbances," 5
Dodaro, Robert, 89, 180, 183
dog, becoming too weakened by the flea, 46n72
domestic political rules, maintaining the status quo, 49
domination, as glory's corollary desire, 95
Donatists
    on Augustine as inadequately Christian, 68
    Augustine defended the Catholic Church against, 67
    Augustine early sought to be a peacemaker to, 104
    baulked against Augustine's appeal to Rome, 105
    comparing Augustine's struggles with to the "war on terror," 114
    Mathewes peculiar reading of Augustine's struggle against, 145
    violence of, 105, 199
Donatus, letter to, 107
"double effect," 153n158, 156
Douglas, James, 29n22
draft, activation of, 62n114
draft riots, understood as class warfare, 62n113
Dresden civilians, firebombed in 1944, 28n21
drone data, as difficult to pinpoint, 189n70
drone policy, morally dubious, 131
drone strikes, releasing results of, 190
drones, 9, 188, 189
dual citizenships, 10, 77
dulce et decorum est pro Patria mori, "old lie," 50
Dulles, Allen, as former UFC president, 32

Dulles, John Foster, 30, 32, 33, 33n33, 34, 35n36
Dulles brothers, 30–31, 32, 33, 33n32

earthly authority, Augustine not demonizing all, 82
earthly city, 77, 125
earthly glory, as always insecure, 87–88
earthly kingdoms, 78, 81
earthly peace, 97, 99, 118, 158
earthly polity, pilgrims making use of, 183
ecclesial courts, of Rome, 73–74
Eckstein, Arthur, 63
economic and military doctrine, as often indistinguishable, 197
economic and military dominance, unmistakable earmarks of empire, 46
economic influence, of the US, 47
economic self-interest, US pursuit of, 169
economic welfare, US prioritizing over foreign freedom and liberty, 45
economics, maintained by military means, 44n67
Eisenhower, Dwight, 30, 32
electoral college, refusal to abandon, 60
electrical plant, uses of, 155
"elephantiasis," political sort of, 85–86
Ellsberg, Daniel, 171n12
Elshtain, Jean Bethke, 117–36
    on altruistic "nation-building," 129
    arguing for a new American imperialism, 200
    on authentic compassion, 180n39
    authoring "What We're Fighting For" in response to 9/11, 127
    diagnosed America with Roman volatility, 122
    getting hands "dirty" to affect a greater good, 136
    hesitancy to embrace earthly peace, 119
    theological apologist for the George W. Bush administration, 114, 200

on unacceptable forms of defense, 121n42
on war as the only possible recourse, 125
Emeritus, the Donatist Bishop of Caesarea, 106
empathy, at least feigning for the electorate, 175
emperor, 58, 100
empire, 83–90
  Augustine on, 10–11
  definition of, 18–19
  demise facilitated by getting too large, 85
  growth of as a gift of God, 86
  as human rule supplanting God's sovereignty, 143
  as most vulnerable at the fringe, 48
  as a neutral concept for Augustine, 193
  as noble opposition to some encroaching evil, 89
  Roman, 58, 83, 97n126, 108, 193n85
  United States as, 18, 46
  in the West raising the specter of Rome, 55
"enemies," growth of the number of, 86
"enemies of the state," Chileans branded as, 38
enemy, 56, 141, 154
"enhanced interrogation," 39–41
"enlightened self-interest," Biggar on, 137
enmity, for the US, 4–5
"enmity with the world," 158
equitable care (*caritas*). See *caritas* (equitable care)
eternal city, founded on the judgment of truth, 88
eternal life, 100
eternal peace, belonging exclusively to the heavenly city, 97
"ethic of responsibility," of Elshtain, 131
ethicists, 14–15, 114
ethics, 1, 191
ethics and sin, as conjoined twins, 1n1
Eusebius, 71, 72, 82

evangelicals, as another extreme political lobby, 182
evil
  Augustine's conception of, 115, 119
  choosing the least, 6
  defined by the absence of good, 115n10
  need for violence to restrain, 112
  not repaying with, 7
  overcoming with good, 181
"exceptional cases to act," 27
exceptionalism, 154
excessive realist, 115–17, 199
executions, in the United States, 2
"executive action," as a euphemism for murder, 33n31
expansionist spirit, of the US, 19, 86
external enemy, in the absence of, 121
"extraordinary renditions," kidnapping suspects, 39
"extreme poverty," 187

"failed state," as ambiguous, 130
faith, in the transformation of the world, 80
fallenness, giving priority to humanity's, 148
"false news," 191
false peace, 119
father
  disciplining his child to death, 142
  disciplining his son, 102, 138, 140, 201
  preferring to correct his child through verbal reasoning, 13
fatwa, 175n25
Faustus, answer to, 91
fear
  among people who have no certitude of a life after this one, 44
  Augustine on rightly ordered, 125
  imperial societies fomenting, 88, 89
  infiltrating an empire, 86
  living with cultivating humility, 90
  turning Elshtain into an ardent jingoist, 201

Federalists, 61n112
Felix of Aptungi, 104
Ferguson, Niall, 25n13, 45–46, 49
fetuses, rights of, 167
"few teeth have been pulled" misappropriation, of the just war tradition, 149
Filipino nationalists, 26
financial, military, and political coercion, convergence of, 10
financial transaction tax, DeFazio advocated, 49n84
fire, eliminating the dross from the gold, 92
fiscal hyperextension, 48
flail, cutting up the straw and cleansing the grain, 92
flea, guerrilla fighting the war of, 46n72
Floyd, George, 132n80
fly, swatting with a sledgehammer, 156–57
followers of Jesus, as nonviolent, 138
food stocks, profiteering generals mismanaged, 69n11
football, 3
force, 100, 159n188
foreign aid, purchasing influence, 47
foreign iniquity, 85, 121
foreign lands, settlers encroaching into, 20
foreign outsiders, castigating as "other" or "ungrievable," 169n9
foreign personnel, hired as defense contractors, 62
foreign policy decision-making, locus of, 10
foreign proxies, direct manipulation of, 197
foreign soldiers, Rome contracted with, 61
foreign usurper, US legacy as, 34
forgiveness, 168n3
founding fathers, in the first anti-colonial revolution, 19
France, withdrew from Vietnam in 1954, 35
Franklin, Benjamin, 57

fraternal justice, not resonating with Augustine's thought, 139
fratricides, characterizing the city of man, 78
free will, Americans exercising, 176
freedom, 15, 53n95, 54, 87
Freedom Partners Action Fund, 49
free-market economy, forces that manipulated, 9
French, wanting everyone else to recognize French superiority, 51
friends, apprehension they may become enemies, 86
frontier, of an empire as indefinite, 49
frui, pursued for their own enjoyment, 98

G-7, members of, 140n111
G-20, accounting for 80 percent of global GDP, 140
Gadsden Purchase, 21
gang, defined, 83
Gates of Janus, remained open during wartime, 96, 97n126
Geneva Accords, divided Vietnam, 35
Geneva Conventions, US played fast and loose with, 39
"Genocide Prevention and the Responsibility to Protect," 152n156
genocides, in Rwanda and Bosnia, 131
genuine peace, underwritten by *caritas*, 194
global fraternity, Biggar's notion of, 140
global markets, manipulated, 46
global order and economy, America's role in, 143
global stage, stabilizing US presence on, 198
globalization, market-state terror as product of and response to, 42n55
glory, 86, 95
God
  alone as good, 204
  conferring authority, 150

confounding Christian moral self-
    justification, 5
failed to restrain the Hutus, 138
Jesus calling his own Father, 179
overseeing the rise and fall of all
    empires, 86
ruling on earth through
    Constantine, 71
God, guns, and glory, Holy American
    Trinity of, 23n9
"God Bless the USA," Lee Greenwood's
    performance of, 4
gods, of Rome grew with the empire, 84
God's people, redemption and
    sanctification of, 148
Goff, Stan, 16, 28n21, 142n118
Gonzalez, Alberto, 39, 136n97
good men, taken by the bad, 88
good Samaritan, parable of, 54
Good Shepherd, 142, 196n3
goods and evils, moral calculus of, 133
gospel, complicating rights as a US
    citizen, 6
gospel peacemaking, 162
Goths, 68–69n11, 146
governance, by Christians as a blessing,
    100
government, 80, 81n63, 121, 122
governors and ministers, self-interested,
    16
grace, understanding over sin, 147
Great Britain, raising taxes on a variety
    of goods, 45
Gregory, Eric, 70
Grotius, Hugo, 146
Guadalupe-Hidalgo, 21
Guam, acquired from Spain, 24
Guantanamo Bay, 25n15
"guarantor of human dignity," US as,
    130
"guardians," of the people of God, 50n86
Guatemala, US intervention in, 32–35
guerrilla warfare, difficulty in, 46n72
gun ownership rights, 204n8

Haas, Michael, 188–89
hacking, 48

Haley, Nikki, 140n112
Hamas, 42n55
Han Chinese empire, Roman empire
    smaller, 63n123
happiness, 89
"hard (militarily or economically
    coercive) power," abundance of
    US, 60
hardness of God, as kinder than the
    softness of men, 105
Harris County, capital punishment
    convictions, 2n4
Haspel, Gina, 40
Hauerwas, Stanley
    on American Christians, 8
    on capitulation to violence, 191
    on the Founding Fathers' intentions,
        53
    on God giving time to learn to be at
        peace, 137n103
    on the honor code of the US
        military, 15
    on September 11 hijackers as "mass
        murderers," 122
    summarizing Yoder's "Constantinian
        problem," 157n177
Hawaii, annexed economically before it
    became a US state, 24
Hawaiian Queen Liliuokalani, 23
heavenly city
    calling forth citizens from all
        peoples, 99
    citizens of, 79–80
    growing through humbling at the
        foot of the cross, 88
    increasing its census when grace
        liberates a former slave from the
        bondages of sin, 77–78
    making use of earthly and temporal
        things, 98
    not needing to withdraw from the
        earthly, 80
heavenly kingdom, as detached from
    history, 159
Hebrew nationalism, returned Jesus's
    conviction and sentence, 184n52
Helms, Richard, 36n39
heresies, writing a catalogue of all, 110

histories, as necessarily selective by nature, 23
history
    American, 9, 65
    Augustine desacralizing human, 185
    between Cuba and the United States, 24n12
    Napoleon on, 23
    Roman, 67
    secularization of human, 185
    US, 59, 64
    of US engaging the "other," 10
Ho Chi Minh, 35
holistically pro-life, 167, 186–93, 204
Holy American Trinity, of God, guns, and glory, 23n9
"holy wars," forswearing, 172
homeland and government, rightly ordered love of one's, 14
Homer, 79
house negro, parable of, 173n18
housing bubble, in the US, 47
Howe, Stephen, 18–19
human authority, exposing the legitimacy of, 181
human body, comparing the empire to, 85
human community, as *civitas terrena*, 115
human history, Augustine desacralizing, 185
humans
    effects of sin in, 115
    God giving power to individual, 81
    as inherently social beings, 160
    sinful nature of, 101
    as social by nature, 120
    striving for earthly immortality as futile, 79
humility, 82, 167–71
Huns, 69n11
Huntsville, Texas, sanctioned executions in, 2
husband, physically coercing his partner, 142
Hussein, Saddam, 38, 124

identification, with one's homeland, 8
ideologues, US assaulted by, 124
Ignatieff, Michael, 129, 147
"illegal enemy combatants," terrorists as, 39
immigration, as a heated political polemic, 169n9
"immortal fame," striving after, 79
immortality, 78, 79
imperial citizen and Christian bishop, Augustine as, 114
imperial city, could not rule over provinces, 115n12
imperial coercion, Augustine's advocacy of, 104
imperial context, conducting ourselves within, 166
imperial dilemma, Augustine's evaluation of, 110
imperial disposition, of the US, 27
imperial expressions, US pivoted from openly classical to unconventional, 29
"imperial necessities," Christian complicity with, 107n176
imperial overstretch, 10, 130, 144–45, 197, 199
imperial pilgrims, 12–13, 165–66, 202–4
imperial practices, US and, 198
imperial pretentions, of the US since its inception, 165, 202
imperial society, impossible to be just, 89
imperial subject, obedient to the gospel, 93
imperial virtue, understanding of, 86–87
imperialism
    American, 9, 22n7, 47, 132, 200, 203
    Augustine's reluctance to embrace or reject, 108
    called freedom, 3
    classic, 24
    classical, 18
    Communist, 34
    defense of, 139
    instability inherent within, 86
    John Howard Yoder on, 71

SUBJECT INDEX

maintaining the apparatuses of the empire, 19
nationalism carrying the same historical baggage, 130n68
as one word certain to reinvigorate animus, 130
as the solution for Elshtain, 129
World War II forced it to evolve, 22
In Defence of War (Biggar), 137, 201
in extremis, 133
"In God we trust," as appropriately written on every dollar bill, 192
in loving God, we also love our neighbor, 120
"inadvertent empire," 114, 143
inalienable rights, 52
the in-between space, with no declared war, 133
"Indian Territory," 20n5
indigenous people, exploitation of America's, 169n8
individual strikes, including the legal basis for, 190–91
influence, non-territorial empire of, 60
infrastructure, of a nation, 155
inhabiting the good, 148
injuries, pardoning rather than avenging, 93
injustices, unconventional means of addressing, 155
the innocent, loving more than the guilty, 154
innocent civilians, compensating the families of, 190
innocent neighbor, distinguishing from the aggressive neighbor, 141
"insoluble dilemma," of Williams, 172n17
instability, inherent within imperialism, 86
"insurrection," Philippine-American War referred to as, 26n17
Internal Revenue Service (IRS), Yoder's letter to, 187–88
international economic policy, determined by prominent countries (the G-7), 140
international lawlessness, imperial pretension of prosecuting, 145
international laws, circumvented, 9
international prerogative, US exercising over "poor stewards," 27
International Telephone and Telegraph (ITT), 36n39
internet, US Department of Defense created, 57n103
Internet traffic, monitoring of, 48
interrogation techniques, in Guantanamo Bay, Cuba, 39
intervention, allies produced by, 34
Iran, 4, 30–32, 32n28, 48, 197
Iraq, 124n51, 125, 195, 201
Iraq War, tragedy of, 132n74
Irish Republican Army, 42n55
Isaac, 78, 101
Isaiah, 168
Ishmael, 78
Islam, 129n66, 175n27
Islamic State (IS), *al Qaeda* replaced by, 9
Islamists, opposing American values, 125–26
isolationism, 130
isolationist heritage, from the framers of the constitution, 19
Israel, apartheid state on Palestinian land, 140

James, Harold, 46
Janus's temple, gates of war, 96, 97n126
Jean, Botham, 132n80
Jeroboam, 81n63
Jerome, 55, 64
Jessen, Bruce, 39
Jesus Christ
admonition against public displays of self-aggrandizing religious practice, 177
bearing witness to the truth, 178
blood of, 78
call to love one's neighbor, 154
came to set us free from the power of sin, 148
with the centurion in Luke 7, 91

SUBJECT INDEX

Jesus Christ *(continued)*
    chose a donkey for his entry into Jerusalem, 195
    command to "not resist the one who is evil," 6
    considered a political rival to Rome, 184n52
    describing a more robust notion of witness, 179
    executed as a threat to law and order, 181–82
    on his relationship with the Father, 179
    interrogated by Pilate, 178
    as Lord, 54
    not hamstringing witness altogether, 180
    not restraining Saul with words but "laid him low by his power," 106
    on our treasures revealing our hearts, 87
    pleased with the centurion who understood authority, 94
    on practicing righteousness" discretely, 79
    refusal to engage in the political power struggles of his day, 196
    refusal to violently defend himself, 138
    response to the mob that brought the adulteress before him, 101–2
    teaching about forgiveness not mentioning a public/private dichotomy, 177
    teachings against violence and resisting evil, 159
    told his disciples to not fear those who kill the body, 88
    used physical and rhetorical violence, 138
    using force and afterwards teaching Paul, 106
Jews, seeking to kill Jesus, 178–79
jihad, authority belonging exclusively to an *Imam*, 176n27
Jim Crow laws, 59n109, 169n8
John the Baptist, 79n57, 87, 91, 93, 179
Johnson, Andrew, 58
Johnson, Chalmers, 48
journalism, as sensationally commodified sell ads, 191
"joy of blessedness," as the church's "peculiar possession," 99
judge, applying torture, 103
Julian of Eclanum, 110
jus post bellum (justice after war), 131, 132
"A Just and Lasting Peace" (Obama), 43–44
just cause, 123–24, 151, 153
just judge, 102
"just occupation," 132
"just peace," 161
"just peacebuilding," 162
"just peace-making," 155, 202
just response, with proportionate force, 156
just war
    Augustine's views on, 111
    Christian church embodying, 151
    as Christian discipleship, 149–50, 152, 155, 202
    criteria, 91, 147
    as an imperial phenomenon, 139
    narrative, 141
    as the prerogative of the most powerful, 198
    principles, 148n142
    reproving domestic and international order, 119
    response, issues obfuscating, 124
    theory, 146, 160
    thinking, 122
    tradition, 43, 91–94, 118, 139, 141, 146, 147, 149, 150, 198
Just War Against Terror (Elshtain), 117, 122, 200
"Just War as a Public Policy Checklist," 147
"just war on terror," 11
"just wars," as the cost of genuine freedom, 52
justice
    Augustine on the administration of, 112

SUBJECT INDEX

demanding when feeling aggrieved, 166
doing, 167, 180
existing for the good of all, 161n193
God's standard of, 92
Greco-Roman philosophy on, 180
love as the crux of, 181
as not a chore to be accomplished, 182
not culminating in preemptive and retributive killing, 186
not found wherever fear of death impedes action, 89
prior to the advent of modernity understood as a virtue, 152
as a profoundly dense construct for Augustine, 180
seeking for others over and above one's self, 153
sense of in the Roman Empire's constitution, 116
witnessing, 178–86
work of enabling, 12
"justice for us," the nation content to settle for, 151
justice system, favoring the wealthy and white, 3
justification, for war without end, 9
justified violence, 54, 160n192, 198

King Kalakaua, signing the "Reciprocity Treaty," 23
Kay, David, 124
Kennedy, John F., 29n22
Kennedy, Robert, 29n22
Kennedy administration, removed its protective hand from Diem, 36
Kerry, John, 12, 186
Khomeini, Ayatollah, Hussein compared to, 38
kill lists, 189, 190
"kill or be killed" binary, 126, 167
killing, 112, 126, 141, 163
"kind harshness," 139
kindness, loving, 167
King, Martin Luther, Jr., murder of, 29n22
kingdom of God, 127, 194
kingdoms, 81, 83, 85
Kinzer, Stephen, 32n28, 35–36, 45
Kissinger, Henry, 36n39, 37
Koch network, political arm of, 49
Korah, opposition to Moses, 104
Ku Klux Klan, 59n109
Kuwait, liberating from Saddam Hussein, 4

labors of birth, 78
law
    blessing of force to uphold, 100
    both religious and imperial producing injustice, 181
    as a diagnostic tool, 170n11
    as reactionary at best, 157
    weightier matters of, 167–68
Lazarus, 184n52
Le Nain de Tillemont, biography of Augustine, 66n5
least evil, choosing, 147
legitimate authority, criterion of, 151
Leithart, Peter, 22n7, 49–54, 72, 193
lesser evil, 147, 148
Lewis, C. S., 105
liberal democracy, 113
liberty, 54
liberty and freedom, as vices, 51
libido dominandi, Rome flushed with, 121
Lieber Code, 28n21, 133n84
life, 158, 186, 204n8
"limited but necessary" use of torture, justifying, 201
Lincoln, Abraham, 28n21, 62n113
listening, repentance as a distinctive kind of, 168
literary legacy, Augustine preserving, 109–10
lives, giving to and for others, 153
Livy, 97
the Lord, disciplining the one he loves, 92

Louisiana Purchase, 21
love
    as the antecedent of justice, 87
    aspects of, 13
    Augustine calling upon, 158
    Augustine making into the norm, 116
    as a communal act, 87n86
    exercising justice, 181
    of God made the heavenly city, 77
    as the mechanism innervating all moral life, 160
    misappropriated to unworthy objects, 13
    motivating violent coercion, 160
    as the nature of the debt owed to both God and neighbor, 180
    of neighbors as the only acceptable end and means for waging war, 157
    people bound together by common objects of, 120
    as the primary driver behind obedience and right action, 13
    privileging the innocent over the guilty, 154
    as the proper motivation for war, 138
    as rarely without sacrifice, 142
    for the recipients of one's violence, 201
    requiring us to cede our "legal right" to reparation, 157
    restraining violence, 155
    as the right intention, 154
    of self made the earthly city, 77
Love Your Enemies: Discipleship, Pacifism, and Just War Theory (Cahill), 158
loved to be "enjoyed" [*frui*], 98
"lowest kind of good," 97
Lucretia, exemplar of Roman vice, 75–76
lust for domination, dominating the earthly city, 77
"lust for power" (*libido dominandi*), originated in Augustine's *City of God*, 33n33
lying, Augustine's view of, 159n186

Machiavelli, 115
Madison, James, 61
Malcolm X, 29n22, 173n18
Mallaby, Sebastian, 129
malum opus, *The City of God* as, 68
Manichaeism, 67n8
"manifest destiny," 20, 26–27, 60
Marcellinus, 6–7, 74, 88–89, 88n93, 92–93
market capitalism, nuancing freedom, 52
market state of terror, 42n55
"market state terrorism," law ill-suited to address, 41–42
Markus, R. A.
    on Augustine's views on "just war," 111
    on Augustinianism as politically radical, 185
    distinction between the two cities as eschatological, 80
    interpreting the just-war tradition, 114
    on just war in the saeculum, 162–64
    on love of temporal goods, 98
    on Roman exceptionalism, 193n85
Marshall Plan, modern-day, 132
martyrs, fear not keeping from worshipping Christ, 103
masculinity, implicated in war, 142n118
Maslow, Abraham, 47
mass shootings, frequency of, 3
Mathewes, Charles, 50–51, 113, 114, 143
Maximian, the Catholic Bishop of Bagai, 106
McCone, John, 36n39
meekness, declaration of, 169
Mercer, Robert, 49n84
mercy, leading to repentance of, 96
Micah 6:8, 166, 167, 180, 203

SUBJECT INDEX

"Middle East," as a pejorative term, 129n63
Milbank, John, 75, 80, 112, 118, 161n192, 199
military applications, for citizenship, 62n117
military bases, network of US, 25n16, 48, 197
military dominance, 63
military draft, 62
"military necessity," sanctioned circumvention of laws, 28n21
military participation, 125, 138
military power, unmatched, 60
military psychologists, designed "enhanced interrogation techniques," 39
military solutions, US prioritizing, 47
military spending, US, 204n8
military strength, 10, 25
military supremacy, Americans having faith in, 16
military targets, legitimate, 155
military technology, evolving faster than international law, 157
"minimally decent state," 132
minimum amount, of force necessary, 156
ministerial guidance, as Augustine's scaffolding, 199
misappropriation, of Augustine to bless the US response to 9/11, 127–28
mission, to eradicate terror, 56
Mitchell, James, 39
modernity, 53–54, 150
Mohammed, Khalid Sheikh, 40, 41
monotheism, Church's adherence to, 68
Monroe, James, 26
Monroe Doctrine, 26, 27, 33
moral casuistry, discredited tradition of, 134
moral compass, church as, 158
moral deficit, pacifists finding themselves in, 137
moral dissonance, caused by competing allegiances, 8
moral duty, to advance liberty and freedom, 51

moral high ground, cost of, 14
moral imagining, few Christians equipped to undertake, 173
moral incongruences, in America, 7
moral judgment, on September 11 hijackers, 122
moral map, Augustine creating, 120
moral self-justification, Christian, 5
moral superiority, hypocritically feigned, 170
moral training, as necessary, 188
morality, synopsis of American, 4
morally deficient practices, 198
morally formed civic character, for just-war thinking, 122
Moses, 179
Mossadegh, Mohammad, 30, 31
mufti, qualifications to be, 175n25
mujahideen (those engaged in *jihad*), 11n18, 35n35, 142n117
murder, 30, 101

Napoleon, 23
nation, supplanting the church as the sacred community, 50
national complicity, democracy introducing, 193
National Rifle Association, political lobby of, 2
"national security," injustices in the name of, 171
National Security Council (NSC)
  creation of, 27–28
  NSC 10/2, 28, 28n21, 29, 30
  organizing a coup, 31
national selfishness, challenging, 170
national sin. *See also* sin
  complicity with, 170, 175
  as not a new idea, 174
  repenting of, 169, 203
national sovereignty, as sacrosanct, 151
national violence, disseminating to all corners of the globe, 3
nationalism, 130n68, 184, 184n52
nationalistic socio-economic reforms, of Jacobo Arbenz, 32
nation-building imperialism, 130

nations, as inherently self-centered entities, 45
nation-state terrorists, 42n55
nation-states, 41n55, 139
Native Americans, 20, 20n5
Native peoples, 21, 22
natural resources, US brought into its sphere of influence by military means, 45
naval stations, Cuban government required to sell or lease land to the United States for, 25
"necessary means of survival," 174
"necessities," Augustine's "wise judge" on, 159n185
neighbor love, 97, 117
neighbors, 97, 148
new Augustinian theologians, 113
New Testament, Biggar's reading of, 138
news, stylized and crafted for a target audience, 191
Nicaraguan Contras, Reagan's support of, 38
Niebuhr, Reinhold, 114, 115–17
Niebuhrian realist paradigm, rejecting, 147
"nihilistic politics," natural end of, 50
"nihilistic realism," Augustine avoiding, 116
9/11, 16, 16n29, 113, 117, 145
Nixon, Richard, 31n27
non-Christians, expectations for Christian politicians, 178
non-citizens, becoming naturalized citizens, 62n117
non-combatant
 deaths, 149
 determining from combatant, 44n66
 immunity, 136
 permissibility of harming, 156
non-intervention, 152, 176
nonviolence, 16–17
normative love, Niebuhr's litmus test for, 116
North, Oliver, 38
North Africa, in the Roman Empire, 65n2
North Korea, 144n128

Northcott, Michael, 51n90, 195
nuclear conflict, 27
nuclear disarmament, US policy to incentivize, 128n62
nuclear weapons program, underwriting Israel's, 129
Numa Pompilius, 97, 97n126
Nye, Joseph, 60n111, 197

Obama, Barak, 9, 43–44
O'Donovan, Oliver, 15, 81n63, 83, 87n86
oil industry, Mossadegh sought to nationalize in Iran, 30
oil trading, still tied to the US dollar, 47
oil-rich nations, US sanctions against, 47
"old lie," translated, 50n87
Old Testament, foretold the New Testament, 91
"ontological priority of peace," 199
"Operation Mongoose," plans to assassinate Castro, 24n12
Operation PBSUCCESS, 29n23, 32–33, 34
Oregon Treaty, 21
original sin, locating the origins of empire in, 143
the "other," 10, 96n123
other cheek, turning when struck, 7
"outsiders within," the empire's borders, 96n123
overly enthusiastic realist, 199

pacifism, 137–38, 201
"pacifist inclinations," of Augustine's contemporaries as non-existent, 164
pacifists, 6, 137
pagans, 68, 199
Pahlavi, Shah Mohammed Reza, 31, 32n27
Palestinian Jews, not responsible for atrocities in the name of Caesar, 174
Palestinians, American support for Israeli oppression of, 176

SUBJECT INDEX

Palin, Sarah, 174n19
"paradoxical norm," in Augustine's just-war theory, 160
pastoral reading of Augustine, 199, 203
"paternal" political entity, as a "father state," 139
patriotism
 author's father's lack of, 4
 including protest, 12, 186
 as a non-negotiable article of faith, 14
 putting forward uncomfortable questions, 166–67
 transfiguring to love of countrymen, 204
Paul
 against being conformed to the world, 183
 on being subject to the governing authorities, 150
 on the "cross" as either folly or the power of God, 195
 forced by bodily punishment to the gospel, 106–7
 on the law and sin in Romans 7, 170n11
 on paying to all what is owed them, 182
peace
 achieved by eliminating one's enemies, 97
 Augustine's esteem of won by words, 94
 coercively ordered love as the essence of, 160
 as a "common object of love," 95
 disturbers of as those who claim to be upholding, 119
 envisaging in a country without war, 188
 genuine as outgrowth of seeking collective good, 153–54
 as a goal, 153
 ingrown nature of, 95
 lacking selfish connotations, 95
 priority of manifested by Augustine, 161n192
 pursuing genuine, 90
 seeking through correction, 96
 striking down the unarmed, 119
 as an uncertain good for empires, 86
 yielding authentic, 153
"peace is seldom simple," as Biggar's primary premise, 137
peacebuilding, 161–62
Pearl Harbor, 23, 24n11
penitence, practices of, 183
penitential posture, in a political landscape, 170
Pentagon, vetting foreign-born recruits, 63n117
Pentagon Papers, smuggled out by Daniel Ellsberg, 171n12
a "people," Augustine's definition of, 87
people of God, political entity treating, 50
Percy, Martyn, 192, 192n79
perfect love, casting out fear, 107
"perpetual dictator," Caesar designating himself as, 57
petrochemical trading, denominated in US dollars, 197
petrodollar monopoly, Russia and Iran fighting back against, 47
Philippines, 24, 26
physical coercion, 93, 139, 199
Pilate, 178, 181, 184n52
pilgrim ethic, 120
pilgrimage, as a follower of Jesus, 3
pilgrims, 80, 100, 120, 169
pillars, of empires, 56
Pinochet, Augusto, 37, 37n40
Platt Amendment, ended occupation of Cuba, 25
plausible deniability, 4, 29, 29n22, 192
Plutarch, on Cato's suicide, 76–77
political culture, of the West, 43
political enemies, sub-contracting assassinations of, 29
political engagement, Christian, 159n185
political ideologies, producing disparate interpretations, 56
political institutions, Augustine not bothered by the form of, 82
political landscapes, as never static, 110

political left, urging people to do good, 204
political marginalization of the church, 150
political order, "desacrificed" through Constantine's actions, 72
political participation, 166, 176, 180
political position, won by violence, 15
political realist, Augustine as a reluctant, 112
political realities, of empires and just wars, 70n17
political responsibility, abdicating all manner of, 185
political rule, 81n62
political space, contemporary congregations participating in, 114
"political theologian," Augustine as, 110
political theology, compromised by the established system, 185
political writings, of Augustine, 184
politician, 14, 183
politics of manipulation and domination, rejecting, 182
polity, 83, 173
poorer classes, enfranchisement and empowerment of, 59
popular base, Diem lacking, 35
Poroshenko, Petro, 128n62
Possidius, Bishop of Calama, 66n5, 108–9
post-Enlightenment political structures, repurposed forceful coercion, 53
post-traumatic stress disorder (PTSD), among drone operators, 189
poverty, 187, 204
Powell, Colin, 39n45, 129
power, 8, 56, 140, 185
praise, courting like hypocrites, 177
preemptive war, 90
present, obscuring Augustine, 162
preventative war, 90, 125
pride, 82, 166
princeps, or first citizen, maintaining the Republican façade, 57
principles, US was founded upon Christian, 3

private contractor, church as to the state, 158
privatization of mass incarceration, 204n8
prodigal son's older brother, thicker sense of justice than of kindness, 167
professional army, Romans reorganized its soldiers into, 61
pro-life, 12, 167, 186–93, 204
proportion, 156, 157
prosperity and markets, securing, 46
Protestant diaspora, leaving the church too hoarse to speak loudly, 157
proxies, installed by the US, 34
Psalm 25:17, as a cry for a deliverance, 107
psychological warfare, 33n29
public confession, of complicity with national sin, 12
"public life," *res publica* as, 84n69
public policy, church affecting change in, 150
public repentance, 177
public testimony, repentance as, 203
Puerto Rico, acquired from Spain, 24
punishment, 96, 102, 108
Purple Heart, 12n21

questions, Christian citizens asking pointed, 13
Quodvultdeus (deacon), 110

racism, pushed underground in America, 22
Ramsey, Paul, 6, 15, 147, 154–55
Reagan, Ronald, 38
realism, of Augustine as "excessive," 115–16
recipient of punishment, failure to love, 102
"Reciprocity Treaty," guaranteeing the US exclusive rights, 23–24
recruitment problem, for James Madison, 61n112
redemptive violence, as unjust violence suffered, 54

SUBJECT INDEX

refugee crisis, 375 AD mismanagement of, 68n11
release process, for detainees, 135n94
religio licita, metamorphosis of Christianity to, 71
religious experience, everyone entitled to a personally tailored, 192
religious faith, used as a partisan tool, 203
religious law (the law of Moses), Jesus condemned by, 181
religious tolerance, American, 50
religiously zealous nationalism, killed Jesus, 184n52
reluctant realist, Augustine as, 199
Remus, 78
Renaissance Technologies, Mercer as a top executive at, 49n84
repentance
    as the best cure for a conscience, 177
    distinguishing genuine, 170
    humility of political, 167–71
    as the initial Christian act of political engagement, 12, 166, 203
    as a peculiar practice to the non-believer, 178
    rarely lauded as a patriotic endeavor, 183
    rejoicing in the second Passover, 168
    safeguarding against tyranny, 184
republic, 55, 57, 84
Republic of Grace (Mathewes), 113
Republican Congress, following the US Civil War, 58
Republican Party, identifying as Christians, 186n59
repurposed violence, exporting to other nations, 53
repurposing, Augustine, 199–202
res publica, 83, 83–84n69
resistance, 7, 166
"Responsibility to Protect" (R2P) clause, 123n50, 131
restraint, Augustine's praise for, 145–46
retaliation, Jesus's teaching on, 93
retribution, 173n17
Revelation's Beast, emulating, 50

Revisions (Retractiones), Augustine's, 109n181, 110
"right authority," 139
right intent, 153
right to declare war, locating the origin of, 150
righteousness, not practicing before other people, 177
righteousness (*dikaiosune*), Pauline notion of, 180
right-leaning pundits, envying Roman pre-eminence, 56
rights, prioritizing our over the right, 151
Roanoke Colony, ill-fated, 19
Roman auxiliary model, US military adopted aspects of, 62
Roman courts, tilted in favour of the wealthy, 73
Roman emperors, aspiring to naked autocracy, 58
Roman empire
    discontent with its domestic peace and security, 108
    emergence from within the Republic, 58
    encompassed with barbarous nations and enemies, 97n126
    no specially privileged place in God's providence, 193n85
    world order based upon a lust for conquest, 83
Roman history, Augustine lived during an extraordinary period in, 67
Roman imperial expansion, occurred under the Republic's rule, 58
Roman law, not permitting execution of the un-condemned, 75
Roman liturgy, deficiency of as Augustine framed it, 84
"Roman predicament," distinctly American as well, 46
The Roman Predicament (James), 46
Roman Republic-turned-Empire, survived over 1,200 years, 60–61
Roman solution, conquer and provide prosperity, 46

Roman-American imperial
    comparisons, 56
Romans
    cherished glory as hope for
        immortality, 78
    defending temples of the gods
        supposed to protect them, 84
    espoused justice as the foundation
        for their endeavors, 87
    innovation in engineering and road
        construction, 56n103
    lived in dark fear and cruel lust, 88
Rome
    benefitting the citizens of the
        heavenly city, 99
    coveted a foreign adversary, 122
    endured just one tribulation, 92
    false conception of "justice," 120
    love of being free metastasized into
        lust to dominate its neighbors,
        11, 13
    as not indispensable for Augustine,
        144
    as an oligarchy before emergence as
        an empire, 59
    origin in God's providence and in
        restraining wickedness, 108
    possessed "hard" and "soft" powers,
        60
    proclaimed all their wars were
        defensive, 121
    "ruling on what constitutes
        orthodox belief and punishing
        dissent," 71
    sack of by the Visigoth army, 54–55,
        64, 92
    similar tact with the Visigoths, 47
    as the symbol of a whole civilization,
        55n99, 64
    waged wars of expansion, 85
Romulus, 78
Roosevelt, Theodore, 27
Roosevelt Corollary, 27
rule of law, 41, 42
rules of the road, 43–44
Russia, 128n62, 140, 152n156
Rwanda, genocide, 201

sack of Rome, 54–55, 64, 92
"sacral" conception of the empire,
    185n54
sacral order, equating America with, 121
sacralization, of national interest, 51
sacraments, performed by *traditors* as
    valid or not, 104
sacrifice, reinterpretation of, 52
saeculum, influencing with the gospel,
    171
safety, disdaining for their savior's sake,
    103
"Saint Augustine's Views on the 'Just
    War'" (Markus), 162
salvation, working out with fear and
    trembling, 5
Samson, 46
Sandinista government, 38
Saudi Arabia, 47
schisms, among God's people as
    calamitous, 104
Schmitt, Carl, 42
Schneider, Rene, 36, 37
schools, gun incidents in American, 3n5
scriptures, as Jesus's witnesses, 179
second Iraq war, Biggar's final verdict
    on, 137
secular version, of the just-war
    tradition, 157
secularization, 185, 185n54
security, obsession with, 16
security council, permanent members
    of, 139–40
"Selective Service System," 62n114
self-defense, 123, 151–52, 176
self-determined governments, US
    willingness to sabotage, 45
"self-evident truths," 5
self-interest, 95, 153
self-interested peace, measured against
    neighbor-loving peace, 86
"self-interested pursuits," advancing, 53
self-perception, nation approaching its
    idealized, 186
self-sacrificial nature of *agape*,
    Niebuhr accusing Augustine of
    obscuring, 116
senate, of Rome led by two consuls, 55

September 11, 2001, 16, 117–18
Sermon on the Mount, 7, 44
Sessions, Jeff, 181n43
sex or murder, learning mechanics of, 14n25
Shah of Iran, 31, 32n27
shalom-wholeness, peace that is, 90
shareholder, citizen as fully vested, 171–78
Sharia just-war theory, Bin Laden's letter and, 175–76
shepherds of flocks, first righteous men as, 80
Sherman, General, loophole for, 28n21
Silver Star, 12n21
sin, 81n62, 169. *See also* national sin
size, as the enemy of empire, 48, 85
slavery, 58n108, 80, 188
slaves, designated as three-fifths of a person, 186n58
Smith, J. Warren, 90
social change, resisting, 119
social ethics, 158, 161
social integrations, 115
social order, 158, 185
social security, 204n8
social structure, 164
social-safety-net programs, 204
society, became intrinsically "secular," 185n54
"soft (culturally or ideologically seductive) power," 60, 60n111, 197–98
soldiers
    enduring and conflated faith in American, 52
    instinctive resistance to killing, 141n114
    need for in Rome, 61
    obedient to gospel command, 93
    undermining the will of a foreign majority, 24
soldiers and citizens, justifying war, 16
sole remaining super-power, US as, 129
Soviet Union, 4, 22
Soviet-Afghan war, 142n117
Spain, 24, 25

special interest lobby, church pigeonholed as, 150
special-interest floodgates, opened beyond their capacities, 49
specter of war, loomed heavily over Rome, 88
spectrum, empires existing on, 50
"splendid vices," of Augustine, 51
stabilizing influence, of the US, 129
stakeholders, citizens of a liberal democracy as, 203
standing army, church not having, 151
"start-up" terrorist cells, venture capitalists for, 42n55
state
    sacralized by the blood of its citizens, 50
    survival as a priority, 153
state law (the laws of the Roman empire), Jesus condemned by, 181
state of exception, 42, 44
state violence, American compliance with, 188
statecraft, distilling violent moral quandaries, 6
state-sanctioned coercion, through "just war," 112
status quo, 170, 185
Stevens, John, 23
subordination, legitimate and illegitimate, 116
success, reasonable chance of versus "probability of success," 155
sugar plantations, foreign-owned in Hawaii, 23
suicide, of Lucretia, 75, 76
suicide attacks, in *jihad* as "golden tickets" to paradise, 79n53
Super PACs, 49, 49n84
superiority, American ethos of moral and racial, 20
supreme emergency, 149
"Supreme Good," seeking, 97–98
supreme value, setting only on God, 98–99
surveillance and communication technologies, 197

suspension of habeas corpus, US use of, 200
Swift boats, captained by Kerry in Vietnam, 12n21

Taber, Robert, 46n72
Taliban, led by Mohammad Omar, 142n117
targeted killing, 132, 133, 200
targets, on a screen, 189
tax dollars, sub-standard stewardship and, 187
taxation, excessive of the American colonies, 45
Taylor, Breonna, 132n80
teaching, of scripture that only God is to be feared, 88
Teaching Christianity (Augustine), 159n184
telescope, being born on the wrong side of, 162
temporal nature, of the city of man, 78
temporal peace, of the earthly city, 97
temporal survival, deifying the state's continued, 172
territorial integrity, as sacrosanct, 151
terror, 9, 127, 136
terrorism, 126
"terrorist," as a subjective term, 11n18
terrorist organizations, galvanization of, 189
terroristic violence, confronting systematic, 131
terrorists, getting rid of, 127
testimony, Yoder giving to government, 188
Texas, capital punishment in, 2
Texas Cession, 21
theism, Americans defining, 53
theodicy, 138
theological ethics, 2n1
thieves, empires as, 83–90
Third Reich, crown jurist of, 42
threats, faced by Augustine from all sides, 199
throne of David, as concession to Israel's weakness, 81n63

Tolstoy, on the meaning of "do not resist evil," 7
"too many teeth" misappropriation, of the just war tradition, 149
torture
  Augustine uncomfortable with, 102
  as a crime against humanity, 136
  Elshtain offering a fuller treatment of, 133
  giving legal form to that which is extra-juridical, 42
  of the innocent, 159n185
  likely to produce false information, 41
  US use of, 200
Torture and Terror in a Time of Troubles (Elshtain), 131, 200
"torture lite," 134, 136
treachery, CIA committing abroad, 29n22
Treaty of Paris, 21
trials and tribulations, enduring, 92
"trickle-down economics," 171
Trojan War, remembered in the work of Homer, 79
Trotsky, 29n23
Truman, Harry S, 27, 33, 172n17
Truman Doctrine, 27–30
Trump, President, 187n63, 189, 192–93, 192n79
Trump administration, drone data report and, 189n70
truth
  bearing witness to gospel, 178
  malleable conception of, 192
  speaking to power, 191, 194
  telling as the most unambiguous witness, 204
truth claims, holding opposed, 7
"turbulent energies," harnessed, 53
two cities, 77–83, 120
two-party cartel, tyranny of, 60

Ukraine, 128n62
"unconventional empire," 18–64
  US as, 9–10, 19, 22, 197
"Unfair treatment of Israel," 140n112

unforgiving servant, parable of, 96
unified voice, not existing for Protestant churches, 150
united church, holistically pro-life as difficult, 193
United Fruit Company (UFC), 32, 33n30, 34
United Nation's charter, Article 51, 123
universal interest, empires as privileged carriers of, 154
universal truths, of Elshtain, 126
universality, aspirations of, 19
unjust, for some men to rule over others, 115n12
unjust weapons, drones as, 188
unmanned aircraft, imperial policing by, 197
unquestioned, making questionable, 163
Untermensch, Nazi use of, 96n123
unthinkable, making thinkable, 163
US (United States)
    as the "already" of the *Novus Ordo Seclorum*, 51
    backed France reasserting colonial authority over Vietnam, 35
    churches ill-equipped to critique Americanism, 51
    citizens calling to account the actions of their government, 175
    companies in Cuba before Batista fled, 24n12
    congruency with the Roman Empire, 55
    deserving an administration acting on behalf of its citizens, 175
    destined to end as it was conceived, 125
    disclaiming responsibility for covert operations, 28
    distancing from empire, 143
    dollar as the world's global reserve currency, 197
    drone policy, 190–91
    as an empire, 46
    in Europe and on the Korean Peninsula, 132
    evolved into an unconventional empire, 9
    filling its military with conscripted soldiers, 62
    giving Israel billions of dollars, 140
    having more guns than citizens, 2
    history failed to produce even one tyrant, 59
    as an indispensable nation, 144, 154
    invaded the *al Qaeda* stronghold of Afghanistan and then Iraq, 145
    killed foreigners to access Asian markets, 26
    knew the body count Pinochet was amassing, 37
    lapses in professed republican principles, 64
    loving an "-ism" with which to galvanize the populace, 89n96
    military advancing the interests of generous corporate donors, 49
    military bases in thirty-eight countries, 48, 143
    military mounting an armed defense of settlers, 20
    military undergoing evolution, 61
    nations challenging slapped with sanctions or worse, 143
    Navy opened ports in the South Pacific, 24n11
    as not an inadvertent empire, 143
    not impervious to the same decline as Rome, 63–64
    obligations in the Middle East, 46
    policy deployed and persisting after the second World War, 197
    replaced the colony with the military base, 197
    rewarded Hussein's invasion of Iran, 38
    "searching abroad for monsters to destroy," 27
    secured the removal of Jacobo Arbenz, 35
    seeking access to the potential of distant lands, 45
    spending on children as near the bottom for developed countries, 187
    spending on defense, 144

US (United States) *(continued)*
    as a standard bearer in the conduct of war, 43–44
    standing between two imperial archetypes, 50
    support for Ngo Dinh Diem, 35
    supported the coup against Ukraine's Viktor Yanukovych, 128n62
    torture and drone strikes executing kill lists, 187
    tripartite equilibrium of power, 55–56
    used nuclear weapons on noncombatants, 128
    withdrew support from the Batista regime in 1959, 24n12
usage of things, as wicked or righteous, 98n135
uti/frui dialectic, Augustine employing, 98
utilitarian approach, on torture, 134

Valens, led an army against the Goths, 69n11
Vandals, 69n11, 108–9
vengeance, 102, 168n3, 181
vice(s), 85, 93
Viet Minh, US equipping and training to expel Japan, 35
Vietnam, political developments in after World War II, 35–36
Vietnam Veterans Against the War, 12
Vietnam war, protestors calling for the end of, 171n12
violence
    as always the last recourse for Augustine, 112
    American obsession with, 2
    bearing the burden of proof in pacifism and just-war thinking, 122
    Christ refusing to defend himself against, 196
    Christians accepting the inevitability of, 7
    devastating effects on other people's lives and societies, 162
    dilemma created for Augustine's epistemology, 160
    enduring without returning it in kind, 196
    as "kind harshness" motif in Augustine, 138
    moral culpability for, 100
    more pervasive among men, 142n118
    as a normative part of faithful obedience to Christ, 138
    not depriving Augustine's flock, 109
    only love should induce, 201
    rejecting, 167
    responses to, 145
violent exception, to the ontological priority of peace in Augustine's writings, 112
violent lynchings, of the Ku Klux Klan, 59n109
violent parallels, between contemporary American context and the Roman empire of Augustine's time, 196
violent world, US fashioned in its own image, 128
Virgil, on suicide, 75n38
virtue, 51, 89, 182, 184
Visigoths, 47, 91
Volusianus, 6–7
voting, 60

Walzer, Michael, 149
war
    as an abstract idea, 148
    assuming many qualifiers, 198–99
    Augustine condemning excessive use of, 96
    as the continuation of commerce, 44–49
    dilemma created for Augustine's epistemology, 160
    investing materially and ideologically in, 144
    "just war" grounds, 149

as a lesser evil, 147, 157
as a means for securing money and sovereignty, 45
as a means to peace, 95
moral reaction in those experiencing it, 16
as normative and a communal good when held far away, 16
as not anathema for Christian soldiers, 93
not incompatible with Christian discipleship for Augustine, 91
as the only option for states with few and fallow alternatives, 155
recalibrating Augustine's contemplations on just war, 199
resist as a euphemism for, 89n96
restraining, 146
slaying by word, 94
as a unique act of judgment, 142
waged in obedience to divine command, 101
waging to acquire peace, 94
war against terrorism, as a police matter, 133
war and torture, Augustine questioned and critiqued, 108
War of 1812, recruitment as a problem for James Madison, 61
"War on Drugs," 89n96
"war on terror"
    as an act of neighbor-love, 123
    Americans feeling as though won, 121n45
    amorphous nature of "combatants," 9
    Augustine as an advocate of, 10
    Augustine's personal, 145
    caused many to revisit the imperial question, 22
    Elshtain comprehending what is at stake, 130–31
    as an imperial endeavor, 10
    as a just war, 122, 157, 198, 200
    moral narrative providing ethical cover for, 118
    seeking to secure American safety, 145

theologians utilized Augustine to interpret, 11
uncertainty on the objective being met, 44
undermining as mythos the "leader of the free world," 39–44
ushered in a permanent state of exception, 43
waging, 8
war crimes committed during, 140
war "without teeth," as an application of just war, 149
warfare, 67, 163, 187
warmonger, Augustine as no, 160n192
Washington, George, 61
waterboarding, 40
watershed moment, of the church's self-understanding of its identity, 110
way of life, preserving, 89
the weak, ultimate weapon of, 195
wealth, American dream of amassing, 8
wealthy, guaranteeing prioritization of the will of, 60
weapons, Iran the largest purchaser of American-manufactured, 31n27
wedding feast, parable of, 105
"What We're Fighting For," letter to Islamists, 127
wheat and tares, 73, 156n172
white Christians, in the Republican party, 186n59
white minority, control of Hawaii's arable land, 23
the wicked, restraining in order to enable the good, 11, 156
Will, George, 52
Williams, Robin, 136n98
Williams, Rowan, 172
witness, 178
witnesses, Christian, 15, 178, 190
witnessing, justice, 178–86
WMD (weapons of mass destruction), 124
wolf, shepherd loving also, 142
Women and War (Elshtain), 122
world police, US role of, 128, 144

World Summit Outcome Document, 152
World Trade Center, people leaping from, 55
World War II, 19, 22
Wynn, Phillip, 111–12

Yahweh, 99, 203
Yanukovych, Viktor, 128n62
Yoder, John Howard, 71, 72, 170, 174, 187

Zahedi, Fazlollah, 31
"zone of war," 133

Scripture Index

Old Testament

Exodus
32:1	104n162
32:6	104n162

Numbers
16	104

Deuteronomy
6	168
6:7	168n5

1 Samuel
8	80
13:14	94n113

Psalms
25:17	11n20, 103n158, 107
61	73

Proverbs
9:10	88n91

Isaiah
6:5	168n4

Jeremiah
29:7	99n139
36:23	104n163

Micah
6:8	166, 167, 180, 182, 203

New Testament

Matthew
5:16	79n57
5:23–24	177n31
5:39	6n11
5:44	154n163
5:46	154n163
6:1	177n30
6:1–4	79n56
6:12	99n140, 169n6
6:14–15	177
8:8–10	94n114
9:13a	178n32
10:16	183n46
10:28	88n92
13:24–40	156
18:21–35	96n121
19:14	181n43
20:16	193n84
23:23b	168n2

Luke

3:14	93n110
7:6–9	94n114
14	105
14:23–24	105n167

John

3:30	79n57, 87n85
5	179
5:17b	178n35
5:18b	179n36
5:19	179n37
5:31	179n37
5:36	179n37
5:39–40	179n37
5:47	179n38
10:17–18	196n3
11:48	183n52
11:50	183n52
15:13	195
18	178
18:23	7n13
18:37	178n33
19:12	183n52

Acts

10	94n115
23	106
23:3	7n13

Romans

7	170n11
12	181, 183
12:3	169n7
12:14	181n44
12:17–19	181n44
12:21	181n44
13	81n63, 181, 181n43
13:1	150n146
13:4	74, 150n146
13:8	181

1 Corinthians

1:18	196n2
1:27–29	196n2
4:7	196n4
6:1–6	73

2 Corinthians

3:17–18	54n97

Philippians

2:12	5n8
3:18–19	38n44

Hebrews

12:6	92n104

1 John

4:18	107

Early Christian Writings

Ambrose

"Duties of the Clergy"

1/27–28, 59	161n193

Aquinas

Summa Theologica

II/II 64.2	156n172
II/II 64.7	153n158

Augustine

Answer to Faustus — 91

22/73	100n147, 101n148
22/74	91n102
22/75	91n101
22/79	91n100

SCRIPTURE INDEX

City of God	10, 68, 74, 75, 77, 80, 82, 88n93, 101, 109n181, 113, 145	XIX/16	96n122
		XIX/17	97nn129–130, 98nn133–134, 99n138
I/19	75, 75n38, 76nn39–42	XIX/21	115n12
		XIX/24	87n86
I/21	101nn151–152	XIX/25	51n91
I/23	76n45	XIX/26	99n139
I/29	80nn58–59	XIX/27	99n140
II/2	55n101	XV/4	97n128
II/19	88n88	XV/7	96n121
II/21	84nn70–71	XXII/6	103n159
III/9	96n124		
III/10	85nn79–80, 97n125, 97n127, 145n134	*Confessions*	
		IX/vi/14	67n8
III/12	84n73	*Expositions of the Psalms*	
III/14	86n81	61/10	73n30
III/17	88n89		
III/28	119, 119n27	*Against Faustus*	
IV/3	88n90	22/78	98n135
IV/3, 4	83n68		
IV/4	83n67	*Letters*	
IV/5	85n75, 98n132	43	104n164
IV/8	84n72, 85n74	43/1–2	104n161
IV/15	85nn76–78, 145n133	51	104
		87	106
V/1, 7	79n55	88/5	104n165
V/12	95n119	88/8	106n171
V/14	78nn49–50	93/2	105n166
V/15	79n56	100	107
V/16	99n137	100/1	107n175
V/17	82n65	104/14	102n157
V/19	100n141	105	104n160
V/21	81n64	105/10	104n164
V/25	100n142	133	74
V/26	100n143	133/3	74n34
XIV/2	78n48	134/2	74n34
XIV/9	100n144	134:3	74nn32–33
XIV/28	77n47	136/2	7n12
XIX/4	87n87	138	84n69
XIX/5	86n84, 90n98	138/9	93n106
XIX/6	11n19, 102, 103n158, 159n185	138/10	83n69, 93n109
		138/13	93nn107–108
XIX/8	86nn82–83	138/14	105n170
XIX/11	98n131	138/15	93n111
XIX/12	95n120	151/7	89n94
XIX/15	80n61, 82n66	153/2	70n17

Letters (continued)	
153/10	100n145
153/15	102n154
153/16	101nn149–150
185	93n112
185/6	104n164
185/22	106nn172–173, 107n174
185/25	105n168
185/26–28	106
189	93–94
189/5	94n116, 158n178
189/6	94n117
221–24, 25*	110n183
224/2, 10*:1	110n182
229	94

Political Writings	
251n4	83n69
253n20	73n31
"Sermon 13," 122	102n156
"Sermon 13," 125	101n153
xix	102n155
xxviii	100n146
	84n69

Revisions	
2/48	109n181
prologue 1, 3	93n112
	109n181

Sermons	
397	91–92
397/4	92n103
397/9	92n105

Teaching Christianity	
III/16	109n181
III/45	159n184
	73n29

The Trinity	
VIII/4	181

Grotius

Rights of War and Peace	
I/XI	146n136

Jerome

Letters	
123/16	64n127
127	55n100

Possidius

108–9

Life of Saint Augustine	
XXVIII, 6–8	109n178

Greco–Roman Literature

Aristides

63

Orations	
26/22	63

Cicero

Annals	
fragments V/1	84n71

The Republic	75
3/14, 24	83n67

Horace

Odes	
III/2.13	50n87

Livy

The History of Rome	
	97n126

Plutarch

"Cato the Younger"	
I	76n43
LXIX	76n44
LXXI	77n46

Lives of the Noble Grecians and Romans
90   97n126

Sallust

The Conspiracy of Catiline
2:2   86n81

Virgil

Aeneid
6/434   75n38
6/438   75n38

Islamic Literature

Hadith   175n25
Quran   175n25, 176n27
Shariah   176n27

www.ingramcontent.com/pod-product-compliance
Lightning Source LLC
Chambersburg PA
CBHW050847230426
43667CB00012B/2185